Crafting Nonfiction

Lessons on Writing Process, Traits, and Craft

Linda Hoyt

Kelly Boswell

*first*hand

HEINEMANN

DEDICATED TO TEACHERS

*first*hand
An imprint of Heinemann
361 Hanover Street
Portsmouth, NH 03801
www.heinemann.com

Offices and agents throughout the world

"Dedicated to Teachers" is a trademark of Greenwood Publishing Group, Inc.

© 2012 by Linda Hoyt and Kelly Boswell

Book and CD resources illustrations © Houghton Mifflin Harcourt/HIP

Permission to use excerpts from *Amazing Bats* (Chronicle Books, 2005) courtesy of Seymour Simon. Cover photograph on page 47 ©Joe McDonald/Bruce Coleman, Inc.

Cover design: Lisa Fowler and Jenny Jensen Greenleaf
Composition: Eclipse Publishing Services
Cover photos: Bill Miller, Larry Crowley, and David Stirling
Text illustration: 3–5 students of Mrs. Hoyt and colleagues

Library of Congress Cataloging-in-Publication Data
Hoyt, Linda and Boswell, Kelly
  Crafting nonfiction intermediate, lessons on writing process, traits, and craft / Linda Hoyt and Kelly Boswell.
     p. cm.
  Includes bibliographical references.
  ISBN 978-0-325-03722-6
  1. Authorship. 2. Authorship--Vocational guidance. I. Title.
  PN145.H693 2012
  808'.02--dc23

                                    2011047791

ISBN 10: 0-325-03722-1
ISBN 13: 978-0-325-03722-6

Printed in the United States of America on acid-free paper
16 15 14 13 12 ML 1 2 3 4 5

To Deb Doorack
You epitomize grace, strength, and vision.
Working with you is an honor.
Linda

To Carson and Brady
Wherever you go, go with all your heart.
Kelly

ACKNOWLEDGMENTS

From Linda

Kelly: From the day I first watched you in action with your students—and later with educators—I knew you were special. Working as your partner on this project has been absolutely wonderful. Thank you for sharing your enormous depth of understanding, your teacher heart, and your considerable writing talent.

Team Heinemann: It is an honor to stand in your shadow. Lesa Scott, Anita Gildea, Kate Montgomery, Deb Doorack, Charles McQuillin, Abby Heim, David Stirling, Lisa Fowler, Stephanie Levy, Heather Anderson, the sales team, and so many more. My thanks and appreciation to all.

To the teachers who tested lessons, provided feedback, and gathered work samples for this resource: Leah Starkovich, Portland, Oregon; April Willard and Kristal Lomax, Thomasville, North Carolina; Debbie Welemin, Burnsville, Minnesota; Jane Olson, Apple Valley, Minnesota; Linda Bozeman, Denton, Texas; Aleisha Fuller-Moore, Denton, Texas; Holly Smith, Sanibel Island, Florida; Kelly Davis, Ellicott City, Maryland; Teachers of East Woods Elementary, Hudson, Ohio; Jan Martin and Eric MeMoine from Kinnaman Elementary, Beaverton, Oregon; Eileen Cronin, Melissa Sidiropoulos, Jennifer Gillingham, Boston Public Schools.

From Kelly

Linda: Thank you for giving me the opportunity of a lifetime. Working with you has been a joy and a delight! I am in awe of your talent, and I am honored to call you a friend.

Kerry Bishop, Sarah Dunkin, Kristy Castor, Michelle King, Melissa Mayes, and Renee Niepoky: You are amazing educators and best buddies from Beaverton School District. Your work with writers inspires me to believe in the power of possibilities. I am privileged to know you.

Sherri Downey, Leslie Whitmore, Sandy Kindt, Roxy Rogers, and Heidi Freeman, teachers and dear friends from Ruder Elementary in Columbia Falls, Montana. Thank you for your friendship, encouragement, and positive energy. Jerry Bauer and Nancy Loeza at Whittier Elementary in Bozeman, MT. Thank you for opening up your hearts and your classrooms to me. The work you do with students is fantastic!

Cory, my sweet husband and my best friend: Your unwavering love and support help me reach for the stars.

CONTENTS

PROCESS

TRAITS AND CRAFT

Teaching Nonfiction Writing

Today's nonfiction writing

brings excitement to both educators and children, fostering a fertile setting in which nonfiction writers can read, think, and write as they explore their innate interest in the world around them.

EMBRACING A MULTIFACETED VIEW OF NONFICTION WRITING

Nonfiction writing comprises the bulk of writing done by adults at home and in the workplace. It also represents the majority of the writing that students will do throughout their years in school. However, nonfiction writing does not have to sound like an encyclopedia! Instead, it can be filled with voice, engaging details, exquisite word choice, and sentences that sound lively and natural to the ear. As nonfiction writers, students have an opportunity to unleash their natural curiosity as they research, investigate, and wonder. As nonfiction writers who are empowered with a view of writing that includes consideration for *content, form, and craft,* students learn to execute writing that is driven by rich language and graced by intriguing visuals, text features, and page layouts. This multifaceted view of nonfiction writing creates a learning environment in which writing becomes an exciting invitation to embrace knowledge about the world while escalating each student's proficiency in the fine points of high-quality writing.

Raising the Bar with Nonfiction Writing

Lucy Calkins once said, *"Lifting the level of writing instruction matters . . . because writing matters"* (*A Guide to the Writing Workshop*, page 2). We agree! And we would like to add that we think this is more true than ever before. Today's schools, in response to increased accessibility of technology, demands of the workplace, and guidance of the Common Core State Standards, realize that nonfiction writing can and should be taken seriously in every dimension of the curriculum. Writers need to have explicit instruction showing them how to write in response to their learning, how to communicate points of view that are clearly supported by facts, and how to create summaries, explanations, informational reports, nonfiction poems, procedures, technical texts, and so much more. But the secret is to help writers also discover that they can make their work infinitely more engaging if they are diligent in applying stages of the writing process and infusing craft elements such as voice, word choice, and sentence variety into the writings they compose.

Just as a florist takes pride in creating the right balance between structural elements, color, and form in a display of flowers, young writers find satisfaction in knowing how to add the artistic touches that craft elements, literary devices, and process bring to nonfiction writing.

DELIVERING DYNAMIC DEMONSTRATIONS

Modeling is one of the most effective of all teaching strategies (Pearson and Fielding, 1991), so we believe that writers of nonfiction should experience modeled writing every day—sometimes more than once! When students see and hear an expert writer in action, they can imagine what is possible in their own writing. They have a clear vision of what their own writing should look like and sound like—and they understand how the writing was constructed. Like the picture on the box for a jigsaw puzzle, modeled writing helps writers see the path they are about to travel and establishes a yardstick for reflecting on progress toward an attainable target.

Modeling Mature, Well-Developed Writing

Modeled writing is an opportunity to set the stage for writers to gain maturity in word choice, sentence structures, or process elements. This means that, with the exception of writing models created to demonstrate drafting and spelling, modeled writing should look like it was written by an adult—not a child. During read-alouds, we read as an adult, delivering the reading selection with fluency, expression, and dramatic interpretation. *We don't read aloud like a child.* So the same high standard for performance and delivery should be evident when we write in front of students.

Modeled writing is a time to pull out all the stops and generate nonfiction text that elevates expectation and paves the way for excellence. This is a time to let writers observe the creation of intriguing nonfiction writing that has fascinating facts plus inviting sentence formations, sizzling interjections, and mood-shifting phrasing. This is

A super cell, characterized by its constantly rotating upward drafts, is a highly dangerous storm system that lasts for hours and may travel hundreds of miles. Winds swirl. Lightning cracks. Skies darken. Alarms begin to shriek.

Modeled Writing Example 1

When explicit modeling and think-alouds are offered every day, writing blossoms into a state of richness that could never be achieved through assignments alone.

We must demonstrate to our students that we are writers, too. It is only through the act of writing that we can show students that we value writing and its role in our learning lives.
—Lynne Dorfman and Rose Cappelli, *Nonfiction Mentor Texts*

When students see and hear an expert writer in action, they can imagine what is possible in their own writing.

a time to create a model that writers can aspire to emulate. By raising the standard for your modeled writing, you will lift expectations for your students as well.

> The frog is hungry after his long sleep, but he waits patiently. Suddenly, his bulging eyes fixate on a dozing fly. His long, sticky tongue darts out and . . . Snap! The unsuspecting insect pops into a greedy mouth.

Modeled Writing Example 2

A Tip:

In advance of a modeled writing lesson, jot the modeled writing that you plan to demonstrate on a sticky note. Then, place the sticky note on the chart where you will be modeling. With that little reminder, you will never have to worry about classroom distractions derailing the quality of your modeled writing.

Through careful observation of their teacher as a writer, writers gain critical understandings that empower them with independence and strategy.

Letting Them See You Struggle

While we certainly want modeled writing to raise the bar and set a standard for excellence, intermediate-age writers can also benefit from occasionally seeing the struggles that adults face as writers. This is especially true of modeled writing opportunities focused on process. When modeling for pre-writing, drafting, and revision, give yourself permission to think aloud about possible topic choices or how to start a sentence, change your mind, and start again. It is okay to show kids the power of rereading and rethinking and then adjust your writing to reflect your new view. It is even okay to show kids that you occasionally throw away a draft and start again with a fresh piece of paper to support a new line of thinking.

Thinking Aloud

Think-alouds, when combined with modeled writing, provide invitations for students to *listen* in on the thinking of a proficient writer. During a think-aloud, the goal is to make your thinking transparent enough that your writers can understand the internal processing that supports the text you are creating. As you write and think aloud, learners are more likely to notice the techniques that empower nonfiction writing and perhaps even hold their breath in awe as they watch how onomatopoeia and creative punctuation bring voice and life to a piece of writing. As close observers unencumbered by paper and pen, writers are free to notice details and see the natural path a nonfiction writer takes as she flows from thinking to writing and back to thinking. Through careful observation of their teacher as a writer, writers gain critical understandings that empower them when they pick up their pencils to craft nonfiction texts of their own. And who could be better at offering those opportunities for close observation than the teacher they know and trust—the teacher who can take their hands and show them how to breathe life into nonfiction writing.

> **Think-alouds** crack open a writer's thinking, making internal processes visible to learners.

Sample Think-Aloud 1

I am rereading this section about bald eagles, and I realize that I need to include more rich details. The writing doesn't have enough details to help readers create a picture in their minds. It says that eagles have talons and beaks, but it doesn't explain what their talons and beaks are used for—or even what they look like. I am going to revise and add some specific details to make my writing come to life. Watch as I scratch out this section and rewrite it to add details that will help my reader to visualize.

Sample Think-Aloud 2

We know that headings serve as mini-titles that are spaced throughout a piece of writing to keep each section clear and organized. Today I want to show you how I can use headings to help me as I draft. I am ready to create a draft about the great white shark. Watch as I make a list of headings to capture the big ideas I want to include in my writing today:

Ancient Predators; Teeth, Teeth, and More Teeth; Powerful Predators. Since the first heading is Ancient Predators, this section of my draft will need to talk about how great whites have been around for a long time. Watch as I write: Long before . . . oceans. Since my heading is about "ancient," did you notice how I focused my draft on providing more information about how very long sharks have been in existence? Drafts and headings are powerful partners.

During a think-aloud, it helps to use phrases such as:

As I think about this, I realize that I can choose to _____ , _____ , or _____. I am going to choose _____ because. . . .

As I think about this, I realize that. . . .

As I prepare to write, I am wondering. . . .

Watch how I. . . .

Notice the way I. . . .

Tune in, writers. I am about to show you. . . .

Keep your eyes on my pen and check out the way that I. . . .

Rereading is a powerful tool, and it just helped me realize that. . . .

In a setting where explicit modeling and think-alouds are offered every day so writers can see what they need to do and listen to a proficient writer think out loud, writing blossoms into a state of richness that could never be achieved through assignments alone. When we have higher expectations for ourselves as writing educators and for our students as developing writers, amazing things are possible.

The important point is that your writers need to watch you engage in modeled writing every day. Empowered by the rich vocabulary and interesting language structures from your modeled

To maximize achievement, writers need to observe explicit modeling and think-alouds every day.

writing, oral language will grow hand in hand with proficiency in nonfiction writing.

PONDERING THE POWER OF A REAL AUDIENCE

While the major purpose of this book is the minilessons that launch writing experiences in the writing workshop and in cross-curricular learning, it is essential that we remind ourselves of the power of an authentic audience. When writers write just to drop their creation into a basket for the teacher to grade, motivation and achievement suffer. Instead, if writers know they will be sharing their writing with a real audience, even a partner, intrinsic motivation and achievement soar! If we want writers to do the hard work of deep thinking, integration of fact and craft, revision, and editing, they must know that their writing will impact an actual audience. So as you investigate the lessons in this resource, we encourage you to always consider the potential for a real audience and wonder:

- Is this writing that is best linked to a writer's notebook and a partner share?

- Is this writing that is worthy of a team conference in which small groups of writers can share their work and discuss the facts, traits, and craft elements they were able to include?

- Is this writing that should be carried through all the stages of the writing process and be presented in a bound book, poster, or electronic text?

When writers write for an authentic audience, motivation and achievement soar!

LEARNING FROM AN EXPERT

Seymour Simon, the award-winning author of more than 250 nonfiction books for young readers, has been called the dean of the children's science book field by the *New York Times*. What is unique about Seymour's work is that he keeps a list of nonfiction craft elements next to him as he drafts as a reminder to integrate the facts that anchor his work with rich descriptions, comparisons, exciting visualizations, and other literary devices. This is significant, as this list of craft elements fuels his work and helps him ensure that the content will be interesting and accessible to readers. When Linda asked Seymour if he would share a few thoughts for inclusion in this book, he wrote the piece that appears opposite.

Like Seymour Simon, you have an opportunity to help your students understand that great writing doesn't just roll off your pen like magic. We encourage you to let your writers know that even famous authors have to think about facts and then decide how to share them with a reader so the facts are exciting to read. Writers need to understand that even the published authors they see as mentors take time to consider interesting ways to open sentences, insert text features, and choose their words. These conscious and deliberate choices that all writers need to make are the difference between flat, monotonous nonfiction writing and nonfiction writing that sparkles.

When writers consciously attend to content, form, and craft, writing takes on depth and richness that cannot be achieved with attention to facts alone.

CRAFTING MY BOOKS

When I write my books about space or animals or weather, I'm always aware of my readers and how my writing must explain and clarify yet still be exciting and interesting. I'm explaining difficult concepts in many of my books so I try to make connections to a young reader's world and understanding. One of the ways I do this is to make comparisons such as this one from my book *Stars:* "With powerful telescopes, we can see that the stars are as many as the grains of sand on an ocean beach." I also try to use strong verbs to dramatize the text. In my book *Icebergs and Glaciers,* I wrote, "When glaciers move, they grind and crush everything in their path."

I try to write effective leads in all kinds of ways, such as getting the reader to participate by doing something physical, writing exciting visualization, drama and suspense, comparisons and analogies. In my book *The Heart,* the first pages open with "Make a fist. This is about the size of your heart. . . . It weighs only about ten ounces, about as much as one of your sneakers." I also like to ask questions of my readers. I use descriptive detail as a story line in many of my texts. In my view, writing exciting nonfiction is not that different from writing exciting fiction.

—*Seymour Simon*

NAVIGATING THIS RESOURCE

Crafting Nonfiction is designed to provide an array of simple, ready-to-use minilessons that can be slipped into the writing workshop or into the nonfiction writing you provide in science, social studies, mathematics, and health. The goal of these lessons is to support you in providing top-quality nonfiction writing instruction that is embedded with craft and graced by process—with a minimum of preparation time.

As you dip into the lessons, you will find that there is a strong emphasis on cracking open the thinking that goes on inside a writer's head as text is created. Samples of teacher language provide think-alouds that invite your writers inside the writing process and expose the joy of crafting text that is both factual and artfully written. You'll also find lessons that provide strong support for trait-based instruction, offering writers tips on word choice, sentence fluency, research, and ideas, voice, conventions, and presentation.

There are no worries about taking the time to create fascinating passages for modeled writing. Samples for modeled writing are right here in these pages to springboard your thinking. You can use them as they are written or use them as a seed from which your own ideas can evolve.

These lessons are, by design, short and focused. Each lesson can and should be completed in 15 minutes or less so that writers have

time to do what they most need to do—write! With these brief minilessons, you may want to power up the writing that you do in science, social studies, and the other disciplines or add variety to the minilessons in your writing workshop. You can also use these lessons with small groups and in one-on-one conferring as a support to differentiation and targeted instruction.

A Few Tips for Using This Resource

This resource is organized into two major sections: Process and Traits and Craft Elements. Within each major section, you'll find subsections that are designed to make lessons organized and easy to find.

Process lessons are grouped according to the stages of the writing process. In Research and Planning, you will find a wealth of resources that range from modeling how to use the key word strategy to using a graphic organizer or planning page layout. In the section on drafting, lessons focus on drafting a persuasion, adding action, and experimenting with leads. Revising is the section where you will find helpful modeled writing lessons on how to tune up sensory images, how to combine sentences, how to maintain main ideas, and how to revise for sentence fluency. In the sections Editing and Presenting, the lessons turn toward audience and a focus on page layout, text features, and page breaks.

The section on traits and craft elements is rich in lessons that focus on the artistic side of writing. In this section, lessons are organized around traits of high-quality nonfiction writing, with craft elements woven into each section. The traits are as follows:

- Content and ideas
- Organization and text features
- Style (word choice and sentence fluency)
- Voice and audience
- Conventions (punctuation, grammar, sentence structure, capitalization, spelling consciousness)

Features of a Lesson

Each lesson is focused on a behavior that writers can absorb and attempt to immediately apply in nonfiction writing. The structure of the lesson is repeated throughout this resource, providing a familiar, predictable routine for both you and your students.

As you view the page, be sure to notice the *When To Use It* feature. This is designed to assist you in lesson selection.

Another feature you will want to notice is *Turn and Talk*. It is important to anticipate that there will be times for students to turn and talk woven into the fabric of the lesson. This is essential processing time when discourse is distributed so all writers are talking, thinking, and reflecting on the learning that you are modeling. It is often helpful to have writers come to your meeting area with a "thinking partner" and for the thinking partners to sit together on the carpet. Since thinking partner match-ups are already in place, you won't need to waste valuable lesson time while students try to find someone with whom to discuss the learning.

Most importantly, be sure to notice the sample modeled writing. This sample can be copied as is and save you the time of getting creative, or you can use the modeled writing as a starter for your own thinking and shift the content toward a subject that is current within your classroom.

Steps of the Lesson:

- *Focus the Learning* is a brief explanation of why this lesson is helpful to primary-age writers, and it often provides tips for ensuring success with the target learning.

- *Modeling* is the heart of the lesson. In this step, you will find think-aloud language that you may want to consider as you demonstrate and consciously show your writers how to infuse the target learning in a piece of nonfiction. The modeling portion of the lesson is divided into two steps to provide a pause for turn and talks.

  This portion of the lesson is essential and is worthy of a bit of advance thought. This is your vitally important opportunity to make your thinking transparent and show your students how proficient nonfiction writers construct a message, take notes, play with different sentence openers, and lift their nonfiction writing so it is not boring! So it is a good idea to read the sample text and think-aloud in advance and decide if you are going to use the think-aloud as is or modify it to make it your own.

- *Analyze* is a time to reread the modeled writing and reflect. Because rereading is one of the most important process tools we can teach writers, you want to make it clear that writers always reread and reflect on what they have created. Let your writers watch you start at the beginning and read aloud, touching each word as you go. Let them hear you notice places in your work where you applied the target learning or places where you are thinking you might revise to make a sentence more exciting or descriptive. Analyze includes a final turn and talk, plus a summary of the lesson that should refocus your writers on the target learning and prepare them to pick up their pencils.

- *Variations* Differentiation is an essential key to lifting nonfiction writers toward the highest possible levels of success. This section has suggestions for less experienced writers and more experienced writers. These tips can be used to modify the overall lesson, support additional lessons if they should be

appropriate, or guide your thinking as you plan for guided writing groups and confer with individuals.

- *Cross-References* Be sure to note the cross-references, as these will give you tips on additional lessons that can be linked to this lesson to provide additional support or offer an opportunity to stretch and extend the learning.

Tools to Have on Hand

Most lessons call for you to model a piece of writing, thinking aloud as you construct the text. Therefore, you will need a good supply of chart paper and markers. Once models are created, you and your students will want to return to them for reference and ongoing support. You'll need a strategy for saving your modeled writing. Some teachers find it helpful to place modeled writing on hangers and simply hang them from a clothes rack. Others use a spiral tablet of charts and flip back and forth as needed.

Selecting Lessons

Selecting a lesson from this resource is like going to a restaurant and preparing to order. As you view the menu, you have the joyful challenge of selecting meal items that best match your personal needs and interests. I encourage you to treat this resource like a menu of possibilities. As you view the menu options, pick and choose from lessons that support observable needs in your learners, lessons that assist you in targeting a particular trait, or lessons that match a particular time of year, content, or unit of study.

Target Specific Needs

Formative assessments, your observations of writers during one-on-one conferences and your analyses of student writing samples, can and should guide your thinking and lesson selection. This resource is an opportunity to do what teachers do best—match instruction to learner need.

Examples of how to analyze a writing sample and then select specific lessons from this resource begin on page 44.

Target a Particular Trait

Your students may benefit from lessons that focus on a particular trait, such as word choice or organization. Knowing that we need to help writers develop across the full spectrum of traits, you may want to work through these sections in order. Or you may see a need in your students, such as creating a clear beginning, middle, and end, that would lead you to a particular trait such as organization.

Most of all, ensure that your writers experience modeled writing and support with an array of lessons representing each trait so their nonfiction writing development is structurally and artistically sound. When students have repeated exposure to high-quality models that demonstrate how to include a particular trait and when they have the opportunity to integrate that trait into their writing, achievement soars!

Organize by Time of Year

Early in the year, when you are establishing routines and under-standings for the writing workshop, you might focus on the lessons for process—especially planning, drafting, and revising. As the school year progresses and writers develop fluency and begin to consider publication, you might add lessons on editing and presenting.

If you are engaging writers in a unit of study on persuasion, report writing, procedural text, or written response, you might select lessons that best support the features of the unit. For example, when students are writing reports, you could select focus lessons that pertain to research or to specific text features such as bold words or a table of contents.

Weave Lessons Through the Day

Across the Curriculum

With so much content crowding our instructional day, we need to integrate content across the curriculum. These lessons can be used to teach writing in connection with science, social studies, health, or mathematics. For example, if students are learning about frogs in science, you might consider choosing lessons that teach students how to research, take notes, and create a labeled drawing. Likewise, if you are engaging in a mathematics unit on graphing, you might choose the lessons that teach how to locate and use facts from a visual or how to create a chart or table.

In the Writing Workshop

Writing workshop is grounded by an opening minilesson. The lessons and modeled writing presented in this resource will slip naturally into your workshop routines, saving you time and elevating your students' nonfiction writing.

To Differentiate

Use the lessons in this guide to support differentiation during small-group writing instruction or when conferring with individuals. Remember that modeled writing and think-alouds become even more powerful in the personalized settings created by a small group or conference. This is a time when you can stretch highly proficient writers to reach even greater heights or scaffold those who need additional support.

However you choose to utilize the lessons in this book, remember that all of them can be used for whole-class minilessons, for small-group supports, or as vehicles to live one-on-one conferences.

ONGOING, FORMATIVE ASSESSMENT: INFORMANT TO INSTRUCTION

Ongoing, authentic assessment is the heart of teaching. However, assessment is only useful when it is used to guide our instructional decisions. As teachers, it's imperative that we become careful observers, collecting writing samples to analyze, listening in on partner conversations between writers, conferring with individuals, and using expert kid-watching skills during guided writing sessions.

When we observe writers, analyzing writing samples and behaviors closely, we can determine which students are integrating the writing technique from modeled writing into their work. Close observation will make it clear which students might benefit from additional support in a small-group writing lesson or a one-on-one conference in which the skill, process, or craft element is modeled again. These careful observations will also guide you to know if the entire class may benefit from another modeled writing focused on the same writing technique.

Each piece of writing that you examine will broaden your base of understanding for your writers and improve the scaffolds you offer in conferences, in guided writing sessions, and in modeled writing demonstrations.

Analyzing Nonfiction Writing Samples: Observe, Reflect, Plan

The following nonfiction writing samples, reflective of those you might see in an intermediate classroom, offer invaluable insights into the development of each writer. As you analyze a writing sample, it is important to first identify strengths of the writer and then to consider teaching moves and specific crafting lessons that will best lift the development of this nonfiction writer.

As with all formative observations, it is important to note that while every writing sample provides valuable information, it takes a review of many samples over time to fully understand the strengths and areas of need for a learner. This is especially true with nonfiction writing, as each text type includes different text structures, features, and conventions.

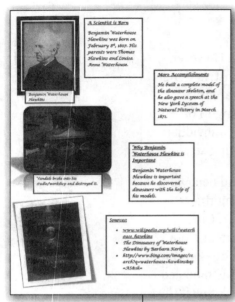

Sophia's Visual Text

Sophia's Visual Text

Strengths of this writer:

Sophia has created an interesting and organized visual text. She has done a nice job of balancing the text and the visuals on the page. She has also included a list of her sources.

Observations and possible teaching moves:

Sophia has provided basic information about Benjamin Waterhouse, but she could benefit from additional teaching in how to add details that make the facts about this fascinating man come to life for a reader. She may also be ready to experiment with combining sentences for improved sentence fluency.

Suggested lessons from this resource:

- Revising, Lesson 9, Combine Sentences
- Ideas, Lesson 3, Jaw-Dropping Details Add Interest
- Ideas, Lesson 6, Anticipating the Questions of Your Reader
- Sentence Fluency, Lesson 2, Rereading to Check Sentence Fluency

Link to the Common Core:

- Develop the topic with relevant facts, definitions, concrete details, quotations, or other information and examples.

Sea Turtle

Strengths of this writer:

Malik has included descriptive words and phrases that evoke strong imagery in the reader's mind (*beak like choppers ready to eat, boney shell, hard leathery skin*). He has experimented with using powerful action verbs to begin a few lines of his poem (*swimming, diving, chomp*).

Observations and possible teaching moves:

This writer is clearly having fun exploring descriptive language, but he may need more modeling on how to write an informational poem. He might also be ready for additional lessons in how temporal words and phrases can add clarity and flow to the piece. He may benefit from a short guided lesson on how using onomatopoeia can add some more voice and pizzazz.

> Sea Turtle
>
> Swimming through the big open sea
> Boney shell
> Hard leathery skin
> Beak like choppers ready to eat
> Suddenly... the turtle realizes-time
>   to breath
> Swimming for its life to get air
> Diving through the water racing
>   after a fish
> Chomp... bye, bye fish
> Flippity, Floppity flippers flop along
>   the sand
> The turtle heads back to the water...
> Laying her eggs

Sea Turtle

Suggested lessons from this resource:

• Word Choice, Lesson 9, Using Temporal Words and Phrases to Signal Event Order

• Word Choice, Lesson 11, Use Onomatopoeia

• Sentence Structure, Lesson 3, Compound Sentences

• Drafting, Lesson 11, Writing an Informational Poem

Link to the Common Core:

• Use appropriate transitions to create cohesion and clarify the relationships among ideas and concepts.

**How Does a Beam
Bridge Work?**

How Does a Beam Bridge Work?

Strengths of this writer:

Lily has effectively organized her information and has displayed it in a visually pleasing way. She has included a diagram and a callout box in which she has placed a "fun fact." As she begins her writing, she speaks directly to her reader and draws the reader in.

Observations and possible teaching moves:

If other writing samples suggest that Lily is having difficulty navigating homophones (such as *too, to,* and *two*), a modeled lesson in a small-group setting might be in order. Lily might also benefit from learning how including actual photographs can boost her nonfiction writing.

Suggested lessons from this resource:

• Sentence Fluency, Lesson 3, Using a Variety of Sentence Beginnings
• Text Features, Lesson 3, Using Photographs
• Spelling Consciousness, Lesson 4, Navigating Homophones
• Sentence Structure, Lesson 4, Opening Element

Link to the Common Core:

• Use appropriate and varied transitions to create cohesion and clarify the relationships among ideas and concepts.
• Engage and orient the reader by establishing a context and point of view.

Maddie's Letter to Luke

Strengths of this writer:

Maddie has constructed an informative, engaging, and delightful letter! She opens with a question—a sure way to hook her reader! Her writing also includes a clear organizational structure (*the first stage, the second stage,* etc.). This makes the writing clear, focused, and easy to read. She shows engagement with her topic when she includes comparisons such as *its mouth is like a tiny vacuum* and the *"young frog" is like a teenager*.

Observations and possible teaching moves:

The writing is clear and organized, but in places, it is a bit choppy. Maddie would benefit from learning how to reread her writing with an ear for sentence fluency. She might also benefit from analyzing each sentence to make sure she has crafted sentences of varying lengths.

Suggested lessons from this resource:

- Sentence Fluency, Lesson 2, Rereading to Check Sentence Fluency
- Sentence Fluency, Lesson 1, Sentences Are of Varying Lengths
- Grammar, Lesson 2, Use Prepositions to Enrich Descriptions

Link to the Common Core:

- Use precise words and phrases, relevant descriptive details, and sensory language to capture the action and convey events.

Maddie's Letter to Luke

> ### Earth feeling the heat
>
> The book Earth feeling the heat by Brenda J. Guiberson has amazing visuals the picture had beautiful nutral colors it made the book come alive. The book had no captoin but the pictures spoke for it. The book made me think I was right next to the animal. The book drew you in. Without or with the captoins I give the book 4stars

Amalia's Book Review

Amalia's Book Review

Strengths of this writer:

Amalia writes convincingly about the visuals in the book and includes some nice descriptive language (*beautiful natural colors*). She has also effectively inserted her own opinion into the evaluation of the book (*The book made me think I was right next to the animal*). This provides a nice personal touch!

Observations and possible teaching moves:

Amalia has a lot to say about the book, but the lack of punctuation and capitalization makes it hard for a reader to follow. She may need a nudge toward identifying complete sentences and punctuating them accordingly. She might also benefit from additional support in combining her sentences to create a smooth and fluent piece of writing.

Suggested lessons from this resource:

- Grammar, Lesson 2, Use Prepositions to Enrich Descriptions
- Punctuation and Capitalization, Lesson 4, Punctuating Onomatopoeia
- Sentence Structure, Lesson 1, Two-Word Sentences
- Sentence Fluency, Lesson 3, Using a Variety of Sentence Beginnings

Link to the Common Core:

- Support the claim with clear reasons and relevant evidence, demonstrating an understanding of the topic.

Kaleb's Explanation

Strengths of this writer:

Kaleb has crafted a piece of writing that is informative and fairly clear. He's included an illustration, complete with a key, which shows that he's thinking about his reader. He also shows that he's becoming comfortable trying more complex sentences such as *After that the Krakawas use sap, rope, and even grasses to keep the wickup sturdy.*

Observations and possible teaching moves:

Kaleb might benefit from a quick refresher on the use of homophones such as *there, their,* and *they're.* It would also be helpful to encourage Kaleb to try using a comparison or even a little humor to show some engagement and bring some of *his* voice to the writing.

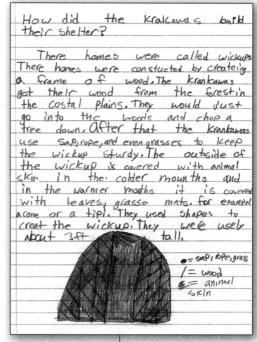

Kaleb's Explanation

Suggested lessons from this resource:

- Spelling Consciousness, Lesson 4, Navigating Homophones
- Grammar, Lesson 2, Use Prepositions to Enrich Descriptions
- Voice and Audience, Lesson 2, Show Engagement with the Topic
- Ideas, Lesson 8, Use Comparisons

Link to the Common Core:

- Include formatting and graphics when useful to aid comprehension.

> Students should have homework every night.
>
> Students should have homework every night because homework extends your learning from school to your home. It is also good practice for remembering what you learned in school. It also provides an educational activity instead of playing a video game or watching television. I think students should have homework every night.
>
> On the other hand, students shouldn't have homework every night because you can go to a museum or have a more fun way of learning instead. Also, lots of students have after school activities that might interfere with their homework. Students will feel rushed when they need to do an activity but they still have homework to do.
>
> In conclusion, to make the majority of people happy, students should be allowed to have homework every night but should have options in the assignments they do each day.

Antoine's Persuasion

Antoine's Persuasion

Strengths of this writer:

Antoine's piece has the beginning of a strong organizational structure. He's organized his writing into cohesive paragraphs, and he's utilized phrases such as *on the other hand* and *in conclusion*.

Observations and possible teaching moves:

Despite Antoine's attempts at organization, this piece is difficult for a reader to follow. He includes an opposing point of view but might need help in how to set up the alternate opinion so that it doesn't distract from his main argument. Antoine may benefit from more exposure to persuasive texts and lessons aimed at strengthening a written argument.

Suggested lessons from this resource:

- Organization, Lesson 9, Using a Persuasive Framework
- Ideas, Lesson 1, Create a Nonfiction Topics List
- Voice and Audience, Lesson 9, Target Voice in Persuasive Writing
- Revising, Lesson 2, Revising a Lead
- Word Choice, Lesson 12, Use Persuasive Language

Link to the Common Core:

- Acknowledge alternate or opposing claims.

Iliana's Personal Narrative

Strengths of this writer:

Iliana establishes the setting for her reader by including some nice sensory images in her opening lines. It's clear that this was a day that she remembers well and one that impacted her.

Observations and possible teaching moves:

Iliana has a lot to say about her day at the beach, but she needs to narrow the topic and develop just one little nugget of her day. For example, a reader would love to hear more about how the wave twisted her knee. She may need a nudge toward finding that one moment in time from that day and developing that into a more focused piece of writing.

> As I walk along the sand I could hear the waves crash aginst the shore and see the dolphins far away in the ocean. I felt the water touch my feet as I walk into the water. The water was warm so I swam in. My foot steped on something slipery and I fell in to the water. When I fell in I swam away as fast as I could because I didn't know what it was. When I got out of the water I ran to my mom to tell her about it. She said she had no Idea what it could have been so I frgot about it and went to look for sand crabs. I found a sand crab by the water and I went to show my mom. She was inpressed that I foand one. I went to go put it back. After that me and my mom crashed into a waved. The wave twisted my knee. The water washed me up on the shore and my mom came running to me and carried me to our unbrella and I didn't go in the water again.

Iliana's Personal Narrative

Suggested lessons from this resource:

- Organization, Lesson 8, Paragraphs
- Grammar, Lesson 2, Use Prepositions to Enrich Descriptions
- Ideas, Lesson 5, Focus on the Main Idea(s)
- Grammar, Lesson 3, Select Precise Verbs
- Word Choice, Lesson 2, Target Powerful Action Verbs

Link to the Common Core:

- Use narrative techniques to develop experiences and events or show the responses of characters to situations.

Mormor

Mormor, my Grandma has a smile that takes all your cares and worries away in a flash. Softly her hand, so worn and yet so soft gently touches mine. The air about her makes you feel loved and elated. Twinkling, her eyes look at me but never get tired doing so. When I am with her I never want to leave.

My Grandma was born on April 11, 1938 in Eveleth, Minnesota, the second child in her family. Her mother died when she was very young after having her younger brother. Later, her father remarried. Her grandparents were immigrants from Sweden and Germany in the 1800's.

Quickly, she grew up and started playing with rubber guns and games like kick the can and baseball in alleyways near her house. One summer the United States notified her that no kids were allowed off their property for the whole summer because of the polio epidemic. Also, a neghbor had a quaretine sign on her house that year because one of the family members had scarlet fever. Her family stressed education a huge amount, so she barely ever missed school except when she was horribly sick.

As she became an adult she worked in many places. Later she married David McCain and lived with him until he was fifty-five when he died of stomach cancer. Not surprisingly she never thought of dating or remarrying. She was a very industrious person that to me is the best Grandma in the world.

Mormor

Mormor

Strengths of this writer:

Alex's first paragraph drips with voice and makes me want to read more. He's done an excellent job of including strong sensory images that make Mormor come to life!

Observations and possible teaching moves:

This piece starts off great but suddenly becomes dry, lifeless, and a bit jumbled. As you confer with Alex, you might show him how to infuse the important facts about Mormor in a way that still maintains the voice and tone of the first paragraph.

Suggested lessons from this resource:

- Organization, Lesson 7, Craft an Ending that Brings Closure
- Presenting, Lesson 2, Inserting Illustrations and Visuals
- Revising, Lesson 6, Tuning Up Concrete Words and Sensory Images
- Word Choice, Lesson 3, Linking Words and Phrases

Link to the Common Core:

- Provide a sense of closure.

Let Your Wings Take Flight

Strengths of this writer:

This writer has used action and some powerful action verbs such as *flaps, gliding,* and *strikes* to engage the reader and paint a picture of this Rufous-tailed Jacamar. As a reader, my heart rate starts to increase with each sentence. What will happen? The colorful illustration also adds a nice touch to this piece.

Observations and possible teaching moves:

After all of the action and suspense in this piece, the conclusion feels a bit like running into a brick wall. You could challenge this writer to create a conclusion that is satisfying and matches the tone of the rest of the piece. You might also nudge this writer to experiment with some additional titles to see if there is one that might be a better fit.

Suggested lessons from this resource:

- Text Features, Lesson 1, Powerful Titles
- Sentence Fluency, Lesson 5, Vary Sentence Beginnings with Adverbs and Adverb Phrases
- Drafting, Lesson 9, Creating a Conclusion
- Word Choice, Lesson 7, Use Metaphor

Link to the Common Core:

- Provide a sense of closure.
- Orient the reader by establishing a situation.

Let Your Wings take flight

The Rufous - tailed Jacamar quickly flaps it's beautiful wings in the air, gliding through the sky. In the corner of it's sharp eyes it spots a delicous Glass wing butter fly. The Rofous - tailed Jacamar strikes torward the Glass wing butter fly but the butter fly senses danger and blends in with it's transParent wings. The Rufous - tailed Jacamar missed and the Glass wing butter fly was lucky. The lime green bird will soon strike again.

Let Your Wings Take Flight

Class Record-Keeping Grid

Writers	Draw pictures before you write	Add labels to drawings	Count the words in a message	Revise to add details	Add words with a caret	Combine sentences (and, so, but, or)	Make the setting stand out	Beginning, middle, end
Ji	9/8	9/16	10/14					
Alina	9/8	9/8	9/16	9/21	9/21	10/1	10/15	
Margetta	10/1	10/4	10/7					
Yolisa	9/8	9/22		10/15	10/1			
Angie	9/7	9/7	9/22	9/22	9/22			10/7
Harvey	10/1	10/4	10/15					
Ryanne	9/21	9/21			10/14			
Dominic	9/15	9/22	10/1		10/1			
Taylor	9/9	9/9	9/9	9/16	9/16	9/21	10/1	10/15
Marcos	9/22	10/7	10/1	10/7				
Brady	9/8	9/22	10/14					
Carson	9/7	9/21	10/4	10/4	10/4			
Angelina	10/4	10/4	10/7					

Class Record-Keeping Sheet

A class record-keeping sheet is a helpful tool for recording and keeping track of your modeled writing as well as your students' attempts to employ process, trait, or craft elements from your demonstrations. All you need to do is list your modeled writing lesson topics across the top of the grid and then note when you observe the target in an example of student writing. You will quickly be able to differentiate instruction, providing extra assistance for those who need it.

LINKS TO CD-ROM:

Demonstration Lesson Tracker: Planning

Planning		Date Modeled		Date Modeled		Date Modeled	
		Whole Class	Small Group	Whole Class	Small Group	Whole Class	Small Group
1	Selecting a Format for Writing						
2	Planning with Text Structure: Explanation						
3	Planning with a Graphic Organizer: Cause and Effect						
4	Planning for Generalizations						
5	Plan to Write with Imagery						
6	Planning an Informational Poem						
7	Planning Page Layout						
8	Using a Flowchart						
Other							

Monitor Demonstration Topics: Keep Track of Your Lessons

A lesson tracker can help you plan instruction and keep an eye on the topics you are teaching. This broad look will help you evaluate the balance of your instruction both across the writing process and within your grouping structures. The Demonstration Lesson Tracker pictured here is one of 17—one for each section in this book—on the accompanying CD-ROM.

LINKS TO CD-ROM:

Use a Scoring Guide to Monitor Progress with the Traits

The scoring guide that follows is designed to support your ongoing assessment of trait development in the writers in your classroom. You can use the guide "as is" or use it as a springboard to create your own scoring guide.

Trait Scoring Guide

	Just Beginning (1) _____	Developing (2) _____	Getting Stronger (3) _____	Wow! (4) _____
Content and Ideas (the meaning and core communication of the piece)	The writer has difficulty selecting a topic and offers few details.	The main idea is present, but there are few details and specifics.	Details are present and related to the broad topic. The writing is focused enough and rich enough in details to satisfy a reader's curiosity.	The topic is narrow and very well developed. Substantial detail is provided in a manner that interests the reader.
Organization and Text Features (the internal structure of the piece and the text and graphic features that support the piece)	The writing lacks a beginning or ending and lacks organization. No text features are included in the writing.	A beginning and ending are present but not well developed. The order and structure are not clear. A few text features, such as title and labels, are used.	The beginning and ending are more clear, and the order and structure are logical. Additional text features are included (labels, title, boldface words, and captions).	The beginning and ending are well crafted. There is a clear order and structure. Numerous text features are included in the illustration and text (labels, title, boldface words, captions, cutaways, diagrams).
Style (rich vocabulary and the way words flow from sentence to sentence)	Vocabulary is basic. Sentences are simple and do not flow together. The writing is choppy or incomplete.	The writing includes functional words but seldom selects words that are interesting. Sentences are of similar length and many start the same way.	Verbs are becoming active and nouns more precise. Sentences have variety in length and beginnings. The piece can be read aloud with ease.	Action verbs and precise nouns are used in a way that adds interest to the piece. Adjectives create clear sensory images for the reader. There is a smooth flow to the writing. The piece invited expressive oral reading.

continued on next page

LINKS TO CD-ROM:

REFERENCES

Anderson, J. 2005. *Mechanically Inclined: Building Grammar, Usage, and Style into Writers Workshop*. York, ME: Stenhouse.

Angelillo, J. 2002. *A Fresh Approach to Teaching Punctuation: Helping Young Writers Use Conventions with Precision and Purpose*. New York, NY: Scholastic.

Barone, D., and L. M. Morrow, eds., 2002. *Literacy and Young Children: Research-Based Practices* (pp. 226–242). New York, NY: Guilford Press.

Boushey, G., and J. Moser. 2009. *The CAFÉ Book: Engaging All Students in Daily Literacy Assessment and Instruction*. York, ME: Stenhouse.

Bridges, L. 1997. *Writing as a Way of Knowing*. York, ME: Stenhouse.

Britton, J., T. Burgess, N. Martin, A. Mcleod, and H. Rosen. 1975. *The Development of Writing Abilities*. London: Macmillan.

Calkins, L., et al. 2003. *Units of Study for Primary Writing*. Portsmouth, NH: Heinemann.

Common Core State Standards. 2010. Washington, DC: Council of Chief State School Officers and the National Governors Association.

Culham, R. 2004. *Using Picture Books to Teach Writing with the Traits*. New York, NY: Scholastic.

Dorfman, L., and R. Cappelli. 2009. *Nonfiction Mentor Texts*. Portland, ME: Stenhouse.

Duke, N. 2004. The case for informational text. *Educational Leadership*, 61(6): 40–44.

Duke, N., and S. Bennett-Armistead. 2003. *Reading & Writing Informational Text in the Primary Grades: Research-Based Practices*. New York, NY: Scholastic.

Glover, M. 2009. *Engaging Young Writers Preschool–Grade 1*. Portsmouth, NH: Heinemann.

Greiner, A. 2007. Eleven research-based tips for improving writing instruction. *Center for Performance Assessment Newsletter,* May 1, 2007. Denver, CO: Center for Performance Assessment.

Hoyt, L. 1999, 2009. *Revisit, Reflect, Retell*. Portsmouth, NH: Heinemann.

———. 2000. *Snapshots: Literacy Minilessons Up Close*. Portsmouth, NH: Heinemann.

———. 2003. *Make It Real*. Portsmouth, NH: Heinemann.

———. 2004. *Navigating Informational Text*. Portsmouth, NH: Heinemann.

———. 2005. *Spotlight on Comprehension*. Portsmouth, NH: Heinemann.

———. 2007. *Interactive Read Alouds, K–1*. Portsmouth, NH: Heinemann.

———. 2007. *Interactive Read Alouds, 2–3*. Portsmouth, NH: Heinemann.

Hoyt, L., and T. Therriault. 2008. *Mastering the Mechanics K–1*. New York, NY: Scholastic.

———. 2008. *Mastering the Mechanics 2–3*. New York, NY: Scholastic.

Hoyt, L, M. Mooney, and B. Parkes. 2003. *Exploring Informational Texts from Theory to Practice*. Portsmouth, NH: Heinemann.

Moline, S. 1995. *I See What You Mean: Children at Work with Visual Information*. Melbourne, Australia: Longman.

Mooney, M. 2001. *Text Forms and Features: A Resource for Intentional Teaching*. Katonah, NY: Richard C. Owen.

Murray, D. M. 1984. *Write to Learn*. New York, NY: Holt, Rinehart.

Newkirk, T. 1989. *More Than Stories: The Range of Children's Writing*. Portsmouth, NH: Heinemann.

Pearson, P. D., and L. Fielding. 1991. Comprehension instruction. In R. Barr, M. Kamil, P. Mosenthan, and P. D. Pearson, eds., *Handbook of Reading Research*, Vol. 2 (pp. 815–860). New York, NY: Longman.

Portalupi, J., and R. Fletcher. 2001. *Nonfiction Craft Lessons*. Portland, ME: Stenhouse.

Purcell-Gates, V., N. K. Duke, and J. A. Martineau. 2007. Learning to read and write genre-specific text: Roles of authentic experience and explicit teaching. *Reading Research Quarterly*, 42: 8–45.

Ray, K., 1999. *Wondrous Words*. Portsmouth, NH: Heinemann.

Ray, K., and L. Cleaveland. 2004. *About the Authors: Writing Workshop with Our Youngest Writers*. Portsmouth, NH: Heinemann.

Ray, K., and M. Glover. 2008. *Already Ready: Nurturing Writers in Preschool and Kindergarten*. Portsmouth, NH: Heinemann.

Routman, R. 2004. *Writing Essentials: Raising Expectations and Results While Simplifying Teaching*. Portsmouth, NH: Heinemann.

Saunders-Smith, G. 2009. *Nonfiction Text Structures for Better Comprehension and Response*. Gainesville, FL: Maupin House.

Simon, S. 2010. Presentation at the International Reading Association Conference, Chicago, Illinois.

Stead, T. 2001. *Is That a Fact? Teaching Nonfiction Writing K–3*. York, ME: Stenhouse.

———. 2003. The art of persuasion. *Teaching Pre K–8*. November/December.

Stead, T., and L. Hoyt. 2012. *Explorations in Nonfiction Writing, Grade 3*. Portsmouth, NH: Heinemann.

———. *Explorations in Nonfiction Writing, Grade 4*. Portsmouth, NH: Heinemann.

———. 2012. *Explorations in Nonfiction Writing, Grade 5*. Portsmouth, NH: Heinemann.

MASTER LESSON CHART

PROCESS

<table>
<tr><td>◯ Research</td><td>3</td><td>4</td><td>5</td><td>Page</td></tr>
<tr><td>1 Selecting the Best Sources for Research</td><td></td><td>●</td><td>●</td><td>46</td></tr>
<tr><td>2 Alphabox: Identify Important Words and Phrases</td><td>●</td><td>●</td><td>●</td><td>48</td></tr>
<tr><td>RELATED LESSONS: Word Choice: Lesson 1, Use Descriptive Words and Phrases</td><td></td><td></td><td></td><td>202</td></tr>
<tr><td>Word Choice: Lesson 2, Target Powerful Action Verbs</td><td></td><td></td><td></td><td>204</td></tr>
<tr><td>3 Taking Notes</td><td>●</td><td>●</td><td>●</td><td>50</td></tr>
<tr><td>RELATED LESSONS: Research: Lesson 2, Alphabox: Identify Important Words and Phrases</td><td></td><td></td><td></td><td>48</td></tr>
<tr><td>Text Features: Lesson 4, Bold Words</td><td></td><td></td><td></td><td>294</td></tr>
<tr><td>4 Use the Key Word Strategy</td><td>●</td><td>●</td><td>●</td><td>52</td></tr>
<tr><td>RELATED LESSONS: Research: Lesson 8, Using a Research Notebook</td><td></td><td></td><td></td><td>60</td></tr>
<tr><td>5 Very Important Points (VIP) Strategy</td><td>●</td><td>●</td><td>●</td><td>54</td></tr>
<tr><td>RELATED LESSONS: Research: Lesson 4, Use the Key Word Strategy</td><td></td><td></td><td></td><td>52</td></tr>
<tr><td>6 Represent Facts Visually</td><td>●</td><td>●</td><td>●</td><td>56</td></tr>
<tr><td>RELATED LESSONS: Text Features: Lesson 5, Cutaway Diagram with Labels</td><td></td><td></td><td></td><td>296</td></tr>
<tr><td>Text Features: Lesson 7, Chart/Table/Graph</td><td></td><td></td><td></td><td>300</td></tr>
<tr><td>7 Pocket Organizers: Collecting Facts</td><td>●</td><td>●</td><td>●</td><td>58</td></tr>
<tr><td>8 Using a Research Notebook</td><td>●</td><td>●</td><td>●</td><td>60</td></tr>
<tr><td>RELATED LESSONS: Research: Lesson 3, Taking Notes</td><td></td><td></td><td></td><td>50</td></tr>
<tr><td>9 Keep a List of Sources</td><td></td><td>●</td><td>●</td><td>62</td></tr>
<tr><td>RELATED LESSONS: Research: Lesson 3, Taking Notes</td><td></td><td></td><td></td><td>50</td></tr>
</table>

<table>
<tr><td>◯ Planning</td><td></td><td></td><td></td><td></td></tr>
<tr><td>1 Selecting a Format for Writing</td><td>●</td><td>●</td><td>●</td><td>66</td></tr>
<tr><td>RELATED LESSONS: Presenting: Lesson 4, Presenting Electronically</td><td></td><td></td><td></td><td>152</td></tr>
<tr><td>2 Planning with Text Structure: Explanation</td><td></td><td>●</td><td>●</td><td>68</td></tr>
<tr><td>3 Planning with a Graphic Organizer: Cause and Effect</td><td>●</td><td>●</td><td>●</td><td>70</td></tr>
<tr><td>4 Planning for Generalizations</td><td>●</td><td>●</td><td>●</td><td>72</td></tr>
<tr><td>RELATED LESSONS: Drafting: Lesson 2, Turning Research Notes into Running Text</td><td></td><td></td><td></td><td>86</td></tr>
<tr><td>5 Plan to Write with Imagery</td><td></td><td>●</td><td>●</td><td>74</td></tr>
<tr><td>RELATED LESSONS: Word Choice: Lesson 8, Select Words that Evoke Strong Imagery</td><td></td><td></td><td></td><td>216</td></tr>
<tr><td>6 Planning an Informational Poem</td><td>●</td><td>●</td><td>●</td><td>76</td></tr>
<tr><td>RELATED LESSONS: Word Choice: Lesson 1, Use Descriptive Words and Phrases</td><td></td><td></td><td></td><td>202</td></tr>
</table>

MASTER LESSON CHART

MASTER LESSON CHART

MASTER LESSON CHART

MASTER LESSON CHART

Organization

Word Choice

MASTER LESSON CHART

MASTER LESSON CHART

Sentence Structure

		3	4	5	Page
1	**Two-Word Sentences**	●	●	●	**274**
	RELATED LESSONS: *Sentence Fluency:* Lesson 1, Sentences Are of Varying Lengths				228
2	**Write Complete Sentences**	●	●	●	**276**
	RELATED LESSONS: *Sentence Structure:* Lesson 1, Two-Word Sentences				274
3	**Compound Sentences**	●	●	●	**278**
	RELATED LESSONS: *Revising:* Lesson 9, Combine Sentences				124
4	**Opening Element**	●	●	●	**280**
	RELATED LESSONS: *Sentence Fluency:* Lesson 3, Using a Variety of Sentence Beginnings				232
5	**Appositive: An Interrupter that Renames or Explains**	●	●	●	**282**
6	**Inserting a Closer**	●	●	●	**284**
	RELATED LESSONS: *Grammar:* Lesson 5, Add Action with Gerunds				334

Text Features

		3	4	5	Page
1	**Powerful Titles**	●	●	●	**288**
	RELATED LESSONS: *Punctuation and Capitalization:* Lesson 6, Capitalize Headings and Titles				322
2	**Effective Headings**	●	●	●	**290**
	RELATED LESSONS: *Organization:* Lesson 5, Using Headings to Group Related Information				188
	Punctuation and Capitalization: Lesson 6, Capitalize Headings and Titles				322
3	**Using Photographs**	●	●	●	**292**
	RELATED LESSONS: *Presenting:* Lesson 2, Inserting Illustrations and Visuals				148
4	**Bold Words**	●	●	●	**294**
	RELATED LESSONS: *Word Choice:* Lesson 5, Using Domain-Specific Vocabulary				210
5	**Cutaway Diagram with Labels**		●	●	**296**
	RELATED LESSONS: *Word Choice:* Lesson 1, Use Descriptive Words and Phrases				202
	Presenting: Lesson 2, Inserting Illlustrations and Visuals				148
6	**Table of Contents**	●	●	●	**298**
	RELATED LESSONS: *Presenting:* Lesson 3, Infusing Text Features				150
7	**Chart/Table/Graph**	●	●	●	**300**
	RELATED LESSONS: *Research:* Lesson 6, Represent Facts Visually				56
8	**Citing Sources**		●	●	**302**
	RELATED LESSONS: *Research:* Lesson 9, Keep a List of Sources				62
9	**Add Captions to Visuals**		●	●	**304**
	RELATED LESSONS: *Presenting:* Lesson 3, Infusing Text Features				150

MASTER LESSON CHART

MASTER LESSON CHART

Research

The Heart of Nonfiction Writing

Research and the gathering of factual information is the heart of nonfiction writing. This is the time when writers explore the world around them, reflect on their learning, separate fact from opinion, and consider how to share their understandings with others. Research may take the form of observation, reading, real-life experience, focused listening and reflection, or Internet and digital sources. In all cases, writers must learn to determine importance, synthesize their understandings, and prepare to transfer their thinking to print.

LESSON	3	4	5	RELATED LESSONS
1 Selecting the Best Sources for Research		●	●	
2 Alphabox: Identify Important Words and Phrases	●	●	●	*Word Choice:* Lesson 1, Use Descriptive Words and Phrases *Word Choice:* Lesson 2, Target Powerful Action Verbs
3 Taking Notes	●	●	●	*Research:* Lesson 2, Alphabox: Identify Important Words and Phrases *Text Features:* Lesson 4, Bold Words
4 Use the Key Word Strategy	●	●	●	*Research:* Lesson 8, Using a Research Notebook
5 Very Important Points (VIP) Strategy	●	●	●	*Research:* Lesson 4, Use the Key Word Strategy
6 Represent Facts Visually	●	●	●	*Text Features:* Lesson 5, Cutaway Diagram with Labels *Text Features:* Lesson 7, Chart/Table/Graph
7 Pocket Organizers: Collecting Facts	●	●	●	
8 Using a Research Notebook	●	●	●	*Research:* Lesson 3, Taking Notes
9 Keep a List of Sources		●	●	*Research:* Lesson 3, Taking Notes

Selecting the Best Sources for Research

WHEN TO USE IT: To assist researchers in choosing the best print resources

FOCUS THE LEARNING

Student researchers can easily assume that if a book is in print, it is high quality and accurate. Establishing criteria for selection of resources results in better-quality research.

Model

Select several resources on a topic of interest, some of which have current copyright dates, and authors who are known experts.

STEP 1: Demonstrate how to consider the usefulness and credibility of a print resource.

Possible Think-Aloud: *To determine the credibility and usefulness of these resources on bats, I need to first look at the copyright dates to see if the information is current.* Amazing Bats *has a copyright of 2005.* Bat Loves the Night *is 2001.* Bat Talk *is 2009.* Bats *is 1986. I may not keep the 1986 resource for my research because it is not very current, but I will check the credibility of the authors to make my final choices. Watch as I look at the back cover and inside of the dust cover. I see that Seymour Simon has written 250 science books for children, more than half of which have won awards from the National Science Teachers Association. That suggests his work is well researched and credible.* Bat Talk *is from the Bat Conservation Society and is written by zoologists. That's good, too.* Bats *is by a group called Adventures Inc. They don't list any references about the author. That makes me suspicious.*

TURN &TALK *Which of these four do you think is worthy of using for research? Support your thinking.*

STEP 2: Show students how you evaluate the usefulness of research materials.

Possible Think-Aloud: *Now it is time to analyze the usefulness of each of these resources. I will skim to examine photographs, labeled diagrams, and visual supports. I see that* Amazing Bats *and* Bat Talk *have powerful photographs. Nicola Davies' book has detailed*

Sample Modeled Writing

VARIATIONS

For Less Experienced Writers: Analyze only one or two elements of the rating tool until students become confident in making high-quality selections for research.

For More Experienced Writers: Apply this rating tool or one the students design to resources on the Internet.

drawings and sketches. *Let's look at text features.* Bat Talk *has a table of contents. And none of the three has an index.*

TURN &TALK *Would you use these books even though they don't have very many text features?*

Analyze

STEP 3: Rate the tools and decide if they should be used.

Possible Think-Aloud: *I am going to use a rating tool for print sources to rate these resources.* (Display a copy of the tool.) *Let's review the decisions we have made and check them off on the chart. Watch as I insert the copyright dates in the second row. The form asks for an analysis, but the only one I need to add a comment on is the 1986 copyright. I will simply write, "too old."* (Continue filling out rows.) *The last row is critical. This is where I decide if I will use a resource and to what degree I will use it. For the first title,* Bat Talk, *I will mark the last option, "absolutely." For the* Bat *piece by Adventures Inc., I will mark the opposite. This one is a definite no. Think together. How would you rate these sources, overall?*

Sum It Up

We can confirm the quality of the resource by looking at the copyright date and the credentials of the author. We can also look at visual supports, text features, and the writing itself.

LINKS TO CD-ROM:
• Rating Tool for Print Sources

Alphabox: Identify Important Words and Phrases

WHEN TO USE IT: To focus writers on collecting content-based vocabulary

FOCUS THE LEARNING

When nonfiction writers collect important words and phrases from their reading and store them in an Alphabox, they have a rich cache of content-specific words to infuse into their writing.

Model

Before the lesson, create an Alphabox on chart paper using a grid that is five spaces across and five spaces down.

STEP 1: Model how to determine importance of content-specific words, and record those words in an Alphabox.

Possible Think-Aloud: *I am gathering research about Harriet Tubman and have learned that she was subjected to cruel beatings when she was a slave. That's terrible! But it is also important to her life, so I want to save "cruel beatings" and "slave" in an Alphabox. Once they are in the Alphabox, those important words will remind me to include these facts in my writing about Harriet Tubman. (Pause and insert words.) The book also says that when she was 12, she was beaten so badly that she had a head injury and suffered from narcolepsy for the rest of her life. Narcolepsy is a brain disorder that causes people to feel overly sleepy—even during the daytime. I will add "narcolepsy" to the Alphabox because that could really affect Harriet Tubman's ability to function.*

TURN &TALK *Use the words that are in the Alphabox so far to summarize what you know about Harriet Tubman.*

STEP 2: Extract words from the Alphabox, and show students how you integrate them into a piece of writing.

Alphaboxes

Topic _Harriet Tubman_

A	B	C Cruel beatings Conductor	D Danger
E Escort	F Freedom	G	H
I Injured her head	J	K	L Liberate slaves
M	N Narcolepsy Network of safe houses	O	P Path to freedom
Q	R Return trips	S Slave	T
U Underground Railroad	V	W	X Y Z

Sample Modeled Writing

Possible Think-Aloud: *To begin a piece of nonfiction writing about Harriet Tubman, I can use the Alphabox to fuel my thinking and remind myself of important words I gathered while I was researching. Watch as I use "slave" and "cruel beatings" to launch my first sentence. "Harriet Tubman was born . . . young." With an Alphabox I am not even tempted to copy sentences from a book. With all these words from my research, writing flows naturally. It is natural to talk about the result of the beatings next, so I will pull "injured her head" and "narcolepsy" from the Alphabox. Check my thinking as I write: "When she was . . . life."*

> Harriet Tubman was born a slave and subjected to cruel beatings from the time she was young. When she was twelve, an overseer injured her head so seriously that she suffered from narcolepsy for the rest of her life. When she finally escaped, she devoted the rest of her life to helping other slaves find the Underground Railroad and escorting them to freedom.

Sample Modeled Writing

TURN &TALK *Examine the Alphabox and select two or three words that fit together. Then, create a sentence about Harriet Tubman. Show me a thumbs up when you and your partner have reached agreement on a sentence.*

Analyze

STEP 3: Reread and reflect.

Possible Think-Aloud: *Let's reread my writing and think together. Have I covered the most important ideas about Harriet Tubman? Are there any other words in the Alphabox that are important to understanding her life?*

Sum It Up

Selecting and saving the most important words and phrases is a key factor in creating powerful writing. With an Alphabox, you have a great tool for collecting and saving content-specific words and phrases. You can use Alphabox words in labeled diagrams, as headings and titles, and most certainly as fuel for strong sentences on your topic.

VARIATIONS

For Less Experienced Writers: Demonstrate how to use a variety of sources for words and phrases to insert into an Alphabox.

For More Experienced Writers: Show writers how to extend beyond literal words taken directly from research and begin to infuse inferences. For example, *The references never said that Harriet Tubman was brave, but **I can infer** that she was very brave since it has been confirmed that she made at least 19 trips back into slave territory to escort runaways to freedom, even though those trips placed her in danger. Inferences can be added to the Alphabox in a different color.*

LINKS TO CD-ROM:
• Alphaboxes

Taking Notes

WHEN TO USE IT: To help writers understand that they don't need to write complete sentences when researching

FOCUS THE LEARNING

Writers can easily become discouraged with research if they are writing too much when taking notes.

Model

Either make copies of "Amelia Earhart" from the Resources CD-ROM, or project it onto a screen with a document camera or projection system.

STEP 1: Demonstrate how to take notes from research.

Possible Think-Aloud: *Writers, one of the tricks that researchers learn is to limit the number of words they use when taking notes. When you find a great fact that you want to remember, the secret is to jot a phrase or make a bulleted list. You don't need to write articles and extra words—just the words that will help you remember the fact. Watch how I do it. The first sentence says that she was a nurse's aide and social worker. I definitely don't need the article, "and." Watch as I simplify and use a dash: "Nurse's aide—social worker." It goes on to say she took her first flying lessons in 1921. I can really shorten that: "1921 first lessons." As the passage continues, it says that she bought a plane and began setting records.*

Amelia Earhart

Nurse's aide—social worker

1921 first lessons

Purchased plane

Newfoundland to Wales—1928 trio— 21 hours.
Set records. Ticker tape parade NY

Atlantic Crossing—1932—Distinguished
Flying Cross

Sample Modeled Writing

TURN &TALK *Think together and shorten that sentence into brief notes with clues to help you remember what you learned in this research.*

STEP 2: Continue modeling note writing.

Possible Think-Aloud: *The next section is about a long-distance flight with two co-pilots from Newfoundland to Wales. That was a record that earned Amelia Earhart a ticker-tape parade in New York. Watch as I write brief notes and cluster them together. By clustering the notes on this event together, I will remember to write about them in the same paragraph when I start drafting. Notice as I write: "Newfoundland to Wales—1928 trio—21 hours. Set records. Ticker tape parade NY." Do you see how "Newfoundland to Wales" is like a heading for the notes on this event? I am thinking it will be good to create a heading for the notes I wrote about her previous occupation, her first lessons, and so on.*

TURN &TALK *Think together and create a heading for the notes about her life before she became famous.*

Analyze

STEP 3: Continue jotting brief notes.

Possible Think-Aloud: *Amelia Earhart became a national hero when she flew solo across the Atlantic Ocean. Watch as I create another heading and cluster my notes about that part of her life. "Atlantic Crossing—1932—Distinguished Flying Cross." Brief notes and headings make research go quickly! Let's reread the passage to be sure that my notes have covered the most important understandings from this passage.*

Sum It Up

Note writing is a text type of its own. You can't use very many words, so you have to focus on giving yourself clues that will help you remember. It also helps to cluster notes together under headings because those will make great paragraphs when it is time to begin drafting.

VARIATIONS

For Less Experienced Writers: Provide coaching in small groups to support determining importance and jotting brief phrases and words.

For More Experienced Writers: Practice taking notes from a short video or other presentation that does not have a written text to use as support in determining importance.

LINKS TO CD-ROM:
• Amelia Earhart

Use the Key Word Strategy

WHEN TO USE IT: To help writers identify key words and phrases when researching

FOCUS THE LEARNING

The key word strategy is one that should reside in a prominent place on the tool belt of every researcher because it helps readers to extract key words and prepare to use them in writing.

Model

You will want to have a copy of *A Drop of Water* by Walter Wick or another high-quality nonfiction resource as the focus of this lesson.

STEP 1: Demonstrate how to extract key words and phrases using sticky notes.

Possible Think-Aloud: *As I read from* A Drop of Water *by Walter Wick, I am going to collect key words and phrases that capture the most important ideas. Once I have collected key words, I can use them to summarize my research about how frost is formed.* (Display the book, page 32.) *The book says that water vapor condenses on cold surfaces, so I will write "water vapor" on a large sticky note. Next, I will take a second sticky note and write "condensation"—another important term. I put the key words and phrases on separate sticky notes so I can move them around and consider ways in which I would like to use them.* (Continue reading and collecting content-specific words and phrases, writing each on a separate sticky note.)

TURN &TALK *I have identified the key word, "condensation," and a phrase, "water vapor." Are those the words you would have selected? Are there any others that I should add?*

STEP 2: Continue modeling how to extract key words, and then begin to use them in writing.

Possible Think-Aloud: (Select six to eight additional key words and phrases to work with.) *Now I can arrange these sticky notes in an order that will help me see relationships in the ideas within my research.* (Show students how you can rearrange the sticky notes into categories.) *I can cluster "frost" and "solid" together because frost is a solid. I could link "condensation," "gas," and "water vapor." Those are ideas that link well together. Watch as*

I move the key words from my research around so I can see the relationships in the ideas. This makes it easier to write sentences. Watch as I write: "Have you ever . . . rained?" Did you notice that I wrote "frost" in bold? That makes it stand out as a key word, which helps my reader.

Have you ever wondered how **frost** forms on windows, even when it hasn't rained? When there is a sudden drop in temperature, **water vapor** will condense on cold surfaces—just like you see on a cold glass of soda on a warm summer day. If the **temperature** drops below freezing, the damp **condensation** that clings to a glass, a window, or even a spider web turns into **frost** because the **water vapor** has changed from a **gas** into a **solid**.

Sample Modeled Writing

TURN &TALK *Examine the key words that are displayed, and think together to construct a sentence that uses key words.*

Analyze

STEP 3: Reread and reflect.

Possible Think-Aloud: *As a researcher, I want to be sure that my facts are accurate and that I bring a reader the most important ideas and details. I also need to be sure that I provide examples that help a reader link new understandings to things that are familiar in their world. Watch as I write sentence two. I will add a dash and "just like you see on a cold glass of soda on a warm summer day." Researchers can find the facts, but those facts will have the most power when they are offered with comparisons that help readers understand. Let's reread and be sure we have both great research and easily understood writing.*

Sum It Up

When researching, read your resources carefully and select only the most important words and phrases. Write each word or phrase on a separate sticky note. Then, experiment with different ways to cluster the key words, creating links between ideas from the research. Once the key words are clustered, your research is ready to become powerful nonfiction writing.

VARIATIONS

For Less Experienced Writers: Work with short passages so writers do not become overwhelmed by large numbers of facts. Once a few key words have been gathered, switch to another book on the same topic, and gather additional words. Then, rearrange the categories, showing writers that there are multiple ways to arrange and use the words they gather in research.

For More Experienced Writers: Extend key words to inferences, offering inferences, such as *Frost is nature's artwork, forming beautiful patterns on clear surfaces.* The text does not say this, but it can be safely inferred from the photos and descriptive text.

LINKS TO CD-ROM:
• Key Word Strategy

Very Important Points (VIP) Strategy

WHEN TO USE IT: To assist researchers in determining importance

The Very Important Points strategy helps nonfiction researchers by limiting the number of details they can mark as important within a given passage.

Model

Display the passage about the octopus using a projection system and your computer, or print copies for the students so they can read along. You will want to use a paper copy of the piece so you can place sticky notes directly onto the page.

STEP 1: Show how to cut sticky notes into thin strips and place them as markers for important ideas in a text or in an illustration.

Possible Think-Aloud: *I am going to use a research strategy called the VIP strategy. That stands for "Very Important Points." As I read, I will be researching and trying to locate the very most important ideas. When I find one, I will use a strip of sticky note to mark the research point I have selected. I am only going to allow myself to use four strips of sticky note material in this passage so I won't be tempted to mark too many things. The passage says that an octopus appears to be all head and arms. That is interesting, but I don't think it is worthy of a VIP—most people know that. The research passage also says that each of the tentacles has two alternating rows of suction cups. Watch as I place a strip of sticky note material on the phrase "alternating rows of suction cups." Those are research points I definitely want to include in my writing.*

TURN &TALK *I have used one of my VIPs. Do you think I made a good choice? Is this a very important research point? Why? Would you have selected a different VIP?*

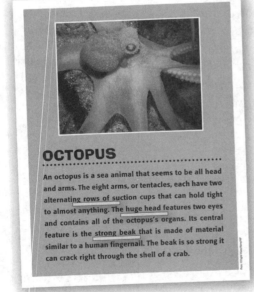

OCTOPUS

An octopus is a sea animal that seems to be all head and arms. The eight arms, or tentacles, each have two alternating rows of suction cups that can hold tight to almost anything. The huge head features two eyes and contains all of the octopus's organs. Its central feature is the strong beak that is made of material similar to a human fingernail. The beak is so strong it can crack right through the shell of a crab.

Sample Modeled Writing

STEP 2: Continue reading and identifying VIPs.

Possible Think-Aloud: *Let's read on and see if there are more research points to mark with VIPs. The next sentence says all of the organs are in the head! That is amazing. Its stomach, its brain, everything is crammed into that huge head. That is definitely a VIP. I need to include that research point in my writing.* (Position a sticky note.)

TURN & TALK *There are two sentences left and two VIPs to use. You may want to consider one VIP for each sentence or use both of them in the same sentence. Read together and identify two VIPs that you think are important research points.*

Analyze

STEP 3: Reread and reflect.

Possible Think-Aloud: *Let's review the research points we have marked with VIPs: "alternating rows of suction cups," "organs in the head," "strong beak." That's only three! We have one left. Good for us for being careful. Now we have an important task. We need to reread and see if there is a good place to use the VIP in this section or decide to save it so we have an extra to spend on the next section of the research. Let's read and think together. Research requires that we determine importance very carefully.*

Sum It Up

Researchers, once you have marked VIPs, you are ready to jot short notes and collect your research findings in a research notebook (see Research, Lesson 8), in your writer's notebook, or even in a pocket organizer (see Research, Lesson 7). When you identify Very Important Points in your research, you are being thoughtful and selective—demonstrating the heart of good research.

VARIATIONS

For Less Experienced Writers: Be sure to model how to mark VIPs in visuals such as photographs, illustrations, and diagrams because these are powerful sources of research information.

For More Experienced Writers: Ask writers to justify their thinking as they select VIPs. Why did they mark point A versus point B? Why is this important to your topic? How might it be used in the writing you will be doing?

LINKS TO CD-ROM:
• Octopus

Represent Facts Visually

WHEN TO USE IT: To help researchers capture important images and words in a visual format

Model

Before the lesson, select a book on volcanoes or a topic of interest to your students to support your think-aloud.

STEP 1: Model how to read and then pause to consider points of research to collect in a labeled diagram.

Possible Think-Aloud: *As I read this selection on volcanoes, I am going to pause frequently to reflect on research points that I think are important. Then, I will work on capturing my research in a labeled diagram. Diagrams are very helpful to researchers, readers, and nonfiction writers. This first section says that a volcano is a rupture in the planet's crust that allows hot magma, volcanic ash, and gas to escape from far below the surface. Watch as I begin a sketch of a volcano.* (Sketch a volcanic cone.) *Now I want to capture important words from my reading and research. I will write "rupture" with an arrow to point where the volcanic cone and the earth connect. I am going to jot "magma," "ash," and "gas" on scrap paper because as I continue my research, I suspect I will learn more about those topics. In reading on, I see that there is a plate of bedrock. Watch as I add a thick layer of bedrock underneath the volcano and then insert a label so I can remember what this layer represents. The next research point I will add is the magma chamber. I will show this as a pool that lies below the bedrock but will run a conduit or natural pipe from the deep magma chamber through the bedrock and up to the top of the volcanic cone.*

TURN &TALK *Partners, look closely at my labeled diagram and identify the facts from research that I have included so far. Think together and summarize your learning, using the elements of the labeled diagram.*

STEP 2: Think aloud as you continue reading, sketching, and labeling.

Possible Think-Aloud: *I will continue reading and researching. Now I am ready to use "magma," "ash," and "gas"—those words that I set aside earlier—because I understand how they all fit together. I already referred to the magma chamber below the surface, but there can also be magma in the conduit. I need to add that label. The vent* (add a label at the top of the cone) *is where the ash cloud escapes. The ash is pushed up by escaping gases, so I need to add the label "gas." Notice as I draw an ash cloud above the vent and add the labels.*

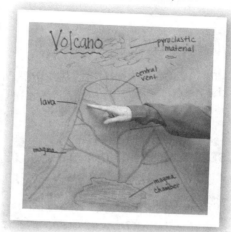

Sample Modeled Writing

TURN &TALK *Evaluate my labeled diagram. Have I included all the key points from the research we gathered from the book? Are there any other details or labels that should be added?*

Analyze

STEP 3: Reread and reflect.

Possible Think-Aloud: *Wow. This labeled diagram is just packed with research facts. I can see that this will be useful in several ways. As I continue to research, I can keep adding details and labels to the diagram. When I begin to write, I can use the diagram to remind myself of the important information I gathered when I was researching. I also think it would be great to include a final copy of this diagram next to the text I will write. That would help a reader, too.*

Sum It Up

Labeled diagrams are helpful tools for researchers. When gathering research with a diagram, you read, pause, sketch, and add labels—then do more research.

VARIATIONS

For Less Experienced Writers: Show writers that research can be collected in a series of sketches, focusing on different categories of information on a topic.

For More Experienced Writers: Show these writers how to use sketches to create a storyboard that organizes research facts and supports a stream of organization for the research.

Pocket Organizers: Collecting Facts

WHEN TO USE IT: To support writers in organizing facts from multiple sources

FOCUS THE LEARNING

Research can quickly become overwhelming if writers don't have an easy-to-use system of clustering and saving facts as they are gathered.

Model

Prepare for this lesson by printing "Ecological Nightmare" from the Resources CD-ROM and identifying two other resources on the same topic. Then, create a pocket organizer with envelopes and a file folder per the photo in this lesson.

STEP 1: Demonstrate how to collect facts on small squares of paper and save them in categories on the pocket organizer.

Possible Think-Aloud: *As we read the readers theater script, "Ecological Nightmare," I am going to collect facts on these small pieces of paper and put them into my pocket organizer.* (Have teams read through "All: Grave danger lurks. . . .") *To collect the research facts, I don't need sentences—just words and phrases. Watch as I use a small rectangle of paper and write a fact: "poisoned by plastic fragments." I will slip this fact into the envelope on the pocket organizer that is labeled "Effect on Sea Life." Another fact that I want to record is that there is danger to our food chain. That has huge implications for people. This time I will use a square and write, "danger to food chain." I will put this fact into the envelope labeled "The Problem." A pocket organizer keeps facts organized inside their envelopes until you are ready to write.* (Have teams continue reading to the end, and then model selection and insertion of facts into the pocket organizer.)

TURN &TALK *Think about the facts that I selected. Would you have chosen them for your own research? If your facts were different, in which pockets would you place them?*

STEP 2: Add additional details from two different resources.

Possible Think-Aloud: *Researchers need to collect facts from multiple sources. Every resource has an author with biases and perspectives, so it is important to read the work of several knowledgeable writers and collect facts from many places.* (Display a new resource on the topic, and begin to read and collect facts, inserting them into the pocket organizer.) *Notice how I can use the same pocket organizer to collect facts even though I am using*

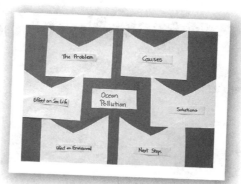

Sample Modeled Writing

different resources. Writers, watch as I empty the envelope on "Effect on Sea Life." I want to analyze it and see if I have a good balance in my facts. I have used two resources so far. Once I analyze the facts I have gathered, I can decide if I have enough information on this subtopic or if I need more. The facts in this envelope include . . . . (Read them or display them under a document camera.)

TURN &TALK *Are my facts strong enough, or do I need to find more on the effect on sea life? Be ready to support your thinking.*

Analyze

STEP 3: Reread and reflect.

Possible Think-Aloud: *Get ready. I am going to take the facts out of another pocket. You will need to analyze them and decide if the research is adequate. If you think there are enough facts, we will work together and construct a paragraph using these facts. If you think we need more information, then back to research we go.*

Sum It Up

Pocket organizers make it possible to merge facts from many sources, organizing them into meaningful categories that will translate to organized paragraphs. The secret is to record facts on rectangles of paper and then slip the facts into the correct envelope in the organizer. It is helpful to remove facts periodically and assess them to determine if there is enough research on the topic or if more is needed.

VARIATIONS

For Less Experienced Writers: Show writers that the rectangles can capture sketches as well as words and phrases to round out the research they can draw from when they begin to write.

For More Experienced Writers: Staple a page to the back of the organizer, and use it as a place to record references that were used in the research.

LINKS TO CD-ROM:
• "Ecological Nightmare"

Using a Research Notebook

WHEN TO USE IT: To help writers organize their research, even when using multiple sources

FOCUS THE LEARNING

Research notebooks are another format for collecting and organizing information. In a simple blank book, one page is dedicated to each subtopic of the research. Then, writers flip to the correct pages to record facts as they are identified in research.

Model

To prepare for the lesson, print "All Wrapped Up" from the Resources CD-ROM.

STEP 1: Demonstrate how to assemble a research notebook.

Possible Think-Aloud: *When I am researching and gathering information for my writing, it really helps to use a research notebook. Watch as I stack 10 half sheets of plain paper and then staple them together. Next, I need to identify subtopics that I expect to encounter in my research and write one subtopic on each page. There should be extra pages because research usually uncovers subtopics that I hadn't thought of before I started. My topic is "Mummies." I can generate subtopics by considering what I hope to learn as well as what I expect to find in the way of categories of information. I know that one subtopic will be "Where have mummies been found?" Another one needs to be "What was the process of mummification used in Egypt?" I need two pages in the research notebook for this one because I know there is a lot of information.*

TURN &TALK *Think together. What are some of the subtopics that I might encounter in research about mummies? What would you want to learn if you were researching this topic? Create a list.*

STEP 2: Write one subtopic on each page of the research notebook, and begin gathering facts.

Possible Think-Aloud: *It is interesting to know that mummies have been found all over the world. This is a fact that I would like to add to my research notebook. This research point doesn't fit with the process of mummification or cultural beliefs. I will add it on the page with the heading "Where have mummies been found?" Notice that as I enter the fact in the research notebook, I don't use sentences.*

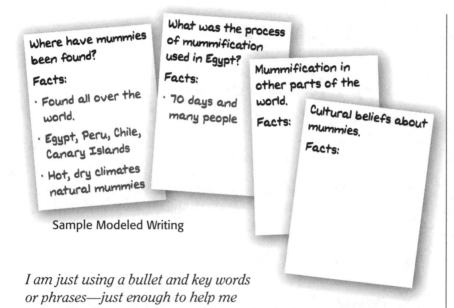

Sample Modeled Writing

I am just using a bullet and key words or phrases—just enough to help me remember later when I go to write. I also find it amazing that the Egyptian process took 70 days and the labor of many people. That's expensive! Watch as I enter that fact with a bullet on the page about mummification in Egypt.

TURN &TALK *How might a research notebook help you when you are researching and gathering facts?*

Analyze

STEP 3: Reread and reflect.

Possible Think-Aloud: *I realize that I need a page for a reference list. I need to be sure to use multiple sources, so I need to write down the ones I use. Watch as I flip to the back of my research notebook and add a page for references. I want to include the title of the piece, the author, and the copyright date for sure.*

Sum It Up

Research notebooks are helpful tools that give writers a way to organize facts and get ready to write. To make a research notebook, you just need plain paper and a stapler. Then, you identify subtopics and related topics you hope to understand as a result of your research. Then, start collecting facts.

VARIATIONS

For Less Experienced Writers: Confer with writers and review their research notebooks with them to be sure that they understand the concept of recording only key words and phrases—not sentences.

For More Experienced Writers: Model how to extract facts from a page and use them to create organized paragraphs.

LINKS TO CD-ROM:
• "All Wrapped Up"

Keep a List of Sources

WHEN TO USE IT: To heighten awareness of the importance of citing sources

FOCUS THE LEARNING

Writers of nonfiction need to cite their sources because this gives credibility to the work and the quality of the information.

Model

To prepare for this lesson, gather an array of nonfiction selections that students can investigate while searching for the copyright date and publisher.

STEP 1: Demonstrate where to find citation information in nonfiction books.

Possible Think-Aloud: *As I prepare to create a list of the sources I used in my research, I have several things to consider. I need to take care and write the title of each resource as accurately as possible and then list the author and the year of copyright. In some cases, I may want to list the publisher as well. If I am typing the list on the computer, I need to italicize the title of the book. If I am writing it out by hand, then the title of the book is underlined. Watch as I write out "Salmon Stream by Carol Reed-Jones." I got that information off the cover of the book. Now I need to look for the copyright date. This can be tricky because the copyright can be found in different places. In a hardcover book, it is usually on the back of the title page. In paperback books, it could be on the back of the title page, on the inside of the front cover, or even on the inside of the back cover of the book. One of the books I found had the copyright on the back cover! Finding the copyright sometimes requires a bit of detective work.*

TURN &TALK *I have passed out an array of nonfiction resources that are similar to those you have been using for research. Work together and find the copyright dates in two of the books.*

STEP 2: Show students where to look for information on the publisher.

> Sources:
>
> <u>Swimmer</u> by Carolyn Gilman, Boyds Mill Press, 2008
>
> <u>Salmon Stream</u> by Carol Reed-Jones, Scholastic, 2000

Sample Modeled Writing

Possible Think-Aloud: *I have decided to add the publisher to my list of sources. In this book, the publisher is on the title page. In a second book, you can see that it is not on the title page, but it is on the back cover. This is another opportunity for some detective work.*

TURN &TALK *Dive into your books again, and identify the publisher of each resource.*

Analyze

STEP 3: Reread and reflect.

Possible Think-Aloud: *A list of sources is important for researchers. You need evidence that you have searched and found reliable facts to incorporate into your writing. When you present a list of sources with your nonfiction writing, a reader can see that your copyright dates are recent.*

Sum It Up

As you move up through the grades, you will be expected to cite, in more formal ways, the sources you've used for research. Citing sources is important because it shows that the facts you include in your writing are true and reliable. A list of sources like the one you've created today can show your readers as well as your teacher which sources you have used to research and support the facts in your writing.

VARIATIONS:

For Less Experienced Writers: Focus on the title and author to provide practice in citing sources without creating stress.

For More Experienced Writers: Have these writers analyze reference lists, citation lists, and bibliographies to note the various formats for reporting sources. Show them how to cite a website with < > and the date the information was accessed.

Planning

Thinking, Organizing, and Preparing to Write

The planning phase of the writing process is one that should be rich in conversations about the purpose for the writing, the intended audience, and the organizational structures that will lead to nonfiction writing that is thoughtfully laid out—bringing maximum impact to a reader. When the planning portion of process writing is given adequate time and attention, writers express themselves more fully and present writing that is thoughtfully constructed and layered in rich detail.

LESSON	3	4	5	RELATED LESSONS
1 Selecting a Format for Writing	●	●	●	*Presenting:* Lesson 4, Presenting Electronically
2 Planning with Text Structure: Explanation		●	●	
3 Planning with a Graphic Organizer: Cause and Effect	●	●	●	
4 Planning for Generalizations		●	●	*Drafting:* Lesson 2, Turning Research Notes into Running Text
5 Plan to Write with Imagery		●	●	*Word Choice:* Lesson 8, Select Words that Evoke Strong Imagery
6 Planning an Informational Poem	●	●	●	*Word Choice:* Lesson 1, Use Descriptive Words and Phrases
7 Planning Page Layout	●	●	●	*Presenting:* Lesson 3, Infusing Text Features *Text Features:* Lessons 2–11
8 Using a Flowchart	●	●	●	

Selecting a Format for Writing

WHEN TO USE IT: To help writers realize that there are many ways to present and share writing

FOCUS THE LEARNING

Writers need to learn how to present their writing in a wide variety of formats that may include posters, multiple-page books, electronic slide shows, visual displays, and even movies.

Model

To prepare for this lesson, utilize a projection system to display the poster, the multiple-page book, and the electronic slide show on the Resources CD-ROM for the students to view.

STEP 1: Introduce writers to a variety of formats they might consider as they plan a piece of writing.

Possible Think-Aloud: *Writers, I am planning a persuasive piece on protecting the earth. I have done the research. Now it is time to decide how I will present my research to others because the format I select will have an impact on the way I structure the writing itself. The first option is a poster. (Display images of posters from the Resources CD-ROM.) Notice that the paper size and the writing fonts are all enlarged. That is because a poster is designed to attract attention. It doesn't use a lot of dense writing, so words and phrases need to carry a big punch. There are also strong visuals.*

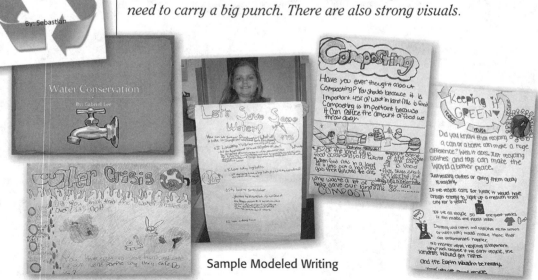

Sample Modeled Writing

TURN &TALK *Put your heads together, and discuss elements that need to be considered if you were to plan for a poster as your format.*

STEP 2: Direct your writers' attention to the issues in planning an electronic presentation such as a slide show or movie created from scans and still images.

Possible Think-Aloud: *Let's look at this electronic slide show on water conservation and consider elements that we would need to think about when planning for writing that takes this form. Each page has a heading and a photograph or clip art. That adds a lot to the visual appeal of the page. I am also noticing that there is a limited amount of text on each slide. That has implications for planning a piece of writing because densely written paragraphs wouldn't fit on the page.*

TURN &TALK *Consider the possibilities of an electronic slide show. What elements need to be included in your planning if you select this format for presenting your research?*

Analyze

STEP 3: Continue exploring formats for planning and writing.

Possible Think-Aloud: *One of my favorite formats is a multiple-page book. In this format, you can explore a topic in depth and support the writing with charts, graphs, and other interesting visuals. Because multiple-page books are bound, like those in the library, they become a treasure you can save over time. In a multiple-page book, I like to include a table of contents listing headings and showing page numbers. It is great to have an attractive cover, a title page, an index, and an "About the Author" page as well. Analyze this format and list the features you would want to consider if you were to plan this type of writing.*

Sum It Up

There are many formats for which you can plan and create non-fiction writing. What is important is that you select a format that matches your purpose and the focus of the writing you intend to create. Then, as you plan, you can set up the organizational structures you need in order to have the best possible writing within the format you have selected.

VARIATIONS

For Less Experienced Writers: Offer only one or two choices of format at a time so these writers do not become overwhelmed.

For More Experienced Writers: Stretch these writers to consider additional formats such as news articles, brochures, movies made from stills such as those you can create with iMovie and Animoto, and letters to an editor that are actually mailed to a newspaper.

LINKS TO CD-ROM:

- Reduce Reuse Recycle PowerPoint
- Water Conservation PowerPoint
- Poster 1: Let's Save Some Water
- Poster 2: Keeping it Green
- Poster 3: Water Crisis
- Poster 4: Composting

Planning for Text Structure: Explanation

WHEN TO USE IT: To help writers plan and execute writing that utilizes the structures and features of a particular text type

FOCUS THE LEARNING

Nonfiction writers need to recognize and know the features of a variety of text structures so they can choose those that best suit their topic, audience, and purpose.

Model

To prepare for this lesson, copy the "Explanation" on the Resources CD-ROM and display the writing. This lesson is based on an explanation, but please see the Resources CD-ROM for a grid showing the features of additional text structures.

STEP 1: Introduce the characteristics and features of an explanation.

Possible Think-Aloud: *We know that there are several distinct text structures, each of which has unique features. Today I will focus on an explanation. An explanation focuses on telling how or why. It could tell how hydroelectric power is generated or why super-cell thunderstorms are so dangerous. Let's read the first sentence of an explanation about the water cycle. "The water cycle sweeps water. . . ." Did you notice that the introduction told you what was about to be explained? A great introduction needs to pique reader interest without giving away details.*

> **TURN &TALK** *Think together and use your writer's notebooks to begin listing the features of an explanation.*

STEP 2: Continue analyzing an explanation and listing its features.

Possible Think-Aloud: *Another feature of an explanation is the use of linking and connecting words as information is added. These words provide several functions. The first is to show order or sequence. These words might include*

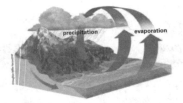

The Water Cycle

The water cycle sweeps water into the atmosphere and back to the earth in a continuing path of circulation. First, condensation in the form of a gas lifts from surface water and collects in clouds above the earth. As soon as the water content becomes high enough, the clouds expel water and precipitation is released. Depending on temperatures in the atmosphere and prevailing weather patterns, this release of moisture can results in rain, snow, sleet, hail, or fog. Evidence would suggest that this cycle of evaporation and precipitation is essential to the survival of life on Earth.

Sample Modeled Writing

Features of an Explanation	Linking and Connecting Words
• Tells how or why • Introduction stating what will be explained • Focus on relationships and interactions between elements or concepts • Conclusion • May include a labeled diagram or explanatory visual	Words to show order (first, next, then . . .): as soon as, as a result, because, to illustrate, once, therefore, since, when, even though, as a result, if . . . then Words to add information: also, because, so, in addition, to illustrate, for example, it should be noted that, a specific example Words of summation: since, because, in conclusion, evidence would suggest, to summarize, therefore

VARIATIONS

For Less Experienced Writers: Guide them in using the tool "Planning an Explanation," from the Resources CD-ROM, to support integration of their content with the features of an explanation.

For More Experienced Writers: Introduce writers to a variety of text structures, comparing and contrasting features so they begin to write with a great range of text types.

"first," "next," "then," "as soon as," and "so on." The second function of linking words in an explanation is to signal that you are adding information: "also," "because," "so in addition," "to illustrate," "to be specific."

TURN &TALK *If you were writing an explanation, what would you include in your planning? What features will you add to your list?*

Analyze

STEP 3: Write a conclusion and reflect on planning an explanation.

Possible Think-Aloud: *Great explanations need strong conclusions. Watch as I use a phrase to launch my summation: "Evidence would suggest that. . . ." That phrase signals my reader. It's a heads-up to pay attention. I also could have used "because," "based on the evidence," or "in conclusion." Come in close as I finish: "this cycle of evaporation and precipitation is essential to the existence of life." Is there anything else you want to add to your list of features for an explanation?*

Sum It Up

When planning a piece of writing, you need to select the text that matches your purpose and topic. Today we focused on an explanation. Will you use this text structure in your next piece of writing?

LINKS TO CD-ROM:
• The Water Cycle
• Planning an Explanation
• Understanding Text Structures

Planning with a Graphic Organizer: Cause and Effect

WHEN TO USE IT: To infuse structural support as writers plan

FOCUS THE LEARNING

Cause-and-effect writing can be richly supported with graphic organizers that emphasize relationships.

Model

STEP 1: Support understanding of cause-and-effect relationships.

Possible Think-Aloud: *When we talk about cause and effect, it is important to understand that most actions cause a reaction, or an effect. For example, if I were to blow air into a balloon, what would that cause to happen? What is the effect? Blowing air into the rubber tube will cause the balloon to expand. The expansion of the balloon is the effect. Now what if I were to take a pin and puncture the balloon? What would that cause to happen? What would be the effect? Life is full of cause-and-effect relationships.*

TURN &TALK *Put your heads together, and identify some causes and effects that you can think of here in the classroom, around the school, or even at home.*

STEP 2: Demonstrate the use of a graphic organizer for planning cause-and-effect writing.

Possible Think-Aloud: *When I am planning a piece of writing that involves cause and effect, it helps to use a graphic organizer. To begin, you can start with an effect and then list the causes. Or you can begin with causes and then list the effects. Watch as I work on a planning organizer for the cause and effect of dumping garbage in the ocean. I will begin with the cause and place it in a text box*

Cause/Effect Organizer 1

Cause	Effect 1	Implications
Dumping garbage in the ocean.	Fish and sea animals are being poisoned.	• Find alternatives for waste. • Recycle. • Protect the food source for animals and people. •
	Effect 2 Beaches are littered.	
	Effect 3 The food chain is affected.	Signal words for cause/effect:

Sample Modeled Writing

to the left. Watch as I write in the text box, "Dumping garbage in the ocean." Then, I will draw arrows to the effects and insert those next. In the effect boxes I will write, "Fish and animals are being poisoned. Beaches are littered. The food chain is affected." Notice that I place each effect in a separate box. To the right, I will draw a box for implications.

TURN &TALK *Think together. What might be the implications of these effects? What might happen if we don't take action? What do people need to do to protect the ocean?*

Analyze

STEP 3: Continue planning.

Possible Think-Aloud: *Another step in planning for cause-and-effect writing is to identify some helpful linking words. This kind of writing requires that we use words that signal a reader that causes and effects are connected to each other. Some of these words might include "as a result," "because," "to illustrate," "therefore," and "this resulted in." Watch as I draw another box on this organizer and make a list of some cause-and-effect words I could include when I start writing.*

Sum It Up

Cause-and-effect writing requires planning that lays out the causes and effects very clearly. It is also helpful to establish implications so the point you are making in the writing is very clear to a reader. Then, when you start writing, you infuse words that signal cause and effect to your reader.

VARIATIONS

For Less Experienced Writers: Begin by having them write causes and effects experienced in real life or in science experiments.

For More Experienced Writers: Stretch writers by having them write cause-and-effect pieces on more complex topics such as the American Civil War, the establishment of the Transportation Security Administration, and food safety practices.

LINKS TO CD-ROM:
- Cause/Effect Organizer 1
- Cause/Effect Organizer 2

Planning for Generalizations

WHEN TO USE IT: To help writers plan for generalizations that are well supported by facts

FOCUS THE LEARNING

Nonfiction writing should not read like a laundry list of facts. It can be enriched with the inclusion of well-chosen generalizations.

Model

Plan to display the facts in the modeled writing on a chart, or use a projection device.

STEP 1: Demonstrate how to create a generalization based on facts.

Possible Think-Aloud: *Generalizations are statements that link readers to big ideas and help them see connections between facts. Generalizations must be supported by real facts. For example, what would you think if I made a generalization that riding public transportation is better than driving your own car? Well, in some cases that might be true. Many people live in places where traffic, parking, and air quality make public transportation a great choice. But what about farmers and others who live in remote places? Is that generalization true for them? No. So when you make a generalization, you need to make it with care and be sure that you have the facts to back it up. Let's do a quick survey and find out who prefers apples and who prefers oranges.* (Have students vote, and base your next comment on the result.) *Based on my survey, I can make the generalization that more students in our class prefer apples over oranges.*

TURN &TALK *Analyze my generalization. Is it supported by facts and/or research? Analyze this generalization: All students like apples better than oranges. Evaluate its quality.*

STEP 2: Show how to build a generalization from facts gathered while researching.

Possible Think-Aloud: *I have facts about the average daily temperatures of some planets in the solar system. The first explains that Mercury is really hot! Three hundred and fifty-four degrees! If I wasn't being responsible, I could say, "All planets in our solar system are* warm." But there aren't enough facts to support a statement like that. Let's add another fact. The dwarf planet Pluto is brutally cold. Three hundred and ninety-three degrees below zero. Let's try a generalization. "The planets of our solar system vary greatly in temperature."

TURN &TALK *Is my generalization adequately supported by facts? Is it true? Could I prove it?*

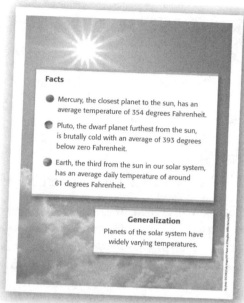

Facts

- Mercury, the closest planet to the sun, has an average temperature of 354 degrees Fahrenheit.
- Pluto, the dwarf planet furthest from the sun, is brutally cold with an average of 393 degrees below zero Fahrenheit.
- Earth, the third from the sun in our solar system, has an average daily temperature of around 61 degrees Fahrenheit.

Generalization
Planets of the solar system have widely varying temperatures.

Sample Modeled Writing

Analyze

STEP 3: Reflect on generalizations.

Possible Think-Aloud: *Let's add some more facts and see where they take us. The average daily temperature on earth is around 61 degrees Fahrenheit. Well, that supports the generalization that planets of the solar system have vastly different temperatures. But let's add more facts and see what you think. If you look at a model of the solar system, you will see that Mercury is the closest to the sun. Earth is in third position. Pluto, the dwarf planet and the coldest, is the farthest away from the sun. Put your heads together. What generalization can you make now?*

Sum It Up

Generalizations can add power to your nonfiction writing, but they must be used with care. While you are planning, check carefully to see what your facts suggest. Then, if you are sure that your facts support your thinking, plan a generalization to rev up your writing.

VARIATIONS

For Less Experienced Writers: While conferring, guide individuals in crafting generalizations from their research notes.

For More Experienced Writers: Show writers that generalizations can make great introductions and headings.

LINKS TO CD-ROM:
- Generalizations Planning Sheet

Plan to Write with Imagery

WHEN TO USE IT: To support descriptive writing that is figurative and engaging

FOCUS THE LEARNING

Imagery can significantly contribute to our sensory connections to nonfiction texts.

Model

STEP 1: Plan phrases that support imagery.

Possible Think-Aloud: *There are not many steam trains left—most are in museums. But it is amazing to think of the difference they made in travel during the westward migration. For this piece of writing, I want to plan a piece with imagery—to showcase the steam train as a respected symbol. As I plan for this writing, I need to start by looking at some visuals and then try to get a mental picture that can guide my thinking. Listen as I close my eyes and share my mental picture. (Pause.) I see the steam coming out from under the cattle guard at the front of the engine—like a beard. The dark armor that covers the front of the engine is for protection from animals on the track and from thieves who would place rocks and explosives in their way. The tracks that stretch out are like an endless road that the train must follow. Watch as I capture this in a list of phrases: "beard of white steam; dark armored face; swirling vapor. . . ."*

TURN &TALK *Describe the visual images that you constructed as I shared my images. What did you think? What did you wonder?*

STEP 2: Show students how you write sentences that contain imagery.

Possible Think-Aloud: *When you plan for writing with imagery, you need to turn your brain into an internal movie theater and play the scene in slow motion so you really see the details. Now watch as I use the phrases I listed to launch my writing. "A beard of white steam frames the dark armored face. . . ."*

Beard of white steam

Dark armored face

Swirling vapor

Endless iron road

Whistle screams

Deep, ancient lungs

Historic Steam Train

A beard of white steam frames the dark armored face. Through swirling vapor, headlights stare down an endless iron road. Suddenly, a whistle screams. Ancient lungs bellow in protest and the wheels begin to turn.

Sample Modeled Writing

TURN & TALK *Writers need to take time to plan, to visualize, and to think about a reader. If you were going to plan for a piece of writing that focuses on using imagery, what would you want to remember?*

Analyze

STEP 3: Continue planning and listing phrases. Then reflect.

Possible Think-Aloud: *Writers, let's reread my list and think about planning for a piece that includes imagery. I know that it is important to look at visuals related to the subject. I also know that I then need to set those aside and create my own mental movie, seeing the subject closely and noticing details. It helps if I visualize a bit of action related to the subject because that adds detail to my mental image. Then, I am ready to list phrases and eventually to write. Think together. Consider the steps you need to follow in planning a nonfiction piece that utilizes imagery.*

Sum It Up

Imagery is a powerful tool that nonfiction writers can use to help readers connect more closely to their topics. To use it, however, takes careful planning. You need to visualize, list helpful phrases, or think of metaphors and similes that will express the images.

VARIATIONS

For Less Experienced Writers: Have these writers focus imagery on real experiences that they have shared in a science experiment, a walk around the school, or a jarring moment when the fire alarm startled them. Emphasize the use of simile rather than metaphor, which is a more difficult concept.

For More Experienced Writers: Stretch to nonfiction poetry with imagery! There are many mentors and models to consider, but free-form poetry filled with rich images can lead writers to communicate information in new ways.

LINKS TO CD-ROM:
• Steam Train

Planning an Informational Poem

WHEN TO USE IT: When writers are planning to write poetry

FOCUS THE LEARNING

Informational poetry is another powerful way to share content.

Model

STEP 1: Create a list of facts for a poem

Possible Think-Aloud: *I am planning to write an informational poem about a coral reef. Because I am planning and this isn't a real draft yet, I want to experiment a bit. First, I need to outline my facts and think of words and images that describe the reef. I also want to put myself in the position of the reef and visualize. What am I made of? What do I look like? What can I be compared to? Watch as I write: "Calcium deposits—polyps—connect in layers—unique shapes— like antlers, trees, or delicate plants—like an underwater city." Notice that I am capturing facts and images. This kind of a list can be helpful when planning a poem. Visualize as I write: "Reef. Laden with coral in wild, wonderful shapes. Undersea illusions of antler, tree, or spiny cactus. Reef-building polyps grow and connect. Layer after layer."*

TURN &TALK *Put your heads together, and share your observations. What facts have you noticed in this early stage of my poem? What mental images can you construct with this poem?*

STEP 2: Continue listing facts and images—experimenting with lines of the poem.

Possible Think-Aloud: *Watch as I add more facts to my list and think about how this poem can teach about coral reefs. I know that skeletons are important to expanding a reef. The skeletons of urchins and sea anemone fall onto the coral, and the mixture of sand, calcium, and continuing polyp growth turns into layers of limestone. This gives strength to*

Polyps—clear branching extensions— connect in layers—unique shapes— like antlers, trees, or delicate plants— like an underwater city.

Skeletons add to layers—extend reach of the reef

Ecosystem

Limestone—colorful algae

Sample Modeled Writing

the reef, and the polyps continue to grow upon a new bed of fragile limestone. I am ready to experiment with those ideas in the poem. "Urchin and anemone skeletons meld into limestone. Spreading my reach. Layer upon layer."

Fabulous Underwater City

Reef

Coral structures in wild, wonderful shapes

Undersea illusions of antler, tree, or spiny cactus

Reef-building polyps grow and connect

Urchin and anemone skeletons meld into limestone

Spreading my reach

Layer upon layer

Enormous underwater city—colored by algae

Teeming with life—an ecosystem

Reef

Sample Modeled Writing

TURN &TALK *It is important that I plan a poem that teaches about the reef. It can use imagery, too, but it also must teach. Analyze my poem so far. Are there enough facts? Should I plan to add more?*

Analyze

STEP 3: Reread and reflect.

Possible Think-Aloud: *Let's reread the poem and see if it sounds poetic when read out loud. That is an important test. As we read, think about the rhythm and the flow of the language. That is part of planning a poem. There needs to be a rhythm—a sense of fluency— that makes it sound good to the ear.*

Sum It Up

When planning an informational poem, it is helpful to list facts and maintain a focus on teaching about the topic. Sensory images can be used, but the facts need to be the heart of the work.

VARIATIONS

For Less Experienced Writers: Have them arrange their facts– words and phrases–in a list and read them as though the list were the poem. In many cases, this informational poem format can result in a lovely poem.

For More Experienced Writers: Focus on adding simile and metaphor to increase comparisons and stimulate sensory images.

Planning Page Layout

WHEN TO USE IT: To help writers understand that layout and page design are important elements of planning nonfiction writing

FOCUS THE LEARNING

Nonfiction writers need to notice and attend to page layouts in nonfiction magazines and well-constructed resources. They need to notice page layout, placement of photos and visuals, integration of text across the page, and so on.

Model

STEP 1: Display an array of nonfiction resources including magazines, leveled reading selections, and other resources. Analyze page layouts and text arrangement on the page.

Possible Think-Aloud: *As nonfiction writers, we have a responsibility to plan great writing but also to plan pages that are visually appealing. A nonfiction writer needs to consider how pictures will be arranged, if text boxes or columns will be used, and how a two-page spread looks from a distance. Join me in looking at this wonderful nonfiction magazine. I see a beautiful two-page layout of Mars. The image of Mars spans the gutter, the place where the left-hand and right-hand pages come together. There is a large cluster of text and a title to the top left, and on the right there are several smaller text boxes with headings.* (Repeat the observation of page layout with additional resources.)

TURN &TALK *Analyze the layouts we have examined. Which ones did you find to be visually appealing? What exactly did you like? What could you do in your planning to move toward pages that look like this?*

STEP 2: Model how to plan a two-page layout.

Possible Think-Aloud: *Looking at the page layouts in the magazine and books really helped me think about planning the use of space on a two-page layout. Watch as I make a vertical dotted line down the center of this page. That is where the gutter would be in a book. I am planning a piece on kayaking. Watch as I place a sketch of a kayak right across the gutter. That is what we*

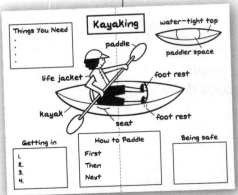

Sample Modeled Writing

saw in the magazine, and I can do it, too. I will draw a text box for the title in the center at the very top and another text box to the left for a bulleted list of "Things You Need." To keep the page in balance, I will add a labeled diagram of a kayak at the top right.

TURN &TALK *Analyze the page layout I am creating and consider its strengths. Reflect on the layouts we examined in the magazines and book, and identify some suggestions that will help me finish planning the layout for this page.*

Analyze

STEP 3: Finish the piece and reflect.

Possible Think-Aloud: *I am going to add text boxes across the bottom so I have room for some writing. On the left, I will write a list with numbered steps for how to get in the kayak. That can be tricky! In the center, I will add a text box for "How to Paddle." So far I have planned a list and two procedures. I need a different text type, so I will plan an explanation on being safe for a text box at the bottom right. Have you noticed that I am not writing the text yet? I am planning. With this page layout sketched out, I will know exactly what to write and the format in which to construct my writing. Writers, put your heads together and analyze the planning I have done. What do you need to remember as you get ready to plan your writing?*

Sum It Up

Nonfiction writers need to think about facts and information, but they also need to think about page layout. Nonfiction resources use a lot of interesting layouts, and so can we.

VARIATIONS

For Less Experienced Writers: Coach these writers and support them in understanding that a picture at the top of the page and writing at the bottom give their work a primary-grade look and feel.

For More Experienced Writers: Engage writers in evaluative analysis of page layouts in a variety of resources. Have them create lists of the features of effective layouts and then implement those features in their own work.

LINKS TO CD-ROM:
- Planning Investigation: Blob Fish Facts
- Planning Investgation: Motorcross

Using a Flowchart

WHEN TO USE IT: To plan a multiple-page book

Model

STEP 1: Demonstrate how to create a flowchart.

Possible Think-Aloud: *A flowchart is a helpful tool that helps you plan out the order in which your writing will flow and also consider placement of visuals. To create a flowchart, I draw a text box. Because I am planning, not drafting, I can jot notes and partial sentences. Watch as I begin planning for a piece on how the respiratory system of a fish works. In the first box of the flowchart, I will write, "Water into the mouth. Close mouth." It is important to understand the intake of water is through the mouth. This is a good place to add a labeled diagram to show the direction in which the water flows. I will make a note in the flowchart so I remember when I begin to draft. Now I will add another text box and an arrow to show the order of the boxes. In this box, I want to emphasize the*

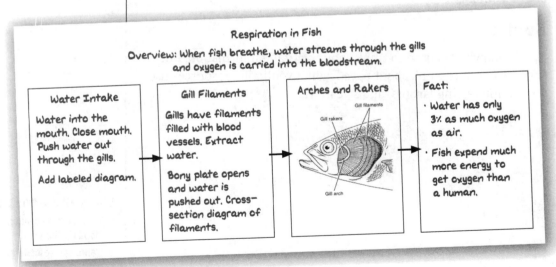

Sample Modeled Writing

structure of the gill and that the water passes through the gills on the way out of the fish's body. "Gills have . . . water." I think this information needs a cross-section diagram to show the filaments. Watch as I make a note in the box.

TURN &TALK *Remember that this is not a draft. I am planning. Consider what separates a planning experience from drafting.*

STEP 2: Continue adding to the flowchart.

Possible Think-Aloud: *I am not going to write in the next box of the flowchart. I found a great photograph online showing the internal structure of the gills with the arches and rakers. That will be important to my writing. In this box, I will write a reminder to insert the photograph or put in a print copy of it with the URL address so I remember the source. The fourth box is for some cool facts that I found. I am going to present this as a bulleted list in the final writing, so I will use bullets as I plan. That will remind me later.*

TURN &TALK *Consider the benefits of a flowchart. Think together and analyze the power of this tool for nonfiction writers.*

Analyze

STEP 3: Reread and reflect.

Possible Think-Aloud: *I realize that I need to add another element to my flowchart—headings. Headings are important, so I am going to add a heading for each box. For the first box, I will use the heading "Water Intake." Put your heads together. Select strong headings for the next two boxes.*

Sum It Up

Flowcharts are powerful planning tools that help a nonfiction writer integrate powerful facts and visuals into a tool that helps writing flow in a logical manner and stay organized.

VARIATIONS

For Less Experienced Writers: Provide a flowchart, such as the one on the Resources CD-ROM, to guide and support planning.

For More Experienced Writers: Show writers how to construct a flowchart on the computer using the "Insert Text Box" feature.

LINKS TO CD-ROM:
• Flowchart Framework

Drafting

Getting Ideas on Paper

Drafting is the time when we pour our hearts into getting a message onto paper, and generate intense intellectual activity. This is a time when nonfiction writers engage in intense intellectual activity. They are likely to be checking their resources for facts, spending time reflecting and thinking, writing a bit, rereading, and then writing some more. This is also a time when writing is and should be a bit messy, as writers must compose quickly to capture fleeting thoughts and secure language on the page.

LESSON	3	4	5	RELATED LESSONS
1 Headings Keep Writing Organized	●	●	●	*Organization:* Lesson 5, Using Headings to Group Related Information
2 Turning Research Notes into Running Text	●	●	●	*Planning:* Lesson 4, Planning for Generalizations *Research:* Lesson 4, Key Word Strategy
3 Stopping to Reread as You Write	●	●	●	
4 Infusing Transition Words and Phrases		●	●	*Sentence Fluency:* Lesson 8, Smooth Transitions with Linking Words and Phrases
5 Underline and Keep Writing	●	●		*Spelling Consciousness:* Lesson 1, Notice When Words Are Not Spelled Correctly
6 Establishing the Setting or Situation	●	●	●	*Organization:* Lesson 6, Create an Inviting Lead *Word Choice:* Lesson 4, Use Concrete Words to Support Visualization
7 Add Action	●	●	●	*Ideas:* Lesson 2, Visualize Action—Then Write *Word Choice:* Lesson 2, Target Powerful Action Verbs
8 Experimenting with Leads	●	●	●	*Organization:* Lesson 6, Create an Inviting Lead
9 Creating a Conclusion	●	●	●	*Revising:* Lesson 3, Checking the Closing *Organization:* Lesson 7, Craft an Ending that Brings Closure
10 Drafting a Persuasion		●	●	*Organization:* Lesson 9, Using a Persuasive Framework *Word Choice:* Lesson 12, Use Persuasive Language
11 Writing an Informational Poem	●	●	●	*Planning:* Lesson 6, Planning an Informational Poem

Headings Keep Writing Organized

WHEN TO USE IT: To help writers draft a clear and organized piece of nonfiction writing

FOCUS THE LEARNING

As readers of nonfiction, headings help give us a focus for reading—they tell us what to expect from a section of writing. As writers of nonfiction, headings can help us craft clear and organized drafts.

Model

STEP 1: Think aloud as you craft a heading, and then use the heading to help you write.

Possible Think-Aloud: *We know that headings serve as mini-titles that are spaced throughout a piece of writing to keep each section clear and organized. Today I want to show you how I can use headings to help me as I draft. I am ready to create a draft about the great white shark. Watch as I make a list of headings to capture the big ideas I want to include in my writing today: "Ancient Predators; Teeth, Teeth, and More Teeth; Powerful Predators." Since the first heading is "Ancient Predators," this section of my draft will need to talk about how great whites have been around for a long time. Watch as I write: "Since long before . . . oceans." Since my heading is about "ancient," did you notice how I focused my draft on providing more information about how long sharks have been in existence? Drafts and headings are powerful partners.*

Ancient Predators
Since long before dinosaurs roamed our planet, great white sharks have hunted in the earth's oceans. Scientists believe that these sharks are such good survivors that they haven't had a need to evolve much in the last 150 million years.

Teeth, Teeth, and More Teeth!
These carnivores never run out of sharp, pointy teeth. They have rows and rows of teeth in their mouth, one behind the other. If one of the great white's teeth is lost, another one moves forward to take its place. In fact, these sharks may grow and use over 20,000 teeth in the course of their lifetime!

Sample Modeled Writing

TURN &TALK

Think together. Analyze this section of my draft. Do my sentences match the heading? Have I provided enough information to explain the heading? Is there anything else I need to do before moving to a new heading and beginning that section of the draft?

STEP 2: Continue thinking aloud as you write.

Possible Think-Aloud: *The next heading is "Teeth, Teeth, and More Teeth!" so I'll use this section to write about the great white shark's amazing ability to grow teeth to replace the ones it loses. I want to be sure to tell my reader that the shark's teeth are sharp and pointy, too. Watch closely as I write, "These carnivores never run out of . . . behind the other." When I think about headings as I'm drafting, it is easier for me to keep the writing focused and clear.*

TURN &TALK *Think together. The next heading is "Powerful Predators." Put your heads together and create some draft sentences that would fit well for this heading.*

Analyze

STEP 3: Reread and reflect.

Possible Think-Aloud: *One of the most important things we do in a draft is continually reread to think about the message, making sure it is clear and organized. This is a time to challenge ourselves as writers to analyze our own work and keep improving the draft. Let's read it together.* (After reading.) *I am so glad that we reread this draft. I still feel good about the headings, but rereading helped me realize that the first section mentions evolving but doesn't explain it. Let's put our heads together and consider some ways to further explain that sharks, unlike many other animals, are much like they were millions and millions of years ago.*

Sum It Up

Today we learned how headings help keep writing focused and organized. Headings tell readers what to expect from a section of writing, which can help make writing more enjoyable to read. Today as you begin drafting, try crafting your headings as you draft, and then use the headings to help you stay organized and focused.

VARIATIONS

For Less Experienced Writers: Less experienced writers may need more support in using the facts they have collected to create effective headings. Consider revisiting Organization, Lesson 5, *Using Headings to Group Related Information.*

For More Experienced Writers: Challenge students to examine a piece of writing from a published writer, for example, *Look to the Stars* by Buzz Aldrin. Discuss the ways in which the writer infused creative headings throughout the piece. Encourage students to experiment with questions, declarative sentences, words, and phrases when constructing their own headings.

Turning Research Notes into Running Text

WHEN TO USE IT: When writers need support in expanding words and phrases into sentences and paragraphs

FOCUS THE LEARNING

As nonfiction writers transition from research to drafting, often they are faced with collections of words and phrases that need to be expanded linguistically. At this phase, they need assistance in thinking beyond the isolated words and focusing on the concepts and understandings behind the words they have collected.

Model

STEP 1: Prepare a group of sticky notes so that each one features a single word or phrase. Model how to cluster them into categories that make sense.

Possible Think-Aloud: *When I researched about box jellyfish, I used sticky notes and collected words and phrases to record my thinking. Now I am ready to start drafting, so I need to organize my sticky notes. I want to group them together in a way that will help me create an organized and interesting piece of writing. I am going to put "Northern Australia" and "coastal waters" together in a group, because these words tell about where box jellyfish live. Now I need to think of a sentence, or even two, for these words. How about "Box jellyfish live in Northern Australia in the coastal waters." Listen as I try it a different way: "The infamous box jellyfish makes its home in the coastal waters off the coast of Northern Australia."*

TURN &TALK *I want my draft to be interesting and informative, so I'll try to use these words and phrases in different ways. It helps to test the sentences out loud before I write them down. Think together and construct a sentence or two that use my sticky notes about the coastal waters and Northern Australia.*

STEP 2: Continue clustering sticky notes and testing sentences that reflect the concepts.

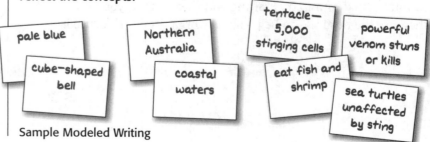

pale blue

cube-shaped bell

Northern Australia

coastal waters

tentacle— 5,000 stinging cells

eat fish and shrimp

powerful venom stuns or kills

sea turtles unaffected by sting

Sample Modeled Writing

Possible Think-Aloud: *I am ready to look at the next group of sticky notes. I want to think about which words might fit together and which ones can be turned into sentences of their own. I am going to put "pale blue" and "cube-shaped bell" together because these words talk about the physical attributes of the jellyfish.*

> The infamous box jellyfish makes its home in the coastal waters off the coast of Northern Australia. This beautiful, pale blue, and deadly creature gets its name from the cube-like shape of its bell. Each tentacle contains 5,000 stinging cells which deliver a powerful and deadly venom that stuns or kills the fish and shrimp it eats. Only the gentle sea turtle is unaffected by the sting of this deadly sea creature.

Sample Modeled Writing

TURN & TALK *Think about "pale blue" and "cube-shaped bell." Design sentences for those sticky notes.*

Analyze

STEP 3: Reread and reflect.

Possible Think-Aloud: *There are many sentences I could write to reflect those facts, but I like "This beautiful, pale blue, and deadly creature gets its name from the cube-like shape of its bell." Did you notice how I took the words and phrases from my sticky notes and turned them into an interesting sentence?* (Continue writing.) *Let's reread and see how this sounds. As we reread, I am going to draw a line under the words that were on the sticky notes so I can see where I placed them in my draft.*

Sum It Up

When we create drafts of our writing, we often need to build sentences from words and phrases that we gathered during our research. It helps to practice saying the sentences in different ways to see which sounds better. If the sentence sounds good when you say it out loud, it is likely to sound great to the person who reads your work! Turning words into sentences is what good writing is all about. As we begin writing today, try practicing your sentences aloud before you write them in your draft.

VARIATIONS

For Less Experienced Writers: If needed, begin by creating a single sentence for each word or phrase collected while researching. The sentences will likely be short and concise, but this exercise can help less experienced writers develop an understanding of how to expand language and describe concepts.

For More Experienced Writers: As these writers turn notes into running text, encourage them to use descriptors to add richness to the writing. Show them how to add adjectives, adverbs, and descriptors to their index cards and see how those additions change the sentences they insert into their drafts.

Stopping to Reread as You Write

WHEN TO USE IT: When you notice that students are not rereading their work as they draft

FOCUS THE LEARNING

Many young writers are not skilled at rereading their work. The goal of this lesson is to draw students' attention to how and why authors stop to reread during the drafting process.

Model

In advance of the lesson, write two or three sentences of modeled writing, like the ones shown below. Slip in some unintended repetitions, contradictions, omitted words, or words that are in the wrong place.

STEP 1: Think aloud as you continue to write, stopping to reread. Show students how you edit or revise, if necessary.

Possible Think-Aloud: *Writers, today I want to show you something that I do when I am drafting. As I write, I take time to stop every now and then to reread what I have written so far. When I stop to reread, it helps keep my writing on track and headed in the right direction. It also allows me to pick up on anything that may need to be changed or fixed. I am going to write about how to create an area where you can collect animal tracks. I've written the first two steps, and now I'm going to stop and reread. (After rereading.) I noticed that I repeated a few words in Step 2. That happens sometimes when you are drafting. Watch as I place a line through the repeated words.*

How to Make a "Track Trap"

1. Locate a dry, flat patch of ground.

2. Using flour, baking soda, or other kind of powder, spread a coating on the patch of ground ~~patch of ground~~ you have chosen.

3. Next, place some bait in the center of your "trap." The bait ^could include any of the following: nuts, peanut butter, vegetables, fruit, or bread.

4. Leave the trap overnight.

5. ~~Come back~~ Return in the morning and examine the trap to see who has been visiting.

6. Trace or draw the tracks in order to save them.

Sample Modeled Writing

TURN &TALK *Join me as we continue to reread what I've written so far. Then, think together: Am I on track so far? Is there anything I need to change or add at this point?*

STEP 2: Continue drafting. Think aloud as you stop to reread again.

Possible Think-Aloud: *Now I'm ready to write about placing the bait in the center of the trap.* (Write Steps 4 and 5, and then stop to reread.) *In Step 5, I wrote, "Come back in the morning. . . ." As I reread that step, I think I want to use a different word to begin that step. I want to say, "Return in the morning. . . ." I'll put a line through "Come back" and write "Return." Let me reread Step 5 again and see if it sounds better now. Sometimes, as writers, it's helpful to reread more than once to make sure the writing is clear and easy to read.*

TURN &TALK *Think together. Is there anything else that you think needs to be changed, added to, or removed from my writing so far?*

Analyze

STEP 3: Reread and reflect.

Possible Think-Aloud: (Finish drafting the remaining steps.) *Let's reread my writing again, but this time, let's all read it aloud. When we read our writing out loud, it allows us to hear the text as a reader would hear it, and it helps us identify areas within the text that could be revised. When I read aloud, I try to imagine that I'm hearing the piece for the very first time. That helps me focus in on any "bumps" in my writing that may slow down the flow of my words and ideas.*

Sum It Up

Today we learned about the importance of stopping to reread as we are drafting. Rereading is an important skill that you'll use through-out your life as a writer. It's part of learning to read like a writer. As you begin writing today, stop every now and then and take a moment to reread what you've written so far. You'll be glad you did!

VARIATIONS

For Less Experienced Writers: Encourage these students to read their writing aloud to a partner and then collaborate with peers as they edit and revise. English Language Learners, in particular, will benefit from the additional practice in oral language as they collaborate.

For More Experienced Writers: Challenge these writers to think about the following questions as they reread: *Do certain phrases sound strange or out of place? Do you stumble over the way something is worded? Does your writing put you to sleep?* Then, show them how you might revise based on the answers to these questions.

Infusing Transition Words and Phrases

WHEN TO USE IT: To insert a specific example

FOCUS THE LEARNING

Transition words and phrases can summarize, give reasons, provide examples, or contrast ideas. This lesson is designed to show students how to infuse transition words and phrases when providing examples related to a topic.

Model

STEP 1: Create a chart with transition words and phrases that might be used when inserting examples. Discuss it with the students. A sample chart can be found on the Resources CD-ROM. Demonstrate how you use the words and phrases from the chart as you craft a short paragraph.

Possible Think-Aloud: *As nonfiction writers, we need to be able to provide our readers with examples that relate to our topic. And we need to create writing that is clear and easy to understand. Transition words can help us do both! I have posted a chart that lists some transition words and phrases writers use when they insert a specific example. I'm going to use this chart as I write about fawns. My first sentence is "Nature has unique ways of protecting fawns." My next sentence will provide a specific example of this. I could use the transitional phrase "for example" and write, "For example, during the fawn's first three weeks of life, they have no scent to them at all." Or I could begin with "for instance."*

Nature has unique ways of protecting fawns. For instance, during the fawn's first three weeks of life, they have no scent to them at all. This means that hungry predators can't sniff them out.

A fawn's lack of scent is not the only way nature protects these delicate babes. Fawns' spots camouflage them as they rest in the tall grass. In fact, many people have been surprised to stumble onto a sleeping fawn nestled in the grasses waiting for the mother doe.

Sample Modeled Writing

TURN &TALK *Think together. Which transitional word or phrase from our chart do you think would work best for this sentence?*

STEP 2: Continue writing and thinking aloud as you infuse transition words.

Possible Think-Aloud: *Sometimes it helps to try a few different transitional words or phrases to see what sounds best. I like the transitional phrase "for instance" for this sentence. Watch as I write, "For instance, during the fawn's first three weeks of life, they have no scent to them at all."* (Finish drafting the first paragraph.) *In my next paragraph, I'm going to tell my reader about another way that nature protects fawns. I'll begin by writing, "A fawn's lack of scent is not the only way nature protects these delicate babes. Fawns' spots camouflage them as they rest in the tall grass." I'm ready to insert another example here: "many people stumble onto fawns unexpectedly." I think I'll choose "in fact." I'll write, "In fact, many people have been surprised to stumble onto a sleeping fawn nestled in the grasses waiting for the mother doe."*

Analyze

STEP 3: Reread and reflect.

Possible Think-Aloud: *Let's reread these paragraphs and look closely at the transition words and phrases I included. What did they do for the writing? Do you think these words will help my reader better understand my message and the examples I included? Adding transition words and phrases helped clarify my message. And they were easy to include when I used the words on our chart.*

Sum It Up

Today I showed you how you can use transition words and phrases when you want to include a specific example. When we use transition words and phrases, it helps to clarify our ideas, and it makes our writing sound more natural when it is read aloud. As you begin writing today, try using some words or phrases from our chart as you include examples in your writing.

VARIATIONS

For Less Experienced Writers: Confer one-on-one with students, and help them to infuse transition words and phrases from the chart as they provide examples related to their topics.

For More Experienced Writers: Challenge writers to examine several quality nonfiction books and analyze how often the author uses transition words and phrases when inserting an example. Talk about the importance of not over-using these words and phrases.

LINKS TO CD-ROM:

- Teaching Chart: Transition Words and Phrases to Use When Inserting Examples

Underline and Keep Writing

WHEN TO USE IT: To help writers make an attempt at spelling an unknown word and keep writing

FOCUS THE LEARNING

To free writers to focus on the content of their writing, it is important to help them become comfortable with making an attempt at spelling unknown words and leaving the corrections for later.

Model

STEP 1: Think aloud as you encounter an unknown word while writing. Show students how you make an attempt to spell it correctly, underline it, and keep writing.

Possible Think-Aloud: *All writers encounter words that they don't know how to spell. This is just part of writing! Today I want to show you one thing you can do when that happens. I'm working on this section of my piece about glaciers. I want to say, "When glaciers erode mountainsides, glaciated valleys are formed," but I'm not sure how to spell "glaciated." Watch as I say the word slowly and write the sounds I hear. I'm not sure "glaciated" is spelled correctly, so watch as I put a line underneath it. When I do that, it reminds me to come back and check that word later.*

TURN &TALK *What did you notice about the way I dealt with that word that I didn't know how to spell?*

STEP 2: Continue drafting. Show students how you make an attempt to spell another word, underline it, and keep writing.

> When glaciers erode mountainsides, <u>glacieated</u> valleys are formed. These trough-shaped, deep valleys usually contain steep vertical cliffs. Circs are formed when glaciers erode backwards into the mountainside, creating <u>vallies</u> that are shaped like shallow bowls.

Sample Modeled Writing

Possible Think-Aloud: *Now I want to tell my reader how glaciers erode backwards to form cirques. "Cirque" is another word I'm not certain of. Watch as I try to spell it, underline it, and keep writing.* (Continue writing, stopping at the word "valleys.") *I'm writing the word "valleys," but it doesn't look quite right to me. I'm going to underline it and come back to check it later. Notice that I don't focus on* **perfect** *spelling when I'm drafting. I want to get my ideas down and keep writing.*

Analyze

STEP 3: Reread and reflect.

Possible Think-Aloud: *Let's reread. Look closely at my writing and the words I attempted to spell. During the drafting phase of writing, I'm focused mainly on recording my ideas and content. I'm not spending a lot of time worrying about spelling. However, when I underline a word that I think might not be spelled correctly, it makes editing so much easier! When I'm ready to polish up this piece of writing, one of the first things I'll do is use my resources to find the correct spelling for the words I underlined.*

Sum It Up

Today I reminded you that when you are drafting, it's important to record your ideas quickly so that you can stay focused on what you have to say. When you are writing a word and you're not sure how to spell it, simply spell it the best you can and then underline it so that you can return at a later time to check the spelling. Who's ready to begin?

VARIATIONS

For Less Experienced Writers: Less experienced writers might benefit from learning how to clap or tap out the syllables in words and then write the sounds they hear in each syllable. This can help them make better approximations of spelling and increase their writing fluency.

For More Experienced Writers: During individual conferences, challenge writers to be sure that their drafts have some cross-outs, insertions, underlined words, and modifications. If drafts are completely clean with no adjustments, writers are not likely to have challenged themselves to reach deeply enough into interesting sentence structures, vocabulary alternatives, and punctuation options.

Establishing the Setting or Situation

WHEN TO USE IT: When writing lacks a setting or when the setting is vague and dull

FOCUS THE LEARNING

Published authors often set the stage by describing the setting or situation in a rich, vivid, and colorful way. This lesson is designed to teach students how to include strong images to make the setting or situation come to life.

Model

STEP 1: Think aloud as you begin writing, considering how to make the setting or situation stand out.

Possible Think-Aloud: *When writers establish the setting or situation, they invite the reader to experience the event. I'm writing about the night that my mom and I saw a huge thunderstorm. I want to set the scene for my reader. I could start by saying, "I saw a huge bolt of lightning and heard loud thunder." That's okay, but I think I can do a better job of establishing the setting and the situation. Sometimes it helps to close my eyes for a moment and try to picture just what that night was like. I'll try to remember how the storm looked and sounded.*

TURN &TALK *Take a moment and try this. Close your eyes and picture a thunderstorm. Tell your partner what you hear, see, and smell.*

STEP 2: Draft sentences that enhance the setting and emphasize sensory images.

> The lightning flashed bright and white through the windows of our small cabin. My mom and I looked at each other with a hushed silence. Then, we waited. When the thunder came, it boomed with such power that the walls shook and the dishes rattled.

Sample Modeled Writing

Possible Think-Aloud: *As I visualized what the storm was like, I remember how the lightning flashed through the window. It was so white and bright! When the thunder boomed, it was so loud that the walls shook and our dishes rattled. Watch me as I add some of those things to my writing to set the scene. First, I'll say, "The lightning flashed bright and white through the windows of our small cabin."* (Continue with another descriptive sentence.)

Analyze

STEP 3: Reread and reflect.

Possible Think-Aloud: *Let's reread my writing so far. Can you picture the setting? Have I established the setting in a way that makes it come to life? If you were the reader of this piece, would you be able to picture the storm? I think I've added some sentences that are descriptive. That helps in establishing a setting that will pull my readers in and make them feel as though they are right there with me.*

Sum It Up

When we establish the setting or the situation, it helps our readers feel as if they are right there with us. As you return to your writing today, try closing your eyes and reliving the moment in time so that you can think about what you saw, smelled, and heard. Then, write about those things to establish the setting. Descriptive writing that is full of sensory details will make your writing even more powerful!

VARIATIONS

For Less Experienced Writers: Engage students in a guided writing experience. Work together to set the scene for a shared experience, such as watching the first snowfall or taking a field trip. Use student suggestions to craft an opening paragraph that describes the setting and the situation.

For More Experienced Writers: Challenge writers to examine how published authors establish the setting and the situation. Then, invite them to try different ways to pull the reader in. Some examples: *Dogteam* by Gary Paulson and *Surprising Sharks* by Nicola Davies.

Add Action

WHEN TO USE IT: When writers need support in how to craft lively and engaging writing

FOCUS THE LEARNING

One of the best ways to boost nonfiction writing is to borrow the techniques that are often used in fiction. One technique is to add an action scene.

Model

STEP 1: Model how to visualize a scene and focus on the action.

Possible Think-Aloud: *Today I want to show you how writers make their topics come to life for their readers. One way they do that is to add a little action. I am planning to write about lions, but I want to open with some action so my reader can visualize the lions. Listen as I close my eyes and visualize a lion stalking his prey. I can "see" the lion slowly creeping from bush to bush. He keeps as quiet as possible while all the while keeping his gaze fixed on the gazelle he is hunting. Could you picture the lion as he hunted the gazelle?*

TURN &TALK *If you were going to write about the actions of the lion, what would you describe? What would you want your reader to know?*

STEP 2: Model writing about the action of the moment.

> The lion slowly and silently creeps from bush to bush, stalking the gazelle he has spotted near the watering hole. Suddenly, with a powerful burst of speed, he pounces on his prey.

Sample Modeled Writing

Possible Think-Aloud: *Visualizing really helped me to picture the action in my mind and then use the action in my writing. I am going to visualize again and see if that helps me add more to the action in this writing. I see the lion as he stalks from cover to cover, and then suddenly, with a final burst of speed, he pounces on his prey. I also visualize his claws. I know he needs those sharp claws to grab the gazelle, so I visualize that he pushes his claws forward as he pounces so they are ready to hook into the gazelle.*

TURN &TALK *I need to turn the rest of my visualization into action in my writing. What should I say about the lion's dive toward the prey?*

Analyze

STEP 3: Reread and reflect.

Possible Think-Aloud: *Let's reread and think about the action in the writing. I need to decide if I described it well enough that a reader could get a mental picture of the way the lion hunted for his food. (After rereading.) What are your thoughts about my actions? Do I need to add more description? Were you able to get a picture of the lion in your mind?*

Sum It Up

Today we learned how to add action to our drafts to make them sound more interesting. Now you know how to visualize about your subject and use that visualization to create an action-packed scene for your reader. When you return to your own writing today, challenge yourself to add a little action.

VARIATIONS

For Less Experienced Writers: Encourage writers to create a list of actions that go along with their topic. For example, if they are writing about sharks, they could make a list of verbs such as "eat," "swim," "dive," "bite," "tear," and "attack." Dramatizing may also provide support for visualizing actions to infuse into writing, especially for English Language Learners.

For More Experienced Writers: Show students how authors include an action scene as a way to begin the piece of writing and hook the reader. Challenge them to try this in their own writing.

LINKS TO CD-ROM:

• Mentor Text: *The Last Living Symbol of the American West*

Experimenting with Leads

WHEN TO USE IT: When writers are beginning a piece of writing and attempting to create a strong and enticing lead to draw the reader in

FOCUS THE LEARNING

This lesson is designed to help students understand that the perfect lead does not fall from the sky into their laps! It takes time and thought to begin a piece of writing in a way that makes the reader want to read more. This lesson is designed to help students understand the need to experiment with several leads before finding one that works.

Model

STEP 1: Think aloud as you begin a piece of writing, crafting several leads before deciding on one.

Possible Think-Aloud: *As I begin this piece of writing about forest fires, I want to think about how to pull my reader in and make him want to read more. I want to create a lead, or a beginning, that is interesting and engaging. Watch as I think about some possible leads and record them on this chart paper. I could begin with, "Most forest fires are started by lightning. The lightning is so hot that it can boil the sap inside the tree." Another lead might be, "Most people think humans cause most of the fires in our nation's forests, but the truth is that lightning can cause just as many, if not more, fires than we can. A lightning bolt is so hot and powerful that it can boil sap inside a tree that it strikes."*

TURN &TALK *Compare these two leads and discuss. Which one is stronger? Which one draws you in, like a magnet? What makes one lead better than the other?*

STEP 2: Continue thinking aloud as you craft another possible lead.

In a flashing instant, a lightning bolt strikes a tree. It does so with such force and heat that the sap inside the tree begins to boil. The fire smolders inside the tree for days before a gentle breeze blows, giving the embers the oxygen they need to erupt into powerful and destructive flames. A forest fire has begun.

Sample Modeled Writing

Possible Think-Aloud: *I'm going to see if I can think of one more lead for this piece. How about "In a flashing instant, a lightning bolt strikes a tree. It does so with such force and heat that the sap inside the tree begins to boil."*

TURN &TALK *Partners, think together. If you were to create a list of attributes of a strong lead, what would be on your list?*

Analyze

STEP 3: Reread and reflect.

Possible Think-Aloud: *I've written three different leads, and now it's time for me to decide which one I think is most powerful. I really like the third lead I tried. I like the way it sounds, and I think my audience will, too. It really helped to experiment with a few different leads before choosing the one that works best for this piece.*

Sum It Up

Writers, today I showed you how I experiment with several leads before choosing one that I think will pull my readers in like a magnet and make them want to read more. As you begin writing today, try using a piece of scratch paper to jot down some ways that you can begin your draft. I'll look forward to seeing what you write!

VARIATIONS

For Less Experienced Writers: Provide more guided practice with creating leads as you work with a small group of writers. As a group or in pairs, experiment with a variety of leads that could be used to write about a shared experience such as a guest speaker or the season's first snow.

For More Experienced Writers: Analyze the way published authors craft leads that draw the reader in. Books with creative leads include *Wings of Light* by Stephen R. Swinburne, *Wolfsnail: A Backyard Predator* by Sarah C. Campbell, and *Kakapo Rescue* by Sy Montgomery. Encourage students to experiment with humor, suspense, surprise, or description as they create leads.

LINKS TO CD-ROM:
• Mentor Text: *Africa's Diverse Landscape*

Creating a Conclusion

WHEN TO USE IT: When writers need practice with writing a clear, interesting conclusion

As writers, we need to recognize that our readers expect an ending to bring about a sense of closure and conclusion. This lesson is designed to show students how to try out several conclusions before choosing one that will work best.

Model

STEP 1: Discuss the importance of writing a powerful conclusion. Then, think aloud as you craft a conclusion for a piece of writing.

Possible Think-Aloud: *When we are ready to craft a conclusion, it's important to remember that this is the part that the reader may remember the most. So we want to write conclusions that are clear and interesting. Readers often expect a conclusion to summarize the main point of the writing, give an opinion, or look to the future. I've finished a piece about wetlands, and now I need to write my conclusion. I could say, "So remember, wetlands are important to people and to animals. We need to protect them!"*

TURN &TALK *What do you think of this conclusion? Is it interesting? Can you think of another way to end this piece?*

STEP 2: Try several conclusions and decide which one is most effective.

> People and animals depend on our nation's wetlands. Wetlands not only serve as filters to remove pollutants from the water in our wells, but they provide habitats and hiding places for a variety of animals. It's imperative that we protect wetlands from people who wish to see them drained or filled. The future of our planet depends on it.

Sample Modeled Writing

Possible Think-Aloud: *Here's another conclusion I could try: "It's imperative that we protect wetlands from people who wish to see them drained or filled. The future of our planet depends on it."*

TURN &TALK *Evaluate this ending. How does it compare with my first try? Which one do you prefer?*

Analyze

STEP 3: Reread and reflect.

Possible Think-Aloud: *I think I'll conclude this piece of writing with "It's imperative that we protect wetlands . . . future of our planet depends on it." Let's reread my final paragraph and see how it sounds. I like the way my conclusion wraps up the piece of writing and makes the reader think about the future.*

Sum It Up

Today we talked about the importance of crafting a strong conclusion. It might be helpful to think of the conclusion as the "wrapping paper" for your writing. The conclusion isn't the main part of your piece, but it can make the rest of your writing look good. When we wrap up a piece of writing with a conclusion, we don't include any new information, but we create a sense of closure for the reader. As you work on your own writing today, think about how you might wrap it up in a way that is interesting and powerful.

VARIATIONS

For Less Experienced Writers: Consider reading the endings from a few quality nonfiction books such as William Kaplan's *One Last Border* or *Keep On!* by Deborah Hopkinson. Lead a discussion about how other authors create a powerful conclusion. Then, demonstrate how you adapt the authors' ideas to craft your own.

For More Experienced Writers: Invite a student or two to offer up their writing for the group to read. Challenge other students to come up with other possible conclusions. Then, allow each author to choose the conclusion he or she prefers.

LINKS TO CD-ROM:
• Mentor Text: *Africa's Diverse Landscape*

Drafting a Persuasion

WHEN TO USE IT: When writers need support in persuasive thinking and writing

FOCUS THE LEARNING

All students need to engage in persuasive thinking and writing to become well-rounded learners and citizens. The goal of this lesson is to help students understand the elements that need to be in place when drafting a persuasive text.

Model

In advance of the lesson, work with the class to create a chart outlining the features of a strong persuasion, and discuss it with the students. A sample chart can be found on the Resources CD-ROM.

STEP 1: Display the chart and demonstrate how you use it as you begin drafting a persuasion.

Possible Think-Aloud: *Writers, today I want to show you how I draft a persuasive piece. When we write to persuade someone or make an argument for our point of view, it's important to remember the features that make a persuasive text strong. I have posted a chart that lists some of those features. I'm going to use this chart as I begin my piece on why the school year should be lengthened. The chart says that a strong persuasive piece draws readers in with the lead. I think I'll begin by describing summer and helping my readers see that summer is good for the soul but not great for the brain. I could say, "Ah . . . summer vacation! The sun, the surf, the swimming—it's good for the soul! However, it is not good for the brain."*

Ah . . . summer vacation! The sun, the surf, the swimming—it's good for the soul! However, it is not good for the brain. Students who spend weeks and months away from school start to lose the skills they gained during the school year. In addition, a summer break puts an unnecessary burden on working parents to find childcare. Furthermore, the traditional school year, with the summers off, was based upon an agricultural model of the past when children needed to have the summer off in order to help on the farm. In short, it is my opinion that the length of the American school year should be lengthened.

Sample Modeled Writing

TURN &TALK *What do you think of this lead? Will it draw my reader in? Can you think of another way to begin this piece?*

STEP 2: Think aloud as you continue to draft.

Possible Think-Aloud: *I like the way that lead sounds, so that's how I'll write it. "Ah . . . summer vacation . . . not good for the brain." Now, in this first paragraph, I'll continue with my introduction. I want to give brief reasons why I think the school year should be lengthened. I'll explore each reason in more depth later in my writing. But, for now, I'm going to give my reader three reasons. The first reason is that students often lose skills over the summer. I'll write, "Students who spend weeks and months away from school start to lose the skills they gained during the school year."*

TURN &TALK *I'm ready to give another reason why I think the school year should be lengthened. Think together and come up with a linking word or phrase from our chart that I could use to connect this reason with another reason.*

Analyze

STEP 3: Reread and reflect.

Possible Think-Aloud: *I think I'll use the transitional phrase "in addition" to begin my next sentence. I'll say, "In addition, a summer break puts an unnecessary burden on working parents to find childcare."* (Continue drafting, using the chart to guide you.) *Let's reread my persuasion so far. Does it sound convincing? Is it clear and organized? Would the reader find it interesting? Determine if I included some of the features we listed on our chart.*

Sum It Up

Today we learned how to include certain features when we draft persuasive texts. When we engage in persuasive thinking and writing, it is important to think about the reader and how he or she will read and understand your arguments. As you draft your own persuasive texts today, use our chart to support your thinking.

VARIATIONS

For Less Experienced Writers: These writers may benefit from additional modeling in how to insert linking words and phrases to make their persuasive writing clear and organized. Show students how you include words and phrases such as "because," "since," "in conclusion," and "based on the evidence."

For More Experienced Writers: Stretch these writers by showing them how to present an opposing view. Coach them as they identify linking statements that point out the opposing view, such as "it could be said that," "some people suggest," and "the opposing view might argue that."

LINKS TO CD-ROM:
• Teaching Chart: Features of a Persuasive Text

Writing an Informational Poem

WHEN TO USE IT: To offer writers another format for sharing their learning

FOCUS THE LEARNING

Nonfiction poetry comes in many formats and organizational patterns, offering writers a wide range of possibilities for communicating about their learning. Best of all, poetry stimulates imagery and style, bringing facts to life in a new and unique way. This lesson is designed to show students how to create a list poem.

Model

STEP 1: Create a list of facts about a topic.

Possible Think-Aloud: *We've been learning about the planets that make up our solar system. On this chart, I'm going to list some words that describe Jupiter. I'll list single words and phrases. First, I'll write, "giant of our solar system," because we learned that Jupiter is the largest planet in our solar system. Jupiter is often shrouded in clouds, and the three rings are only visible when the planet passes in front of the sun. So next I will write "shrouded in clouds, three faint rings." I'll add "many, many moons," too. My goal is to gather terrific words and phrases so I can read this as a list poem when I am finished.*

TURN &TALK *Examine my list of words and phrases. Then, think together. What other words and phrases do you think we should add?*

STEP 2: Continue adding words and phrases.

Possible Think-Aloud: *Do you remember how we learned that there are hurricane-like storms taking place almost constantly on Jupiter? I am going to add "powerful winds" to my chart. I also want to add "orbiting" because Jupiter orbits the sun. Let's finish by adding "storming" and "dense ball of gas."*

Jupiter

Giant of our solar system

Shrouded in clouds, three faint rings

Many, many moons

Powerful winds

Orbiting

Storming

Dense ball of gas

Sample Modeled Writing

TURN &TALK *Are there any other words and phrases we could add to our list about Jupiter?*

Analyze

STEP 3: Reread and reflect.

Possible Think-Aloud: *Let's reread, and this time, let's read our list like a poem. When we do that, we read it with a lot of expression and drama.* (After rereading.) *Wow! It really did sound like a poem, didn't it? A poem is a fabulous way to organize nonfiction writing.*

Sum It Up

List poems are created by listing facts, words, and phrases about a topic and then reading the list like a poem. There are all kinds of ways to share nonfiction information, and now you have one more way to share your topics with others.

VARIATIONS

For Less Experienced Writers: Show students how to use rich descriptions as they craft their list poems. The power of a list poem can be further heightened by having students create a phrase that stimulates sensory images and use it as the ending for their poems.

For More Experienced Writers: Stretch these writers by showing them how to craft narrative nonfiction poetry. *Tiger of the Snows* by Robert Burleigh and Ed Young is a powerful example of this kind of nonfiction poetry.

Revising

Polishing the Message

Revision is the time when writers challenge themselves to reach deeper and put themselves into the role of a reader. This is a time when they wonder about the clarity of the message and challenge themselves to reach for more interesting words and sentence structures, making the message the best it can be.

LESSON	3	4	5	RELATED LESSONS
1 Revising to Add Precise Words	●	●	●	*Word Choice:* Lesson 1, Use Descriptive Words and Phrases *Word Choice:* Lesson 2, Target Powerful Action Verbs
2 Revising a Lead		●	●	*Organization:* Lesson 6, Create an Inviting Lead
3 Checking the Closing	●	●	●	*Organization:* Lesson 7, Craft an Ending that Brings Closure
4 Main Idea Maintained Throughout	●	●	●	*Ideas:* Lesson 5, Focus on the Main Idea(s) *Organization:* Lesson 4, Main Idea Maintained Throughout
5 Revising for Sentence Fluency	●	●	●	*Sentence Fluency:* Lessons 1–9
6 Tuning Up Concrete Words and Sensory Images	●	●	●	*Word Choice:* Lesson 4, Use Concrete Words to Support Visualization
7 Revising with a Writing Partner	●	●	●	*Revising:* Lesson 8, Using a Revision Checklist
8 Using a Revision Checklist	●	●	●	*Revising:* Lesson 7, Revising with a Writing Partner
9 Combine Sentences	●	●	●	*Sentence Structure:* Lesson 3, Compound Sentences
10 Cut and Tape Revisions	●			

Revising to Add Precise Words

WHEN TO USE IT: When the writing is too vague and lacks rich details

FOCUS THE LEARNING

Specific and accurate details add both richness and texture to a piece of writing. Our goal is to support writers as they reread their writing through the lens of supporting details.

Model

STEP 1: Read First Draft of your modeled writing, and think aloud about the details you have infused. Is there enough information that the reader can get a vivid mental image?

Possible Think-Aloud: *I am rereading this section in my piece about bald eagles, and I realize that I need to include more rich details. The writing doesn't have enough details to help readers create a picture in their minds. It says that eagles have talons and beaks, but it doesn't explain what their talons and beaks are used for. I am going to revise and add some specific details to make my writing come to life.*

TURN &TALK *Partners, think together. When you think about an eagle's beak and talons, what mental images come to mind? What details might I include?*

STEP 2: Continue revising, using carets to add additional details.

First Draft:

Eagles have talons and beaks. They hunt fish, snakes, frogs, small mammals, and even other birds.

Second Draft:

sharp   dagger—like
Eagles use their ∧talons and ∧beaks to capture fish, snakes, frogs, small mammals, and other birds. ∧Their excellent eyesight helps them to spot their prey from up to a mile away.

Sample Modeled Writing

Possible Think-Aloud: *I heard some great ideas! Some suggested that I use some adjectives to describe the talons and beak. I'll add "sharp" to describe the talons and "dagger-like" to describe the beak. Marcos and Juan suggested adding a detail that tells more about how they hunt. I'll write, "Their excellent eyesight helps them to spot their prey from up to a mile away." Notice that I don't recopy the sentence. When I revise for details, I can insert the extra words.*

Analyze

STEP 3: Reread and reflect.

Possible Think-Aloud: *Let's reread. Examine my writing and the details I have added. How did the details strengthen my writing?*

Sum It Up

When we add details to our writing, it helps our readers get a picture of what we are trying to say. One of the best ways to ensure we have done this is to reread and revise. Today as you read your work with fresh eyes, I know that you will find places that could benefit from additional details. Challenge yourself to revise with your readers in mind.

VARIATIONS

For Less Experienced Writers: Gather a small group of writers, and ask them to underline words and phrases that are descriptive and create a clear, vivid mental image. If students can't find many, coach them as they revise to add descriptive details.

For More Experienced Writers: Challenge partners to engage in a question-based revision exercise. Partner A reads his or her writing aloud to Partner B. Partner B listens carefully and then writes down three questions. Partner A uses the questions to revise his or her writing. Have partners switch roles and repeat.

LINKS TO CD-ROM:
• Using Precise Descriptions

Revising a Lead

WHEN TO USE IT: To add interest to openings

FOCUS THE LEARNING

Over a period of a week or two, pause for a few minutes at the end of each nonfiction read-aloud to wonder with your students about the lead—the first sentence or two—in the book you just read. Encourage your students to consider leads that they think are great and make them want to read more. Collect great leads on sentence strips, and post them in visible places to support your writers.

Model

In advance of the lesson, create a chart with the first draft of the lead as shown in Step 1.

STEP 1: Reread the first draft of your writing, and think aloud about the lead. Consider: Is the lead inviting? Does it make us want to read more?

Possible Think-Aloud: *As I reread this piece on my grandmother's rocking chair, I am thinking about the leads we have been collecting from our read-alouds. I know that a strong lead is like a magnet that pulls a reader into the rest of the selection. I am thinking about the creaking sound that the old rocking chair made as we rocked. My lead could say, "Creak-creak. Creak-creak."*

TURN &TALK *Think together. If this were your piece of writing, how might you begin? What suggestions do you have?*

STEP 2: Continue revising by changing the original lead.

First Draft:

I will always remember the old wooden rocking chair in my grandmother's house. We spent countless afternoons rocking together while we sang old hymns.

Second Draft:

Creak—creak. Creak—creak. I will always remember the old wooden rocking chair in my grandmother's house. We spent countless afternoons rocking together while we sang old hymns.

Sample Modeled Writing

Possible Think-Aloud: *I am going to select "creak-creak" as my lead. Onomatopoeia makes great leads, and "creak-creak" definitely makes me want to read more. Watch as I revise and insert my new lead.*

Analyze

STEP 3: Reread and reflect.

Possible Think-Aloud: *Let's reread together and make those sound words come to life! Think together. Is my writing better with this new lead? Did this revision improve my writing? Why is this lead more interesting than starting with, "I will always remember . . ."?*

Sum It Up

Today we learned that when we revise, we can also rewrite. We can make our leads like magnets that pull our readers in and make them want to read more. As you begin writing today, take a moment to check on one of your leads. See if you can think of any ways that you can revise that lead to make it more interesting to a reader.

VARIATIONS

For Less Experienced Writers: Provide more practice by gathering students in a small group and showing them how to browse books in the classroom library to find strong leads. Add the leads to an ongoing chart displayed in the classroom.

For More Experienced Writers: Together, create a list of other ways to jazz up a lead such as "focus on the setting," "open with action," and "use onomatopoeia."

LINKS TO CD-ROM: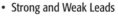
• Strong and Weak Leads

Checking the Closing

WHEN TO USE IT: When the closing lacks a clear sense of conclusion

FOCUS THE **LEARNING**

Over a period of days, read aloud several examples of great endings from a variety of nonfiction texts. Collect powerful endings on a chart, and post it in a visible place to support your writers.

Model

In advance of the lesson, create a chart with the first draft of the ending as shown in Step 2.

STEP 1: Reread the first draft and think about the ending. Consider: Would the reader feel satisfied with the ending? Is it interesting?

Possible Think-Aloud: *As I reread the last paragraph of my persuasive piece on limiting sugar in our diet, I am thinking about the powerful endings we've been collecting from books. I know that I need to come up with an ending that will wrap it all up, and I'm not sure I'm satisfied with the ending I have.*

TURN &TALK *Partners, talk together. What ideas do you have for closing this piece? If this were your writing, what would you do to wrap it up?*

STEP 2: Continue revising by changing the original ending.

First Draft:

Furthermore, the plaque that lives on your teeth feeds on sugar. When the bacteria eat the sugar, it creates acid. This acid can cause painful, expensive cavities. Sugar can be really bad for you.

Second Draft:

Furthermore, the plaque that lives on your teeth feeds on sugar. When the bacteria eat the sugar, it creates acid. This acid can cause painful, expensive cavities. So before you pop another Hershey's kiss in your mouth, remember: not everything about candy is sweet.

Sample Modeled Writing

Possible Think-Aloud: *I remember that sometimes authors speak right to the reader when they are ending a piece. My ending could tell my reader to think twice before eating another piece of candy. Watch as I revise and try a new ending.*

Analyze

STEP 3: Reread and reflect.

Possible Think-Aloud: *Let's reread my writing and think together. Is my writing better with this new ending? Will this revision help my reader feel as though my piece is all wrapped up? Why is this ending better than my first attempt?*

TURN &TALK *Writers, think about a piece of writing that you have been working on. Talk with your partner about your ideas for ending the piece. Offer suggestions to each other. Two heads are often better than one!*

Sum It Up

Writers, we know that endings are important. They are your last chance to make a lasting impression on your reader. As you look at your own writing today, take a moment to focus on the ending. Challenge yourself to think of some ways that you can revise the ending to make it more interesting.

VARIATIONS

For Less Experienced Writers: Collect high-quality endings from nonfiction books, and pair them up with books that have less satisfying endings. Invite students to discuss the attributes of a powerful ending.

For More Experienced Writers: Encourage students to try out a few different endings. Once they have a few endings written down, encourage them to read them to a partner and choose the one that works best.

LINKS TO CD-ROM:
- Strong and Weak Endings

Main Idea Maintained Throughout

WHEN TO USE IT: When the main idea is unclear or when the writer has included additional or unrelated ideas that distract the reader

FOCUS THE LEARNING

Writers often start out focused, but as they continue to write, unrelated information may creep in. Our goal is to teach students how to reread with an eye and ear for clarity.

Model

STEP 1: Post the sentences from First Draft so that all students can see them. Display one sentence at a time, asking students whether the piece has stayed focused up to this point.

Possible Think-Aloud: *When we really get on a roll writing about our topics, it can be easy for our writing to get off track and lose focus. When that happens, our writing suffers and it confuses the reader. Let's take a look at this piece of writing about earthworms. As we look at each sentence, consider where the writing gets off track.*

TURN &TALK *Writers, where do you think the writing lost focus? How do you know it got off track? What sentences do you think should be taken out?*

STEP 2: Model how you delete a sentence that strays from the main idea.

First Draft:

Earthworms can be very beneficial to soil. They not only mix up the layers as they eat their way through it, but they deposit "castings," which have many nutrients that plants need to grow. Plants can grow broad, thick leaves or narrow and thin leaves.

Sample Modeled Writing

Second Draft:

Earthworms can be very beneficial to soil. They not only mix up the layers as they eat their way through it, but they deposit "castings," which have many nutrients that plants need to grow. ~~Plants can grow broad and thick leaves or leaves that are narrow and thin.~~

Possible Think-Aloud: *As I was listening to your conversations, it sounds like many of us think that the writing stayed pretty focused until the sentence that talks about plants growing broad, thick leaves. If I just take that sentence out, my writing would be more clear and focused. Watch how I just put a line through that sentence to take it out.*

Analyze

STEP 3: Reread and reflect.

Possible Think-Aloud: *Let's reread together. What do you think about the writing now? Does the writing stay focused on the main idea? How did taking this sentence out help my reader?*

TURN &TALK *Partners, think together. Have you ever noticed yourself getting off track as you write? Do you have any tricks that help you stay focused on your main idea?*

Sum It Up

Today we learned how to reread our writing with the goal of making sure our writing stays on topic. When you look at your own piece of writing today, see if there are any sentences that need to be taken out to keep your writing as clear and focused as it can be.

VARIATIONS

For Less Experienced Writers: Invite partners to read their writing sentence by sentence. Ask the listening partner to visualize what is being read and to make sure that the mental image fits the main idea.

For More Experienced Writers: Ask individual students to offer up their writing for the group to revise in order to ensure that the main idea is maintained throughout the piece.

Revising for Sentence Fluency

WHEN TO USE IT: When the writing sounds choppy and lacks a natural rhythm and flow

FOCUS THE LEARNING

When students write nonfiction, they often become so focused on facts that they forget about how their writing sounds. Our goal is to encourage them to read their writing with an ear for sentence fluency.

Model

STEP 1: Display First Draft and demonstrate how you read it aloud to focus on sentence fluency.

Possible Think-Aloud: *When I feel like I'm finished with a draft, one of my important jobs is to focus on how my writing might sound to a reader. It should have a smooth and natural sound when it is read aloud. I need to examine my sentences and ask myself, "Are my sentences different lengths? Do I use a variety of words to begin my sentences, or do they all start the same way?" Let's look at this part of my writing.*

TURN &TALK *Partners, think together. What do you notice about how this section sounds when it is read aloud? What revisions would you suggest for this section?*

STEP 2: Demonstrate how you combine sentences to improve the fluency.

First Draft:

Hummingbirds are very small birds. They move their wings rapidly. They also migrate when the weather turns cold. They don't migrate with groups, since they are solitary birds.

Second Draft:

Hummingbirds are very small birds that have the ability to move their wings very rapidly. When the weather turns cold, individual hummingbirds migrate to warmer weather.

Sample Modeled Writing

Possible Think-Aloud: *I heard some fantastic ideas! Some of you suggested combining some sentences to create some variety in the length of my sentences. That way, this section will include some short sentences along with some longer sentences. Others of you suggested that I change the beginning of my sentences so that they don't all start the same way. That's another way to improve my sentence fluency. Watch me as I combine the first two sentences and the last two sentences.*

Analyze

STEP 3: Reread and reflect.

Possible Think-Aloud: *Let's reread my writing now. Does my writing sound more natural? Do my sentence beginnings have a little variety now? How do you think these revisions strengthened my piece?*

Sum It Up

Today we learned that one way we can improve the way our writing sounds is to combine shorter sentences and use different words to begin our sentences. Today as you look at your own writing, see if you can revise to strengthen the fluency of your writing. I will look forward to reading your revisions!

VARIATIONS

For Less Experienced Writers: Collect or write several short pieces of writing that are either strong or weak in sentence fluency. Read the selections and discuss which pieces are fluent and why.

For More Experienced Writers: Challenge partners to take a short and choppy piece of writing and revise it. Demonstrate how to combine sentences to add flavor and variety while keeping the content intact.

LINKS TO CD-ROM:
- Sentence Fluency Checklist

Tuning Up Concrete Words and Sensory Images

WHEN TO USE IT: When writing is too vague and lacks vivid images

FOCUS THE LEARNING

Writers need to learn how to reread their writing with a focus on making sure they have crafted a piece that will create vivid images in the minds of their readers. This lesson is designed to support students in that process.

Model

Prepare a chart of the first draft in advance. Skip lines so there is room for revision.

STEP 1: Read the first draft of your writing, and think aloud about the topic. Show students how you wonder about adding some descriptions that involve the senses.

Possible Think-Aloud: *I am rereading this sentence from my piece about snow, and I'm asking myself, "Have I included words that show my reader how snow feels, tastes, looks, smells, and sounds?" I have shared a fact about snow, but the writing doesn't really help the reader create a vivid image of what I'm describing. I am going to revise and add some words that give more description. That will make my writing sparkle!*

TURN &TALK *Partners, work together to come up with some words that describe how snow feels, tastes, looks, smells, and sounds. Close your eyes and create a picture in your mind of playing in the snow. What words could I add?*

STEP 2: Continue revising.

First Draft:
Snow falls from the sky.

Second Draft:
The silent snow falls from the sky and lands lightly on my hat and coat. I stick out my tongue to taste the icy cold crystals.

Sample Modeled Writing

Possible Think-Aloud: *I heard some fantastic ideas for words that I could add to boost my writing. Some of you suggested that I add the word "silent" to describe how snow sounds. I think I can add that in the first sentence. Hannah and Tristan were talking about how snow feels light and tastes like ice crystals. As writers, we need to use words that help our readers get a picture in their minds.*

Analyze

STEP 3: Reread and reflect.

Possible Think-Aloud: *Let's reread. What do you think of the writing now? I think my favorite parts are the words that describe how the snow tastes. I can really visualize the light snowflakes falling on my tongue. Think together. How did adding the words about sound, feeling, and taste improve the writing?*

Sum It Up

As writers, we need to be sure we think about the picture we are helping a reader create in his or her mind. I know I can count on you to help your readers visualize. As you write, use your senses and help your reader "see" what you see and "hear" what you hear.

VARIATIONS

For Less Experienced Writers: Choose three or four short poems. Some should create strong mental images and some should not. Read the poems several times, and ask students to think about which poem creates the most vivid mental images and why.

For More Experienced Writers: Challenge partners to take a dull and lifeless piece of writing and revise it to include concrete words and sensory images. Invite partners to share their revisions with the rest of the group.

Revising with a Writing Partner

WHEN TO USE IT: When students are ready for feedback on a draft

FOCUS THE LEARNING

When we ask students to provide feedback to another writer in the class, the feedback is often shallow. When we teach students how to ask probing questions, we help them give more meaningful feedback.

Model

STEP 1: Ask a student or a colleague to serve as your writing partner. Read a partial or finished draft, and ask your partner to write down any questions he or she has.

Possible Think-Aloud: *As writers, it's helpful to get feedback from a reader. It often leads us to revise. I've finished writing a short section of my piece about renewable energy. Watch as I read my writing to my partner. As I read, my writing partner has two jobs: She needs to 1) listen carefully to my draft and 2) use a sticky note to write down any questions she has about my piece.* (Read writing.)

TURN &TALK *Partners, think together. If you were going to write down some questions for me, what would they be? What are you, as a reader, curious about?*

STEP 2: Listen as your writing partner shares his or her questions, and think aloud as you use the questions to revise your writing.

First Draft:

Throughout history, people have harnessed renewable energy from the sun, wind, and water. We still harness these sources of energy today.

Second Draft:

Throughout history, people have harnessed renewable energy from the sun, wind, and water. As long as 4,000 years ago, the Babylonians and Chinese were using wind power to pump water that would irrigate their crops. Greeks and Romans used reflective surfaces to capture the sun's rays in order to set fire to enemy ships.

Sample Modeled Writing

Possible Think-Aloud: *Now I'm ready to read my partner's questions and think about how I might revise my writing. My partner asked, "Who harnessed renewable energy throughout history? Can you give some examples?" Aha, so my reader is curious to know more about my first sentence. As I researched my topic, I read about how the Babylonians and Chinese used wind power to pump water to their crops. I also read that the Greeks and Romans harnessed the sun's rays to set fire to enemy ships. I could add those examples and really boost my writing. Watch as I do that.* (Revise writing.)

Analyze

STEP 3: Reread and reflect.

Possible Think-Aloud: *Let's read my revised draft. What do you think of my writing now? Did thinking about the questions my partner asked lead me to revise? When I read my partner's questions and thought about what a reader was curious about, it helped me to focus on what I needed to add.*

Sum It Up

Today we learned how to utilize a writing partner when we are ready to revise. As you return to your drafts, consider asking a partner to listen to your writing and write down some questions. Then, use those questions to help guide you as you revise to make your writing powerful and effective for your reader.

VARIATIONS

For Less Experienced Writers: Provide a common text, and guide students as they ask questions and use those questions to engage in a whole-group revising experience.

For More Experienced Writers: Challenge students to analyze the questions presented by their partners. Ask them to categorize the questions by writing trait. Are the questions addressing **ideas**, **voice**, or **organization**? Encourage students to revise their writing with these traits in mind.

Using a Revision Checklist

WHEN TO USE IT: When writers have completed a draft and are ready to revise independently

FOCUS THE LEARNING

Revision checklists remind writers of elements of high-quality writing they have learned. It is essential to use revision checklists that list only those elements you have modeled and supported through explicit instruction.

Model

STEP 1: Provide each writer with a revision checklist and model its use.

Possible Think-Aloud: *Writers, revision means looking again at what I have written to see how I could improve it. I am going to use a revision checklist to guide me as I revise. The first point on my checklist says, "Reread to check that my writing stays on topic." That helps me make sure that I have maintained the main idea throughout my piece. Watch as I do that and then place a check mark next to that item on the checklist.*

TURN &TALK *Partners, examine your revision checklists together. What is the next item on the list? Think about what I should do next in order to revise my writing.*

STEP 2: Reread for another revision point.

Nestled safely on his father's feet, the baby penguin peeks out into the ice world around him. The frozen ice field ^is^ just inches below the new baby, but he is kept warm and dry in his safe hiding place.

Sample Modeled Writing

Possible Think-Aloud: *The next item on my revision checklist is adding extra words if I need them. (After rereading.) Look at the sentence that starts with, "The frozen ice. . . ." This doesn't make sense. I need to add the word "is." I will use a caret and insert it. Now watch as I add a check mark next to "add extra words" on the checklist.*

Analyze

STEP 3: Reread and reflect.

Possible Think-Aloud: *We have reread this piece of writing several times now, and I found some sections that needed some revision. When we take the time to reread and think about our writing, our work continues to improve.*

TURN &TALK *Partners, think together. What do you think of this checklist? Are there other things we could add that would help us as we revise?*

Sum It Up

Today we have learned how a revision checklist can help when we are ready to revise. I'll put several versions of a revision checklist in the writing corner so that you can select one that is right for the kind of writing you are doing. When you are ready to revise, you now have another tool that can help you make sure your writing is the best it can be.

VARIATIONS

For Less Experienced Writers: Create a revision checklist that includes words and **pictures** to provide additional support. Refer to this checklist when you revise your piece of writing and work with writers in a small group to choose just one or two items on which to focus.

For More Experienced Writers: Once writers become comfortable with using a revision checklist, work with a small group to create new revision checklists that are appropriate for different genres.

LINKS TO CD-ROM:
- Revision Checklist A
- Revision Checklist B
- Revision Checklist C

Combine Sentences

WHEN TO USE IT: When students are writing in short, choppy sentences

FOCUS THE LEARNING

When writers learn to link short sentences together, they increase their control over creating writing that sounds like natural language. Sentence combining has a very strong research base that supports its use, but it is important to remember that one lesson isn't enough. This is a skill that needs to be encouraged and supported over many lessons and many topics as writers mature.

Model

In advance of the lesson, post the short sentences of First Draft in a pocket chart. Using scissors, show how you can cut and move words around to combine two short sentences into one that is longer and more interesting.

STEP 1: Combine two short sentences.

Possible Think-Aloud: *I am going to combine sentence one and sentence two into one sentence that is a bit longer and more interesting. Watch as I insert the word "and" after "body." I will also take the scissors and cut out the words "they" and "have." This new sentence says, "Female black widow spiders have a shiny black body and a red hourglass shape on their abdomen." This is a combination of sentence one and sentence two. I turned two short sentences into one longer sentence that tells my reader a lot more.*

TURN &TALK *What did you notice as I combined those two sentences? Identify the steps I followed to create one longer sentence out of two shorter ones.*

STEP 2: Cut and rearrange the next two sentences to combine them.

First Draft:

Female black widow spiders have a shiny black body. They have a red hourglass shape on their abdomen. Black widows are cannibals. They will eat each other. Black widows spin a thick and jumbled cobweb. They catch beetles, flies, grasshoppers, moths, and other spiders in their webs.

Sample Modeled Writing

Second Draft:

Female black widow spiders have a shiny black body and a red hourglass shape on their abdomen. Black widows are cannibals, which means they will eat each other. They catch beetles, flies, grasshoppers, moths, and other spiders in their thick and jumbled cobwebs.

Sample Modeled Writing

Possible Think-Aloud: *The next two sentences are about how black widows will eat each other. I think I can combine these sentences as well. This time, instead of using "and," I'll insert the words "which means." My new longer sentence now reads, "Black widows are cannibals, which means they will eat each other." Did you notice that I also added a comma where the period used to be? To combine short sentences, you need to change the period to a comma and then select a connecting word like "and," "but," "so," or "or." Sentence combining is easy, and it makes my writing flow much more smoothly.*

Analyze

STEP 3: Reread and reflect.

Possible Think-Aloud: *Let's reread together and think about the way our newly combined sentences sound when we read aloud. (After rereading.) I am noticing that our new longer sentences sound more like talking. We speak in long sentences, so sentence combining can make our writing sound more like talking. Think together. What do you need to remember about combining sentences?*

Sum It Up

Sentence combining is an important skill for writers. When we revise, it is important to be on the lookout for short sentences that can be combined into longer, more interesting sentences. Sentence combining is fun, so I know I will see you combine sentences as you revise. That's what good writers do!

VARIATIONS

For Less Experienced Writers: Using a pocket chart, begin by combining two short sentences with conjunctions such as "and," "but," "or," and "so." Less experienced writers can easily remove a period and insert a conjunction and a comma to create a compound sentence. An example: "Frogs can jump. They leap long distances." Combined sentence: "Frogs can jump, and they can leap long distances."

For More Experienced Writers: Begin a list of different ways to combine sentences, and post it as a chart to assist writers during drafting and revising.

Cut and Tape Revision

WHEN TO USE IT: To help writers revise without rewriting the entire piece

The more writers learn about their topic, the more information they may wish to add. When students learn how to revise by cutting and taping, the task becomes more manageable.

Model

STEP 1: Show how to cut apart a prepared piece of writing and insert new paper to make room for more writing.

Possible Think-Aloud: *I've been working on a piece about matter. I have been reading more about my topic, and I want to include some more information. Let me show you a smart way that I can make room to add facts about my topic. My first two sentences say, "Matter is all . . . air you breathe is matter, too." I want to include a definition of matter after my second sentence. I'll use scissors to cut my original piece of writing, and then I'll use tape to insert a new piece of paper right in the middle. Now that I have room, I can write, "Matter is anything that takes up space and has mass."*

TURN &TALK *Writers, what do you think of my cool way to add ideas and information? How might cutting and taping help you with your writing?*

STEP 2: Insert another new piece of paper, and revise the next sentence.

First Draft:

Matter is all around us. Your dog is matter and the air you breathe is matter, too. There are 3 major states of matter.

Second Draft:

Matter is all around us. Your chair is matter and the air you breathe is matter, too. Matter is anything that takes up space and has mass. There are three major states of matter. They are solid, liquid and gas. Each of these states is also called a "phase."

Sample Modeled Writing

Possible Think-Aloud: *Writers, the next sentence tells my reader that there are three major states of matter. I think I can add more information about that, too. Watch again to see how I cut my paper after the word "matter" and tape on a new strip of paper. I have room to revise and add, "They are solid, liquid, and gas. Each of these states is also called a 'phase.'" Revising this way is fun, and it really boosts my writing!*

Analyze

STEP 3: Reread and reflect.

Possible Think-Aloud: *Let's reread my writing and think together. Is there any other new information that will help make my piece more clear or interesting? I have paper, scissors, and tape, so I am ready for more ideas!*

Sum It Up

Writers, when we revise, we can cut and tape to make room for new information. When we do that, it helps to strengthen our writing. Now that you know this smart way to add bits of writing, I'm ready to admire you as you give it a try!

VARIATIONS

For Less Experienced Writers: Work with writers individually or in a small group so you can coach their thinking as they decide where to cut and insert additional information.

For More Experienced Writers: Challenge writers to work with a partner to use cut-and-paste revision as a way to incorporate information they gain from a new book on the same topic.

LINKS TO CD-ROM: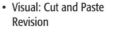
• Visual: Cut and Paste Revision

Editing

Being Polite to Your Reader

Editing should not be seen as a function of correctness or that step writers "have" to take before publishing. Instead, it should be a joyful infusion of possibility in which artistic punctuation, jaw-dropping grammar, and carefully spelled words add the final touch of elegance to a piece of writing. At the intermediate grades, special care should be taken to ensure that internal punctuation and complex sentences are clearly present.

LESSON	3	4	5	RELATED LESSONS
1 Focused Edits: Reread for Each Editing Point	●	●		*Editing:* Lesson 2, Using an Editing Checklist
2 Using an Editing Checklist	●	●	●	*Editing:* Lesson 1, Focused Edits: Reread for Each Editing Point
3 Express Lane Edits	●	●	●	
4 How to Peer Edit	●	●	●	
5 Use Spelling Consciousness	●	●	●	*Drafting:* Lesson 5, Underline and Keep Writing *Spelling Consciousness*: Lesson 1, Notice When Words Are Not Spelled Correctly
6 Paragraphs and Indentations	●	●	●	*Organization:* Lesson 8, Paragraphs
7 Use Copyediting Symbols to Support Editing		●	●	

Focused Edits: Reread for Each Editing Point

WHEN TO USE IT: To help students edit with greater accuracy

FOCUS THE LEARNING

It is often said that rereading is the heartbeat of good writing. With a focused edit, writers reread their work one time for each editing point, reading once for spelling, another time to check subject-verb agreement, a third time to verify punctuation, and so on—addressing editing concerns one at a time.

Model

STEP 1: Prepare the modeled writing in advance, and demonstrate how to reread with a single editing point as your focus. Then, explain that you are changing your focus, and read the entire piece again for a new editing purpose.

Possible Think-Aloud: *In a focused edit, you read a piece of writing and only think about one editing point. For example, you might only look at spelling. Once you think you have spelling under control, you go back to the top and reread again for a different purpose such as checking punctuation. In this procedural text, I am going to start by editing to be sure that each numbered step starts with a verb. That is really important when you write a procedure. When you are using numbered steps, each sentence needs to start with a verb. Come in close and watch as I begin. (Read the beginning of each numbered step, and touch the verb.) Look at Step 2. The verb isn't the first word. It is the second word. I accidentally used the word "then," so I need to take it out. I don't need both a number and a sequence word. For my next focused edit, I will go back to the top and read to check spelling. The first word in the supply list looks right to me, but "spoul" doesn't seem right. Watch as I check it in a dictionary. Aha. It should be "spool." I will edit and change that word.*

TURN &TALK *Partners, think together and read the rest of the piece to check the spelling. This focused edit is for spelling only. You may see other problems, but just focus on spelling.*

STEP 2: Reread for additional editing points.

Possible Think-Aloud:
The next focused edit is for pronoun agreement. That means a singular subject needs a singular pronoun—a plural subject needs a plural pronoun. It looks good until Step 4. "Kite" is singular, but check out the pronoun. This says "them."

TURN &TALK *Consider the options. What should be done to adjust the pronoun in this step?*

How to Fly a Kite

Supply List
· Kite
· ~~Spoul~~ Spool of string
· Wind

1. Assembl the kite.

2. ~~Then,~~ attach the spoul of string.

3. Roll out 3 to 4 fete of string run into the wind

4. Releese the kite and allow them to raise with the wind

5. Have fun!

Sample Modeled Writing

Analyze

STEP 3: Continue rereading and editing with a different focus point for each read.

Possible Think-Aloud: *You know a lot about editing. Since I am going to publish this piece as part of our science display on wind power, it needs to be right. Put your heads together and consider: What other editing points should we include in this focused edit? What else should we check to be sure that this is ready to be presented in a public way?*

Sum It Up

Focused edits are a powerful way to ensure that your editing is top-notch. With a focused edit, you read the entire piece of writing with just one editing point in mind. Then, you select a new editing point and start back at the top with a new purpose. Continue until all editing concerns are addressed, one at a time.

LINKS TO CD-ROM:
• Writer's Self-Reflection

Use an Editing Checklist

WHEN TO USE IT: To guide writers in working on familiar conventions

FOCUS THE LEARNING

It is important to remember that editing checklists do not teach. They simply remind writers of those things they already know how to implement. As a result, it is essential to utilize editing checklists that list only those elements you have modeled and supported through direct instruction.

Model

You will need a piece of writing displayed on a chart to use as the focus for editing. You and the students will also need copies of one of the editing checklists from the Resources CD-ROM. This lesson is based on Editing Checklist II.

STEP 1: Provide each writer with a copy of an editing checklist that is carefully matched to editing strategies that you have already modeled and supported in class.

Possible Think-Aloud: *Today I am using an editing checklist to help me remember the various elements that I want to check as I edit my work for publication. Notice also that I am using a pen that is a different color than my writing so my editing really stands out. The first element on this checklist is to check ending punctuation. The first sentence is, "Did you know that thundrclouds. . . ." Clearly, this should have ended with a question mark. Watch as I quickly repair that. The other sentences are all statements, so I can check off ending punctuation on the checklist. I spotted a spelling error, too, but I am going to ignore that until I come to spelling on the checklist. Item two on the checklist is internal punctuation. That means that I need to check for commas to separate introductory elements and closers, place commas in a series, and so on. I will go back to the top and reread with internal punctuation as my focus. In the first sentence, "hot" and "humid" are both adjectives describing days. They need to be separated by a comma. I'll add that quickly and move on.*

Did you know that thundrclouds forms on hot humid days. Inside the clouds. As condensaytion builds water droplets and ice cristals rubbed together making posutive and negative electric charges. Lightning are most likely to result when their is both positive and negative charges within the same clous.

Sample Modeled Writing

TURN &TALK *It's your turn. The next item on the checklist is complete sentences. Work together to be sure there is a subject and a verb for every sentence. Ask, "Who or what did something? What did they do?"*

STEP 2: Reread for additional editing points.

Possible Think-Aloud: *The next item on this Editing Checklist is checking for subject-verb agreement. A singular subject needs a singular verb. A plural subject needs a plural verb. In the first sentence, the subject is "thunderclouds." That is plural. The verb, "forms," ends in "s." Oops. "S" endings on a verb are usually used with singular subjects. I could say that "a thundercloud forms." Then the "s" would be fine. If I leave this as a plural form, "thunderclouds," the verb should be "form."*

TURN &TALK *Editors, the next item on the list is to check for spelling and misplaced homophones. Read each sentence for spelling and homophones. Be ready to report your findings.*

Analyze

STEP 3: Reread and reflect.

Possible Think-Aloud: *The next item on the list is maintaining verb tense. Let's check. In sentence one, we just worked on the verb form, so we know it is present tense. In sentence two, "As condensation . . . ," the verb is "rubbed." I used present tense in sentence one, so I have to stick with present tense. I will change "rubbed" to "rub."*

Sum It Up

Editing Checklists are tools that need to constantly change as we become proficient in new understandings about writing. The secret to using a checklist effectively is to read the entire piece of writing with just one editing point in mind. Then, when you move to the next editing point, go back to the beginning of the writing and start all over again. This continuous rereading will improve your editing and help you create writing pieces that are polished and sophisticated.

VARIATIONS

For Less Experienced Writers: Select an Editing Checklist with few items, making absolutely sure that every item on the checklist has been the subject of a modeled writing and coaching experience.

For More Experienced Writers: Challenge these writers to create their own Editing Checklists, modifying existing checklists or designing checklists that match writing purposes and particular text types.

LINKS TO CD-ROM:
- Editing Checklists I, II, III, IV
- Editing Reflection Sheet: Capitalization and Punctuation

Express Lane Edits

WHEN TO USE IT: To focus editors on the things that they are doing well

FOCUS THE LEARNING

Express Lane Edits, originally designed by Jeff Anderson, offer students an opportunity to focus on catching themselves getting it "right" rather than emphasizing correction and repair.

Model

Prepare the modeled writing in advance so you can focus on the editing process.

STEP 1: Explain an Express Lane Edit, and begin modeling.

Possible Think-Aloud: *An Express Lane Edit, like the express lane at the grocery store, is quick and focused. With this kind of "express" editing, you don't worry about a huge number of things. You select two or three, and you are done! Notice on my T-chart on the left side, it says, "Shopping List." This is where I will list the items that I will look for today. Since I can only have a short list—this is the express lane—I will select homophones, subject-verb agreement, and commas. Next, I will take a felt pen and highlight every time I catch myself using one of these targets correctly in my writing. If I repair something in my writing, I can highlight it after it is repaired because it is correct.*

Shopping List	Receipt
· Homophones	I am feeling really good about this edit because I can see that I have improved in subject-verb agreement and using commas correctly. I still need to work on homophones.
· Subject–verb agreement	
· Commas	

TURN &TALK *When would you use this type of editing? What are the advantages of an emphasis on getting things right—instead of just looking for errors?*

STEP 2: Continue highlighting, thinking aloud and focusing on things you are doing well.

Sample Modeled Writing

Possible Think-Aloud: *Now I will start over and read to check for subject-verb agreement. In sentence one, "loggerheads" is plural. It ends in "s." "Lumber" agrees with the plural subject. It does not have an "s" or a plural ending! Watch as I highlight the "s" on "loggerheads" and "lumber." This sentence has subject-verb agreement. In sentence two, "turtles" is plural and "cover" has no "s." I get to highlight this one, too!*

Several times a year, female loggerheads lumber onto the beach and, ˢᵉ̲ lay a cluster of 100 or more eggs. Digging, smoothing, and sweating salty tears, the turtles carefully cover their tracks to give the babies a better chance of survival.

Sample Modeled Writing

TURN &TALK *The next item on my shopping list is commas. Start at the beginning, and analyze the commas in this piece. Are they used correctly? Identify those that need adjustment and those that are ready to be highlighted.*

Analyze

STEP 3: Reflect and write the receipt—a reflection.

Possible Think-Aloud: *When you go to the grocery store, you get a receipt. For this editing receipt, you stop and reflect on what you have highlighted and on your progress in creating well-edited writing. Watch as I write: "I am feeling really good about this edit because I can see that I have improved in subject-verb agreement and using commas correctly. In an Express Lane Edit, you focus on what you did right. Think together. What should you remember about the steps in an Express Lane Edit?*

Sum It Up

An Express Lane Edit is quick and focused. You select a small number of targets that you have been working on and then catch yourself doing it right! By highlighting what is correct, instead of just focusing on what is wrong, you are reinforcing the good writing habits that you are developing. Then, you can consider how you did on this piece and targets for future writing.

How to Peer Edit

WHEN TO USE IT: To encourage partners to think together and focus on higher levels of proficiency in editing

FOCUS THE LEARNING

When writers work with a partner to co-edit writing, they help each other notice details.

Model

STEP 1: Use a projection device to display a copy of a peer-editing checklist, or provide students with paper copies of a checklist. Display a piece of writing that has a few errors in spelling, punctuation, or other elements that are appropriate to your writers. Identify an editing partner—a student, the principal, or another teacher— before the lesson begins. Each partner will need a highlighter in a different color.

Possible Think-Aloud: *My partner and I are going to use a peer-editing checklist to help us as we edit this piece of writing. The first item on the checklist is spelling. Watch as we both use our highlighters and place dots above the words we want to check. Partner A: "What did you notice about the words that you have marked?" Partner B: "What words did you find that may need attention?" Writers, it is important that both partners get a turn to share observations and also that they carefully listen to one another. Once we have shared our thinking, my partner and I will use resources and adjust spellings as needed. (After adjusting spelling.) Writers, watch as my partner and I sign off on spelling on the peer-editing checklist. We check off the box and both insert our initials.*

Did you knew that reptiles such as lizards, snakes, turtles alligators and crocodiles have dry scaley skin and a bony skeleton? While these creetures look touph. It is interesting to note, that it cannot generate heat within their own body.

Sample Modeled Writing

TURN &TALK *Peer editing is a powerful partnership. What are you noticing about the way we are working together? What do you see us doing? What do you notice in our behavior toward each other?*

STEP 2: Continue modeling the conversation and peer editing process, using the checklist as a guide.

Possible Think-Aloud: *Now we are ready to look at the sentences— to be sure that they are complete and have a subject and a verb. Partner A: "I see that in sentence one, the subject is "reptiles." The verb is "have." Sentence one looks complete to me." Partner B: "I agree. As I look at sentence two, I see that "creatures" could be the subject and "tough" the verb, but this doesn't sound right. "While these creatures look tough." I think the problem is the first word, "while." What do you think?"* (Work together to repair sentences two and three.) *We now have adjusted so all sentences are complete—no fragments! Let's sign off on this section of the peer-editing checklist.*

TURN &TALK *Analyze this piece of writing and the peer-editing checklist. What should we edit for next?*

Analyze

STEP 3: Reread and reflect.

Possible Think-Aloud: *My partner and I are going to reread my writing one more time and double-check the peer-editing checklist. If we see something we still need to check, we will use our highlighters and make another dot. If we agree that we have done everything we can, we will both sign off at the bottom of the page. This part is really great because before we sign, we both write one compliment about the writing. That helps the editing process become both a celebration and a chance to lift writing quality. Put your heads together. If you were going to offer a compliment about this writing, what would you say?*

Sum It Up

Peer editing is fun. It is a chance to use multiple perspectives and observations to improve writing quality. When you are ready to edit, select an editing partner and one of the peer-editing checklists. You are sure to find that two editors can notice much more than any one of us could manage on our own.

VARIATIONS

For Less Experienced Writers: Provide peer editing experiences with a small number of editing targets to limit the range of behaviors editors are analyzing. This will allow the partners the opportunity to focus on taking turns, making sure both partners get to speak, practice using a checklist, and so on

For More Experienced Writers: Extend the process to peer revision or peer publishing to help writers understand that partner work helps to expand their thinking and broadens the creativity of their work.

LINKS TO CD-ROM:
• Peer-Editing Checklist
• Peer-Editing Celebration

Use Spelling Consciousness

WHEN TO USE IT: To heighten awareness of spelling within messages

FOCUS THE LEARNING

When editing, writers need to learn to trust their intuition and notice when words don't look quite right.

Model

You will need a prepared piece of modeled writing, a ruler, an index card, and a felt pen in a different color than that of the written draft.

STEP 1: Point out that spelling is important when we publish because correct spelling makes the work accessible to others while making the writing look more sophisticated.

Possible Think-Aloud: *As I edit this thank-you letter to the school cook, I am going to focus on "spelling consciousness." That means that while editing, I need to notice when words don't look quite right. To do this, I need to slow down and focus on the visual aspects of each word. Sometimes it even helps to place a ruler under the line of text. This can help my eyes really connect to individual words rather than skimming for meaning. Watch as I place a ruler under the first sentence and begin. Notice that I look at each word by itself. "Today's—pizza—was. . . ." Slowing down like this helps me notice spellings and look at word parts. If I find that I am still reading too fast because I already know what the text says, I can hold an index card to the right of each word to stop my eyes from moving on. Watch as I demonstrate. (Use an index card to slowly uncover each word in the sentence—one word at a time.) "Stupendus" doesn't look right to me. I can write a little "sp" just above it or draw a line under it. That will remind me to check it with a dictionary or spell checker.*

TURN &TALK *I am going to slide the ruler down to the next line of text and use the index card to force my eyes to stop after each word. Read slowly with me and use spelling consciousness. Put your heads together, and share what you notice about the spelling. Identify words that awakened your sense of spelling consciousness.*

STEP 2: Continue modeling and thinking aloud.

Possible Think-Aloud: *Let's continue with the third sentence. I can quickly see that "incluzion" needs some work, so I will draw a line under it and check the dictionary. I am also picking up two homophones in this sentence that I want to be sure to check: "hour" and "to." Those are tricky words, so I have to identify the meaning before I can select the spelling that matches. "Hour" refers to time, so watch as I draw a line through "hour" and change it to "our."*

> Dear Mrs. Miller,
>
> Today's pizza was the most stupendus lunch ever. While are cuisine at school is usually tastey, the homemade pizza was tastier then normal. The whole-wheat crust tasted great and we loved the incluzion of veggies from hour school garden, to.
>
> With appreciation,
> The students in Mr. Allen's room

Sample Modeled Writing

TURN &TALK *"To," "two," and "too" are definitely homophones. Think together. Which one do you think is correct here? Use your spelling consciousness.*

Analyze

STEP 3: Reread and reflect.

Possible Think-Aloud: *We used spelling consciousness along with a ruler and an index card to check the spelling in this letter to the head cook. We slowed down our reading to give our eyes a bit of help in focusing on word parts and appropriate use of homophones. Put your heads together. What are the benefits of slowing down and using spelling consciousness while editing?*

Sum It Up

When we edit, we need to use spelling consciousness and decide if words look right or not. You can use tools such as a ruler or an index card, but the real secret is learning to trust your intuition and think about what looks right. Spelling consciousness is a great support to editing.

VARIATIONS

For Less Experienced Writers: Focus writers on underlining words that do not look right. If there are a lot of words, ask these writers to select three to six words they would like to bring to full correctness. A smaller number of words is more likely to be remembered and retained in long-term memory.

For More Experienced Writers: Remind writers that each syllable should have a vowel. When they apply spelling consciousness, they can then look at each syllable and ensure that there are enough vowels.

LINKS TO CD-ROM:
- Spelling Consciousness Checklist A
- Spelling Consciousness Checklist B

Paragraphs and Indentations

WHEN TO USE IT: When students are editing to be sure that structural elements are in place

FOCUS THE LEARNING

Paragraphs give structural support to messages by organizing ideas into meaningful units. During editing, writers need to check the structure and ensure that all sentences in a paragraph provide unity and coherence and contribute to well-developed ideas. They also need to examine surface features such as titles, headings, indentations, and justification to the left.

Model

Before the lesson, find resources with different styles of presenting paragraphs—one that indents and one in block style that justifies to the left margin with a double space between paragraphs. If possible, display the modeled writing using a projection device.

STEP 1: Review the steps in editing a paragraph.

Possible Think-Aloud: *When I am getting ready to edit a paragraph, I need to watch for both structural and surface features in the writing. First, I need to be sure that all sentences in a paragraph are connected to and contribute to the main idea of the paragraph. Then, I need to check the surface features such as a title, headings, and the way the paragraph is laid out on the page. Here is a paragraph from a piece on driving safety, titled "Hang Up the Phone." The heading tells me that this is an argument for people to hang up the phone while driving. I am going to read it aloud and confirm that all of the sentences are about this one central* idea. (Read the passage.) *Sentence one provides a rationale for hanging up the phone. It has unity with the heading—and so does sentence two. The research makes an important argument.*

Hang Up the Phone

Did you know that talking on a cell phone while driving can quadruple your chance of having an accident? Research has shown that accidents occur because drivers become distracted by the phone call—and lose their concentration on driving. Many states have now instituted laws for hands free cell phone use, requiring that drivers keep both hands available for controlling the car. That may help with steering, but distracted drivers can still be a danger on the road. Many people find that monthly plans are more economical than pre-paid plans.

Sample Modeled Writing

TURN &TALK *Read the rest of the sentences together. Pause after each one and ask, "Does*

this sentence show unity to the heading? Is it cohesively connected to the main idea of this paragraph?"

STEP 2: Model how to review surface structures.

Possible Think-Aloud: *Now I need to look at the paragraph's surface structures. As I edit this piece, I am happy to see a heading in place. The next editing point is on another surface structure— the way the paragraph is laid out on the paper. There are many options for layout. Many sources say that you should indent the first line of each paragraph by five spaces. When you indent, you don't need to double-space between paragraphs, because the indentation shows exactly where a new paragraph begins. Look closely at this resource that didn't indent. The author and publisher justified the text to the left margin and used double spacing to show where one paragraph ends and the other begins.*

TURN & TALK *Compare and contrast these two treatments of layout for a paragraph. What do you notice?*

Analyze

STEP 3: Experiment with indentation.

Possible Think-Aloud: *So I need to decide if I should indent or not. Once I make a decision, I need to be consistent with all the paragraphs in the entire piece of writing. Watch as I use the tab key on my computer and indent the first sentence of the paragraph. With this format, a new paragraph could start right after the first—no extra line is needed to separate paragraphs. Now observe closely as I remove the indentation from the first sentence. With this format, you must add an empty line between paragraphs so you can tell where one ends and the next one begins. Think together. Which layout do you think would be better for this piece of writing?*

Sum It Up

You need to edit paragraphs with two kinds of thinking in mind. First, do all sentences connect to and support the main idea? Second, are headings and indentations done thoughtfully and uniformly used throughout the writing?

VARIATIONS

For Less Experienced Writers: Confer with these writers individually to coach them as they analyze their paragraphs for sentence unity.

For More Experienced Writers: Guide these writers in checking for sentence unity in paragraphs that do not have headings, forcing them to infer the main idea of each paragraph and confirm that sentences still match.

LINKS TO CD-ROM:
- Editing a Paragraph
- Reference Chart: T.I.P.S. When to Start a New Paragraph

Use Copyediting Symbols to Support Editing

WHEN TO USE IT: To offer writers another set of tools to use when editing

FOCUS THE LEARNING

Copyediting symbols can speed up the editing process by providing a uniform set of symbols that writers can insert themselves or understand in the work of another writer.

Model

Prepare a piece of modeled writing in advance so you can show students how to insert copyediting symbols into drafts while editing. Provide writers with a copy of the copyediting symbols from the Resources CD-ROM.

STEP 1: Display and explain copyediting symbols.

Possible Think-Aloud: *The copyediting symbols you see on the chart are helpful tools that can assist editing. If we all use the same symbols when editing, we'll each know exactly what the symbols mean. As I look at this piece of writing on the GPS, I will insert copyediting symbols as I read. When it is time to create a final published piece, I will know how to make adjustments. In sentence one, I see that "positoning" is not spelled correctly. Watch as I write SP just above it. I also notice that the word "thing" doesn't fit. Watch as I insert the symbol for "take it out."* ✂

TURN &TALK *Examine sentence two. There are several places where copyediting symbols are needed. Identify the changes that are needed, and then talk together about the copyediting symbols that would be needed for this sentence.*

STEP 2: Continue copyediting and using symbols from the chart.

GPS Text

Here is a text you could use for small-group practice on integrating copyediting symbols into writing.

A GPS, global positoning system ~~thing~~.
can help find your way almost anywhere on
earth. for ease of use many of today's new
cars and cell phones are equiped with GPS
supports. This allows you to ask for directions
to an address, find a city, or direct you to
safety if you get lost.

Sample Modeled Writing

Possible Think-Aloud: *When I am editing, sometimes I change my mind. At times I have inserted symbols to remove words, check spelling, or insert more words—and then decided that I liked a sentence better in the original form. The copyediting symbol for "keep it the same" is STET. I find myself using that a lot because when I edit in pen, it isn't easy to return the text to its original state. You might want to take special notice of that copyediting symbol on the chart. Look closely as I continue with sentence three. Sentence three begins with "this." That doesn't sound right. The antecedent is "GPS supports." That's plural. Since a pronoun needs to match the case of the subject it refers to, I need to delete "this" and insert "they."*

TURN &TALK *Analyze the copyediting symbols. Many of them will be familiar to you—like a caret. Identify the symbols that you already know and understand, and then set a goal for trying out two or three new ones. Share your thinking.*

Analyze

STEP 3: Have students apply the symbols while editing their work.

Possible Think-Aloud: *Spend the next few minutes editing a piece that is in your writing folder or your writer's notebook. Use the copyediting symbols that are on the sheet. When I give the signal, you are going to trade papers with another writer and identify the changes that writer wants to make by reading the copyediting symbols that he or she has inserted. This is a great way to see how powerful these symbols can be and how they can improve your editing prowess.*

Sum It Up

Copyediting symbols are like a uniform language for editors. They make it possible to quickly and easily identify needed changes without overloading a page with long notes. Keep this page of copyediting symbols handy because I know you will use it often.

VARIATIONS

For Less Experienced Writers: Have writers create personalized posters of copyediting symbols, selecting those that they feel will most help them.

For More Experienced Writers: Provide an opportunity for students to teach younger students how to use copyediting symbols.

LINKS TO CD-ROM:
- GPS Text
- Copyediting Symbols

Presenting

Preparing Our Work for Others

Presentation and distribution are like the icing on a cake or the moment of the final performance at a recital. It is the final touch that lifts a work to a higher level and makes it memorable. Presenting work to others is a subject to be taken seriously, as careful handwriting, spelling, conventions, spacing, visuals, and electronic displays are expected of writers in future schooling and the workplace. When presenting is not given the attention it deserves, barriers are formed between writers and readers, affecting comprehension and appreciation of the work.

LESSON	3	4	5	RELATED LESSONS
1 Experimenting with Page Layout	●	●	●	*Planning:* Lesson 7, Planning Page Layout
2 Inserting Illustrations and Visuals	●	●		*Text Features:* Lesson 3, Using Photographs *Text Features:* Lesson 5, Cutaway Diagram with Labels
3 Infusing Text Features	●	●	●	*Text Features:* Lessons 2–11
4 Presenting Electronically	●	●	●	*Planning:* Lesson 1, Selecting a Format for Writing
5 Creating Page Breaks		●	●	*Planning:* Lesson 8, Using a Flowchart

145

Experimenting with Page Layout

WHEN TO USE IT: When students are ready to work on page layout before publishing

FOCUS THE LEARNING

Writers benefit when they see how a proficient writer (that's you!) experiments with various ways to present information on the page. Our goal is to teach students that page layout matters to readers. Therefore, we need to take the time to make sure our writing is polished and pleasing to the eye.

Model

Gather an array of nonfiction books with visually appealing page layouts, and show them to your writers before this lesson begins.

STEP 1: Use a projection device to show students how you use text boxes and visuals to enhance page layout.

Possible Think-Aloud: *I am ready to present my writing about deserts to an audience. I want to think about page layout and visuals that will help make my writing easy to understand and delightful to read. When I'm using a computer, one trick I use is to place sections of my writing into text boxes. When the writing is in a text box, I can move it around on the page, change the size and shape of the text box, or insert a photograph or diagram. Watch me as I take my cursor and drag the text box with my writing inside to a new position on the page. Now I can enlarge this photograph of the desert that I downloaded from the Internet. This allows me a lot of flexibility as I experiment with different ways to arrange the page.*

Life in the Desert

The desert is one of the most fragile and mysterious of all ecosystems. Scientists still aren't certain how so much life can exist in what appears to be a barren wasteland of sand.

The Thorny Devil lives in the Great Sandy Desert in Australia.

Sample Modeled Writing

TURN &TALK *Think about the way the page looks. Do you like the placement of the text boxes and the visuals? What do you think about the size of the visuals? What else could I do to make this look really polished and professional?*

STEP 2: Continue experimenting with page layout.

Possible Think-Aloud: *In the nonfiction books I have on display, I notice that authors often add captions to the photographs they include on the page. I think adding a caption would enhance my page layout. Watch as I add a smaller text box to the left of the photograph of the Thorny Devil. Now I can type my caption inside that text box. I'll make the font smaller because it's a caption.*

Analyze

STEP 3: Reread and reflect.

Possible Think-Aloud: *Watch as I take a minute and review the layouts in the published resources I have on display. I notice that one has a lot of photographs clustered closely together. I see another that is rather boring, with the picture at the top and the writing at the bottom of the page. Here is one that has a huge picture on the left and lots of smaller pictures with captions on the right. Is there anything else I could do to make my page layout even better? Nonfiction writers need to have great content, interesting visuals, and carefully planned page layouts.*

Sum It Up

Publishing and presenting is an exciting time for writers as we get to enrich our drafts with interesting page layouts full of writing, visuals, and photographs. Today I showed you how to experiment with page layout by creating text boxes and inserting interesting visuals. As you return to your writing, try different ways to make your pages informative and interesting.

VARIATIONS

For Less Experienced Writers: Together with a small group of writers, examine the books, magazines, and web pages that students have used for research. Guide students in gleaning ideas about page layout from these resources. Also consider revisiting Text Features: Lesson 11, *Text Boxes*.

For More Experienced Writers: Once writers become comfortable experimenting with page layout in one genre, show them how to create an electronic slide show showcasing their topic.

Inserting Illustrations and Visuals

WHEN TO USE IT: When students are preparing a piece for publication

FOCUS THE LEARNING

A picture (or visual) is worth a thousand words, especially when you are creating a nonfiction piece in which illustrations and visuals often provide additional information. Once students are ready to share a piece of writing with a larger audience, they are ready to learn how to infuse interesting illustrations and visuals that will enhance the words on the page.

Model

Writers will need clipboards, paper, and writing implements for this lesson.

STEP 1: Display a finished section of writing like the one shown below. Think aloud as you insert a diagram.

Possible Think-Aloud: *As I prepare to present my writing to others, I want to think about the kinds of illustrations and visuals I can include to make my topic come to life. As I examine the nonfiction books in our classroom library, I notice fascinating illustrations, photographs, diagrams, and maps. These visuals support the writing and add richness to the selection. I am looking at a diagram here that would fit nicely with my piece about the rainforest. I want this visual to support the text on the page. (After rereading.) I will add the diagram on this page, since the text describes the different layers of a rainforest. Now I'll write a caption for this visual. I could say, "The rainforest is made up of four different layers." Watch as I write it just below my diagram.*

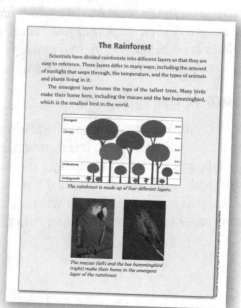

Sample Modeled Writing

TURN &TALK *Partners, think together. Identify the attributes of an effective illustration or visual, and consider ways in which these can enhance the writing.*

STEP 2: Display some photographs and think aloud as you add them to the writing.

Possible Think-Aloud: *Adding the visual and caption gave this page visual power, didn't it? I found this great photograph of a macaw and another photograph of a bee hummingbird. I think my reader would appreciate seeing what these birds look like. Watch as I add them to my writing. Now I'll need a fantastic caption for these.*

TURN &TALK *Put your heads together. Use your clipboards to list the attributes of a powerful visual such as a photograph, illustration, or diagram. What differentiates really great ones from others that are just okay?*

Analyze

STEP 3: Reread and reflect.

Possible Think-Aloud: *In looking at these visuals, I realize that I can write one caption that would work for both photographs. I wouldn't want to do this all the time. Often visuals need their own captions. Watch as I write, "The macaw (left) and the bee hummingbird (right) make their home in the emergent layer of the rainforest." Notice how adding the words "left" and "right" directs my reader to the correct visuals. Now let's reread this page and analyze the visuals I have used. Wonder together: Do they support the text on this page? Will my reader find them interesting and informative?" Use the lists you created of attributes for visuals, and decide if these visuals are powerful rather than just average.*

Sum It Up

Today we talked about the importance of inserting illustrations and visuals into our writing. When you look through your own writing today, identify a few places that would benefit from a detailed illustration, diagram, photograph, map, or other visual. If you've already added some visuals, look back at them and ask yourself if they are effective and pleasing to the eye.

VARIATIONS

For Less Experienced Writers: Show writers how to examine the visuals and illustrations that authors include in published books. Consider: What can we learn from these authors? Then, have students analyze their own writing to consider visuals and illustrations that might be added.

For More Experienced Writers: Challenge more experienced writers by inviting them to create detailed illustrations, diagrams, and maps to power up their presentations. If needed, demonstrate how to scan, or copy and insert, visuals into a finished piece of writing.

Infusing Text Features

WHEN TO USE IT: When writing lacks nonfiction text features

FOCUS THE LEARNING

Nonfiction text features are helpful adaptations that enhance readability and improve the organization of nonfiction selections. They include tools and features such as tables of contents, headings, page numbers, graphs, tables, boldface words, bullets, and more. The goal of this lesson is to help students see that infusing text features makes their writing more professional and presentable.

Model

STEP 1: Display a finished piece of writing like the one shown below. Demonstrate how you can create a diagram with labels from the information you have written.

Possible Think-Aloud: *Today I want to show you how authors use text features to improve their writing and prepare for publishing. Text features include tools such as headings, diagrams, bullets, and boldface words. On this page, I've written about the heart, so this is a good place to insert a text feature—a diagram. Watch me as I carefully draw a picture of a human heart and then draw a line from the part of the heart to the label that tells what that part is.* (Complete the diagram.)

TURN &TALK *Analyze the way I created the diagram and the effect it has on my writing. Can you think of any other text feature I could add to this page?*

STEP 2: Continue adding text features.

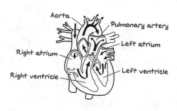

The Heart

The human heart may be small (about the size of your fist), but is a powerful muscular organ that pumps blood through the body.

Oxygen-poor blood comes into the **right atrium**. Then, the blood is pumped into the **right ventricle** and through the **pulmonary artery** until it reaches the lungs. The lungs enrich the blood with oxygen.

The blood, now oxygen-rich, is now carried back to the **left atrium**. The blood pumps to the **left ventricle** and then through the **aorta** to the rest of the body.

Sample Modeled Writing

Possible Think-Aloud: *Let's look at this page again. I am feeling really good about the diagram I have created, but I think I can include another text feature. I remember that boldface words serve as a signal that a word is either important or featured in a glossary. On this page, there are some words that I could make bold. The words "right atrium" should definitely be bold. The right atrium is an important part of the human heart. I think "right ventricle" should be bold, too. Watch as I make those words bold. Notice how the dark print makes them stand out.*

TURN &TALK *Analyze the rest of the writing on this page. What other words should be written in boldface?*

Analyze

STEP 3: Reread and reflect.

Possible Think-Aloud: *I'll make "pulmonary artery," "left atrium," "left ventricle," and "aorta" all bold words since they are important words that pertain to the heart. Now let's look at this page again. I have added a diagram and some boldface words. Now that I've added these text features, I think my writing looks more like a polished published piece of nonfiction!*

Sum It Up

When we add text features to our writing, it enhances the message and helps a reader navigate. As nonfiction writers, we need to remember that text features should be included in most forms of nonfiction writing. As you work to prepare your writing for publication, challenge yourself to include several different kinds of text features.

VARIATIONS

For Less Experienced Writers: Choose some nonfiction leveled books at the "just right" level for these writers. Examine the text features that the authors included to enhance the meaning and help a reader navigate. Together, create a list of text features, along with an example. Display the chart and encourage writers to reference it when writing.

For More Experienced Writers: Challenge experienced writers to add text features they may not have tried before to enhance their work. These writers might want to create a table of contents, a glossary, or an index or insert captions, headings, and so on.

Presenting Electronically

WHEN TO USE IT: When students are ready to learn about another option for presenting and publishing their work

This lesson is designed to show students how to create an interesting and informative electronic slide show.

Model

STEP 1: If possible, display your computer screen using a projection device so that all students can see. Then, think aloud as you create an electronic slide show.

Possible Think-Aloud: *As I prepare to publish and present my piece about the layers of the atmosphere, I am going to turn it into an electronic slide show on the computer. Watch as I create the first slide in my slide show. This slide should include the title and my name, since I'm the author. I also want to include a photograph or illustration to grab the reader's attention and make the slide pleasing to the eye. I think I'll include this visual I found from a free (public domain) source on the Internet. It shows the layers of the atmosphere in an interesting way. Watch as I click on "insert" and then choose "picture." I am going to include this picture from a file, so I'll click on that and then choose the picture.*

TURN &TALK *Think together. What did you notice about how I created this first slide? What might I add to my next slide?*

STEP 2: Continue demonstrating how to create an electronic slide show.

Possible Think-Aloud: *When I'm presenting my writing electronically, I want to be careful not to place too much text on one slide. I also need to make each slide clear, organized,*

The Layers of the Atmosphere
by Mrs. Boswell

Sample Modeled Writing

informative, and interesting. On this slide, I'll add the introduction to my show. Watch as I place "In order to better . . . several different layers" into a text box. Did you notice how I started by creating a text box? Once the text is in the box, I can move it around on the slide. Next, watch as I add a visual to the slide. I can move both the visual and the text box around until I find the arrangement that I like best.

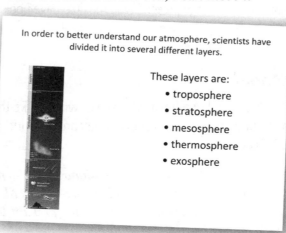

In order to better understand our atmosphere, scientists have divided it into several different layers.

These layers are:
- troposphere
- stratosphere
- mesosphere
- thermosphere
- exosphere

Sample Modeled Writing

Analyze

STEP 3: Reread and reflect.

Possible Think-Aloud: *Let's take a look at my electronic slide show so far and analyze it. The title page, like the cover of a book, has the title, the author, and an interesting visual. That's good. The next page has a short introduction and a bulleted list. The bullets are good. But I think I will also add animation! Watch as I go to "animation" on the menu bar and select which entrance effect I want to use. Now when I show this slide show, the bullets will pop up one at a time! Adding text and visuals—plus animation—is pleasing to the eye and really helpful when you are presenting your writing electronically.*

Sum It Up

Today you explored some options for creating an electronic slide show. As you return to writing today, consider how you might create an electronic slide show using the writing you have crafted. Be sure to focus on the content, visuals, and animation as you consider the possibilities for presenting your work electronically.

VARIATIONS

For Less Experienced Writers: Engage students in a guided writing experience with individual computers, or gather the group around a smart board or projection screen. Work together to add more slides to your modeled writing sample, pausing to allow students to add text boxes, photographs, diagrams, and other visuals. Then, have students work on their own slide shows while you are close for support and coaching.

For More Experienced Writers: Challenge experienced slide show creators to insert transitions between slides, add animation to headings and visuals, create their own layouts using blank slides, experiment with making an image for the wallpaper and placing text on top, and so on.

LINKS TO CD-ROM:
- The Layers of the Atmosphere PowerPoint

Creating Page Breaks

WHEN TO USE IT: To support and encourage presenting in multiple-page book formats

FOCUS THE LEARNING

Page breaks are important in nonfiction selections because they show transitions between key ideas and guide a reader in processing information. This lesson is designed to show students how to present a draft in a multiple-page format so that each page can support a unit of meaning.

Model

STEP 1: Display a finished piece of writing like the one below, but without page breaks. (An example can be found on the Resources CD-ROM.)

Possible Think-Aloud: *When professional authors publish informational books, they use multiple pages—each filled with interesting content and rich visual features. Today I want to show you how I create page breaks in a draft before I present it to an audience. I've written about the tundra, and I'm ready to share it with an audience. As I look at my work, I notice that all of my writing is on one page. I need to create some page breaks that would make my writing easier to read and understand. First, I need to reread what I've written and think about where I could insert a page break.*

(After rereading.) *I think I could insert a page break after the word "wildflowers" since this first part describes the tundra and the next part describes the animals that live on the tundra. Watch as I add a page break after "wildflowers." Notice that I am using a double slash "//" to mark the draft and show where the page break needs to go. I will also slip in "p. 1" to remind myself that this will be the end of page 1.*

The Tundra: Cold, Dry, and Windy

The harshest and coldest of all biomes is the tundra. The tundra is a treeless region found on the tops of mountains and in the Arctic, where the wind blows often and rain scarcely falls. During most of the year, the tundra is covered with snow. However, during the short summer season, the tundra comes alive with a burst of wildflowers.// Despite the treeless landscape and harsh conditions, many animals find their home in the tundra. Sheep, marmots, and mountain goats all live in the tundra. They spend their days feeding on the low-lying plants and the insects that reside there.// Global warming is dramatically changing the Arctic tundra each year. As southern animals, like the red fox, move onto the tundra to escape rising temperatures, it competes with the Arctic fox for food and territory.

Sample Modeled Writing

TURN &TALK *Think together about the steps in creating page breaks in a draft. Why do you think this is an important consideration when you are presenting work to a reader or an audience?*

STEP 2: Continue examining text and inserting page breaks.

Possible Think-Aloud: *As I continue to reread and examine my writing, I see that I can insert another page break after the word "there." This would place the section about how global warming is affecting the tundra on a new page. That would help a reader transition to the new subtopic. Watch as I do that. With page breaks, it also helps me realize that I could add some additional writing on these pages and provide more information. There is room to add some illustrations or other visuals as well. That would make the writing more interesting when I present it to an audience.*

Analyze

STEP 3: Reread and reflect.

Possible Think-Aloud: *Let's reread my book so far. Did creating page breaks improve the look and feel of my writing? How does it compare to my first draft? I think adding the page breaks helped to make my writing more interesting to read. It helped to reread often and think about where a page break would make the most sense.*

Sum It Up

I know you are ready to create page breaks to make your writing more interesting when it is presented to an audience. If you examine the informational books in our classroom library, you'll see that when authors plan page breaks, they have to think about content, visuals, text features, and layout. Each page needs to support an idea with maximum interest for a reader. Creating writing that has multiple pages is what nonfiction authors do! The best part of all is that multiple-page books look fabulous when they are bound.

VARIATIONS

For Less Experienced Writers: Provide more guided practice by typing up the words of a page or two from an appropriately leveled nonfiction book. As you type the text, do so without denoting the page breaks. Provide partners with copies of the text, and challenge them to decide where the page breaks should be placed. Then compare their estimates with the page breaks that the author chose.

For More Experienced Writers: Teach more experienced writers to analyze the page breaks they create. Encourage them to work in pairs to ensure that the breaks support units of meaning. They could also create lists of the features that multiple-page books should include such as a table of contents, numbered pages, title page, and glossary.

LINKS TO CD-ROM:
• Teaching Tool: Modeled Writing Example Without Page Breaks

Ideas

The Content and Focus of the Writing

Ideas make up the content of a piece of writing. When the ideas are strong and the content is rich in facts and imagery, nonfiction writing sparkles with possibility. When writers focus on ideas, they quickly learn that narrow topics, rich details, action, and descriptions entice their readers and lift nonfiction writing to greater heights.

LESSON	3	4	5	RELATED LESSONS
1 Create a Nonfiction Topic List	●	●	●	
2 Visualize Action—Then Write	●	●	●	*Grammar:* Lesson 5, Add Action with Gerunds
3 Jaw-Dropping Details Add Interest	●	●	●	*Voice and Audience:* Lesson 2, Show Engagement with the Topic
4 Use Details to Highlight Attributes		●	●	*Word Choice:* Lesson 4, Use Concrete Words to Support Visualization *Ideas:* Lesson 3, Jaw-Dropping Details Add Interest
5 Focus on the Main Idea(s)	●	●		*Organization:* Lesson 4, Main Idea Maintained Throughout
6 Anticipating a Reader's Questions and Answering Them	●	●	●	*Voice and Audience:* Lesson 3, Open with a Question
7 Focus on One	●	●	●	
8 Use Comparisons	●	●	●	*Word Choice:* Lesson 6, Use Simile *Word Choice:* Lesson 7, Use Metaphor
9 Develop a Persuasive Text	●	●	●	*Drafting:* Lesson 10, Drafting a Persuasion
10 Creating a Biographical Poem		●	●	

Create a Nonfiction Topic List

WHEN TO USE IT: To help writers find and personalize writing topics

FOCUS THE LEARNING

Writers benefit from the flexibility they gain when they have a ready-to-use list of writing topics, generated by wide reading and personal investigation.

Model

Have an array of nonfiction selections available representing science, social studies topics, sports, health, or other topics of interest. Students will need a clipboard or their writer's notebooks with copies of the nonfiction topic list from the Resources CD-ROM.

STEP 1: Generate topics from nonfiction resources.

Possible Think-Aloud: *Selecting topics for nonfiction writing can be a lot of fun because the best ideas often come when I am reading. As I look at this book about sports, I start thinking about baseball superstars like Babe Ruth. Watch as I write my thinking on this topic list. Sports is the big global topic. The subtopics that help me narrow and focus a piece of writing are even more important. Watch as I write some of those in column 2. Next, I need to consider some possible formats and text types that might be a good match for this topic. I could do a collection of biographies, with a biography and photo on each page. My mind keeps going back to the book* Baseball Saved Us. *The children in the Japanese internment camps of World War II needed baseball. I think that topic could be important. Watch as I go back to column 2 and put a star next to that topic.*

TURN &TALK *It is helpful to continue developing lists over time. Then, when you are ready for a new topic, you have a great list from which to select ideas. Think about sports. What topics and writing formats would you add to my list?*

Nonfiction Topic List

Writer _____

Possible Topic	Subtopics	Ideas for the Writing (format, text type, unique visuals, etc.)
Sports	Baseball: Babe Ruth, Willie Mays Little League Women's League in World War II ★ Baseball in the Japanese Internment Camps of World War II Women in Sports: Wilma Rudolph Hockey: The rules	A collection of biographies in a single book, a poem like Robert Burleigh's Home Run, personal narrative, report with real photos
		Procedure
Life in a Soddie	Construction of the soddie, ★ Realities of Lifestyle	Electronic slide show with primary-source photos of soddies and people of that time, Explanation
Manatee	Habitat, Attributes, Fragile with Unique Needs	Persuasion on Protection

Sample Modeled Writing

STEP 2: Continue adding to the nonfiction topic list.

Possible Think-Aloud: *In this book about westward migration and life on the prairie, I am particularly struck by the idea of living in a soddie with dirt walls, a dirt floor, and grass for a roof. I will add that to my topic list. It is important to think of subtopics so I can consider ways to focus and fine-tune my writing—broad topics seldom make great writing. I could write about construction of the soddie or, better yet, realities of the lifestyle—the bugs, animals, and constant dirt. Watch as I add those to the chart. I am going to put a star next to realities. That is a topic that most interests me. For a format, I could do a slide show with real photos, or an explanation and explain how they survived.*

TURN &TALK *Analyze my nonfiction topic list. How might a list like this help you as a writer? How can you remind yourself to keep adding to and modifying the list?*

Analyze

STEP 3: Explore and reflect.

Possible Think-Aloud: *I have a wonderful collection of nonfiction resources for you and a partner to explore together. Take a few minutes to look through some books and start a topic list. Remember that column 2, the subtopics, is critical because that is the column that will help you create a focused piece of writing. Take time to think together about formats and text types that you want to consider as well.* (Have partners explore and begin developing topic lists. Then provide time for them to share with another partner pair.)

Sum It Up

Nonfiction topic lists are helpful tools that are constantly growing and changing. Hopefully, you will be adding to and adjusting them every day. Then, when you are ready for a new writing topic, you will have a fabulous array of ideas from which to draw.

VARIATIONS

For Less Experienced Writers: Focus on columns 1 and 2, and emphasize the importance of finding narrow subtopics for column 2.

For More Experienced Writers: Guide these writers in examining columns 2 and 3 in depth, considering if subtopics are pieces of writing that could stand independently or if they would be good headings. In column 3, help these writers expand the range of formats and text types that they are considering.

LINKS TO CD-ROM:
• Nonfiction Topic List

Visualize Action—Then Write

WHEN TO USE IT: To improve descriptive detail and inclusion of action

FOCUS THE LEARNING

Writing is significantly improved when action is emphasized for a reader.

Model

Project the visual of the mustangs from the Resources CD-ROM, or print a copy for writers to view.

STEP 1: Model how to visualize and list words and phrases that capture action.

Possible Think-Aloud: *I find wild mustangs to be fascinating. It is amazing to me that they continue to thrive in spite of the fences that now surround ranches and the constant threat of capture. As I write about them, I will start by visualizing the action of mustangs running across the sagebrush. I visualize hooves pounding into dry soil, clouds of dust flying around their hooves. Watch as I quickly write some words and phrases to capture the action that I visualize. "Hooves pound. Tearing up dusty sagebrush. Galloping." Notice that I am not trying to write sentences. I am just gathering words and phrases that capture action.*

TURN &TALK *Join me in visualizing wild mustangs racing through a high desert. What words and phrases capture the action for you?*

STEP 2: Continue visualizing and capturing action.

Possible Think-Aloud: *I am going to focus on visualizing the mane that runs down the neck of a horse. As the mustang runs, I see the action of the mane floating, rippling— moving like waves on the shore. Watch as I write: "Mane floats . . . shore." That will help me remember to include the action of the mane in my writing. I am going to focus*

Hooves pound

Tearing up dusty sagebrush

Galloping

Wild and strong

Mane floats—rippling— like waves on the shore

Straining muscles ripple

Bunching, stretching, racing from a threat

Sample Modeled Writing

my visualization now on the amazing muscles of the mustang. As it runs, the muscles strain and ripple. They bunch and stretch as they work together.

TURN & TALK *What words and phrases would you add to capture action related to the mustangs? Visualize together—focus on action.*

The ground shakes as the racing hooves of the mustangs pound deep into dry soil—sending up clouds of dust and tearing up dusty sagebrush.

Sample Modeled Writing

Analyze

STEP 3: Reread listed words and phrases, and then write.

Possible Think-Aloud: *Let's reread the list of words and phrases together. The list really helped me capture action. That is important so a reader will be drawn into the situation. Watch as I begin to incorporate these action images into a piece of writing. I am going to link some of the words and phrases from the list into my writing. I will start with "The ground shakes" so a reader gets the sensory image of the movement. Next, I will add "as the racing hooves of the mustangs pound deep into dry soil— sending up clouds of dust and tearing up dusty sagebrush." Think together and analyze the writing. Does this focus on action? Can you visualize the situation or the setting?*

Sum It Up

To focus on action, it helps to begin by visualizing. Create a movie in your mind of what is happening—focus on the details. Then, make a list of words and phrases that capture movement and details. You may find it helpful to visualize a bit, write some words, and then go back to visualizing another element of the action.

VARIATIONS

For Less Experienced Writers: Encourage writers to focus first on verbs to keep their attention on the action. Then, branch out to other details that support sensory imaging and description of action.

For More Experienced Writers: Show writers how action can be an exciting lead for a piece of writing and then shift to become explanatory or descriptive. Some "-ing" words can be helpful in launching an exciting, action-packed lead as well. See the lesson on using gerunds on page 334.

LINKS TO CD-ROM:
- Mustangs
- Mentor Text: *The Last Living Symbol of the American West*

Jaw-Dropping Details Add Interest

WHEN TO USE IT: To heighten reader interest

FOCUS THE LEARNING

Students often fall into the trap of thinking that nonfiction writing is the simple listing of facts. Fascinating details create interest for a reader.

Model

STEP 1: Model and think aloud.

Possible Think-Aloud: *I am writing about earthworms. I have great books on the structure of an earthworm and their importance to farmers. I will want to include those details, but first, I need to make my reader curious. Watch as I write: "Did you know that. . . ?" I hope this will make my readers wonder why they should care if worms are high in protein. Now the jaw-dropping details: "These amazing creatures . . . pain." It is pretty incredible to think about worms as medicine. But that's not all. Here is another jaw-dropping detail: "In Vietnam, worms are made into a special . . . holiday treat."*

TURN &TALK *Put your heads together. What is the impact of my jaw-dropping details on your curiosity? Do they make you want to read more? If so, what element of these sentences hooked you and drew you in?*

STEP 2: Continue modeling.

Possible Think-Aloud: *Since this is the opening, or the lead, to my writing, I need to set the stage for the rest of the piece. Watch as I write: "While you may not elect to eat one for dinner tonight. . . ." Now I need to tempt my reader to keep going and wonder how or why. Here is another detail: "Earthworms have been called some of the most valuable creatures on earth."*

Did you know that earthworms are high in protein and low in fat? These amazing creatures are used in China to make a soup that helps to stop pain. In Vietnam, worms are made into a special patty that is fried as a holiday treat. While you may not elect to eat one for dinner tonight, you may want to understand why earthworms have been called some of the most valuable creatures on earth.

Sample Modeled Writing

TURN & TALK *I added two jaw-dropping details, and then I tried to make my reader curious. Analyze this lead. Are the ideas strong and interesting? Is there enough detail? Did I leave you wanting more?*

Analyze

STEP 3: Plan the next steps, and then reread and reflect.

Possible Think-Aloud: *I found another jaw-dropping detail that I can add. Did you know that you can freeze a worm, and if you defrost it very slowly, it doesn't die? Isn't that amazing! That means that if the ground freezes, worms will survive and become active again when the ground warms up—a jaw-dropping detail, for sure. Think together and consider where that detail should be added. Should I place it in the introduction or add it to liven up the section on benefits to farmers?* (After students discuss placement of the jaw-dropping detail.) *Let's reread and analyze what I have written.*

Sum It Up

Jaw-dropping details can add a lot of interest for readers. Details stimulate curiosity and entice readers into reading on. Today as you write, think about jaw-dropping or highly interesting details that you can use to capture the attention of a reader.

VARIATIONS

For Less Experienced Writers: Assist writers in collecting details that enrich and expand basic information so they have richer ideas to develop in their writing.

For More Experienced Writers: Show writers that a jaw-dropping detail can be written so it is lifeless and boring. The trick is in how you present it to a reader. Practice rewriting dictionary-like sentences so the details spring to life. An example: "Pandas don't drink much water." Rewrite: "Sitting upright, like a human, pandas consume enormous amounts of water-filled bamboo. As a result, pandas rarely need to drink water!"

LINKS TO CD-ROM:
• Jaw-Dropping Details Organizer

Use Details to Highlight Attributes

WHEN TO USE IT: To help writers enrich descriptions

FOCUS THE LEARNING

When writers provide rich descriptions of their subject, readers notice attributes and features they might miss when descriptions are sketchy or underdeveloped.

Model

STEP 1: Model how to infuse details in a way that highlights attributes.

Possible Think-Aloud: *I am writing about pipistrelle bats, but I don't want to write something like "Pipistrelle bats are no bigger than your thumb. They have small eyes and fragile wings." That kind of writing is okay, but I want to draw my reader in so details and ideas really stand out. I want readers to really notice the attributes of my subject, the pipistrelle. Watch as I use a situation as the focus, including details as I go. "Evening swirls softly into night, and the pipistrelle bats begin to wake. Hanging upside down with bodies no larger than your thumb, beady eyes spring open, and tiny ears twitch."*

TURN &TALK *My goal is to highlight attributes of my subject with details using a situation to draw in my reader. Think together and analyze this writing.*

STEP 2: Continue thinking aloud and modeling.

Possible Think-Aloud: *I am fascinated by the wing structure of bats. The bone structure is much like that of a human hand, and there are no feathers, just extremely thin skin that almost allows you to see the bones inside. Watch as I begin inserting those details while continuing to focus on the situation. "Fragile wings unfurl with*

Evening swirls softly into night, and the pipistrelle bats begin to wake. Hanging upside down with bodies no larger than your thumb, beady eyes spring open, and tiny ears twitch. Fragile wings unfurl with skin so thin it seems transparent, and pipistrelles drop like tiny umbrellas into the darkness. Hunting time has begun.

Sample Modeled Writing

skin so thin it seems transparent. . . ." I know that when a bat lets go with its feet, the wings have to pop open instantly, like little umbrellas, or the bat would land on the ground on its head. Watch as I continue and add that detail: "Pipistrelles drop like tiny umbrellas into the darkness."

TURN &TALK *Compare this writing with the writing that I could have done: "Pipistrelle bats are no bigger than your thumb. They have small eyes and fragile wings." Evaluate the differences.*

Analyze

STEP 3: Reread and reflect.

Possible Think-Aloud: *The goal of this writing is to use details to highlight attributes of the pipistrelle. As we reread, I am going to start a tally and make a mark for each detail that is included in the writing. I will set it up like a little T-chart with details about the situation in column 1 and details about the bat in column 2. My main objective is to provide details about the bat, but I need some details about the situation so my reader*

Situation Details	Bat Details
///	/////

becomes engaged. In the first sentence, "Evening swirls softly into night, and the pipistrelle bats begin to wake," I can tally one under situation because this sentence tells it is night. I can tally one under bat because of the detail that the bat is waking. I can add another tally under bat because this sentence helps a reader to infer that the bat was asleep during the day since it is just waking up. Get ready to read the next sentence. Let's tally the details.

Sum It Up

Nonfiction writers need to include a lot of details to help a reader picture attributes of a subject, but it also helps to establish a situation. When details are woven into descriptions of action, readers feel a stronger connection and are better able to visualize.

VARIATIONS

For Less Experienced Writers: Use photographs and visuals to coach writers in noticing and listing details they can use in their writing. Then, establish a situation that could be common to the subject.

For More Experienced Writers: Have students form partnerships and read their descriptions to each other. Have the listener consciously focus on visualizing and attending to details and then retell what he or she remembers. This will help writers understand that the reader's understanding is the ultimate goal.

LINKS TO CD-ROM:
• Details Chart

Focus on the Main Idea(s)

WHEN TO USE IT: To help writers stay focused on central ideas

FOCUS THE LEARNING

As writers advance into lengthier pieces of writing, it is easy to lose track of main ideas. To maintain focus, it is helpful to teach them to pause often and remind themselves of the key points they are trying to make.

Model

Prepare a chart with the first sentence of the modeled writing and the headings, leaving room to write during the lesson.

STEP 1: Demonstrate the importance of pausing and reflecting on main ideas.

Possible Think-Aloud: *I am writing about Yellowstone National Park—one of my favorite places in the United States. My two central ideas are the geothermal activity and the amazing wildlife. To help myself be organized, I have listed headings that I plan to cover, and as you can see, I have written the first sentence in the section on geysers. This piece is informational—like a report. Watch as I begin sentence two: "The most famous . . . steam." I need to pause and think about my main ideas. This is a section on the geysers. Is everything in these two sentences focused on that main idea, and is it written in the style of an informational piece? It is, so I can keep going. "Once we went to watch the geyser, but there were so many people we couldn't find a place to park."*

TURN &TALK *I will pause again and ask two important questions. Is this sentence focused on the main idea of this section? Is it written in the style of an informational piece? Analyze this sentence.*

Geysers

Yellowstone National Park has long been appreciated for its amazing hot springs and geysers. The most famous geyser, Old Faithful, erupts into action approximately every 90 minutes with a scalding tower of water and steam. ~~Once we went to watch the geyser, but there were so many people we couldn't find a place to park.~~ The secret of this geothermal activity lies far beneath the surface of the earth.

Supervolcano

A Variety of Wildlife

Sample Modeled Writing

STEP 2: Demonstrate how to delete the unfocused sentence and return to the main idea.

Possible Think-Aloud: *I definitely need to cross out that last sentence. I had a memory about Yellowstone that doesn't match the main idea here. Parking and crowds of tourists were in my head because of an experience, but that is not the main idea here. The other problem with that sentence is that it belongs in a personal narrative in which you write about an experience you have had. This kind of sentence is not what you see in great informational writing. So, let's go back to the main idea of this section, geysers. Watch as I write: "The secret of this geothermal activity lies far beneath the surface of the earth."*

TURN &TALK *Okay. You know what to do. We are pausing to wonder if this sentence fits the main idea of this section and if it is written like an informational text. Analyze, evaluate, and be ready to report your thinking.*

Analyze

STEP 3: Identify main ideas that should be covered within a heading.

Possible Think-Aloud: *I am ready to begin writing about the supervolcano that has been found far underneath Yellowstone Park. Scientists now know that this volcano is what causes the geysers and hot springs to push to the surface of the park. It is believed that the supervolcano erupted 640,000 years ago and that activity in the geysers and hot springs is increasing—suggesting that the deeply seated volcano is picking up steam. Put your heads together. I have a heading, supervolcano. What main ideas should I cover in this section?*

Sum It Up

Maintaining the main idea of a piece of writing, or even a section, requires that you really pay attention. You need to pause often and ask yourself, "Is this sentence tightly linked to the main idea? And does this sentence reflect the type of writing that I am doing?" If you slip away from your main idea, catch yourself, cross it out, and get back on track.

VARIATIONS

For Less Experienced Writers: Use the graphic organizer on the Resources CD-ROM to guide writers in carefully planning how main ideas and details will fit together. Then, provide them with reminder notes to place on their desks to pause often and check to make sure they are sticking to the main idea.

For More Experienced Writers: Engage writers in partner reflections that have them reading together and asking the two key questions about main idea and writing style.

LINKS TO CD-ROM:
- Main Idea and Details
- Reflecting on Main Ideas
- Writing Samples

Anticipating the Questions of Your Reader

WHEN TO USE IT: To broaden the base of ideas writers use when drafting

FOCUS THE LEARNING

Books like *How Do Flies Walk Upside Down?* or *Why Don't Haircuts Hurt?* by Melvin and Gilda Berger make great mentors for anticipating reader questions.

Model

STEP 1: Begin generating questions that a reader might ask.

Possible Think-Aloud: *Today I am going to be writing about a carnivorous plant, the Venus flytrap. These are fascinating plants that, unlike most other plants, need to eat insects to be healthy. This is because the Venus flytrap tends to live in very poor soil conditions, and it can't get enough nutrients from the soil and air to be healthy. To gather ideas for writing on this topic, I am going to focus on questions that I think readers might have about this fascinating plant. Watch as I begin my list: "How does the Venus flytrap capture insects?" "What would attract an insect to this carnivorous plant?"*

TURN &TALK *Think together about the Venus flytrap, and generate questions that you would want answered if you were going to read something on this topic.*

STEP 2: Demonstrate how to identify bullet points under each question.

Possible Think-Aloud: *We have some great questions that we anticipate a reader might have on this topic. Now it is time to gather ideas to use in the answers. For the question "How does a Venus flytrap capture insects?" I will need to write about the trigger hairs*

How does the Venus flytrap capture insects?
- trigger hairs
- cilia
- trap closes

What would attract an insect to this carnivorous plant?
- sweet-smelling juice
- flower-like colors

How does the flytrap digest an insect?

What are the physical attributes of a Venus flytrap?

Sample Modeled Writing

©Joel Sartore/National Geographic/Getty Images/HIP

that sense when an insect has landed, the cilia that are like bars on a jail cell and keep the insect inside when the trap closes, and the trap itself. It's like a clamshell and can close in less than a second when it senses an insect. Watch as I use bullet points to list key words that I will want to include in my answer: "• trigger hairs • cilia • trap closes."

TURN &TALK *Anticipate that you are writing this piece. Which of the questions in the list would you choose to answer next? Which one would give the best support to reader understanding?*

Analyze

STEP 3: Reread and reflect.

Possible Think-Aloud: *This is a good time to review my resources and make sure I have considered all the best possible questions that a reader might ask on this topic. I want to be sure that I have selected the best and most important questions around which to focus the ideas in my writing. As I turn the pages of this resource, think together and consider any additional questions we should be developing.*

Sum It Up

Writers, when you anticipate the questions that a reader might ask about a topic, it helps you to organize and gather ideas. This approach also helps you tune into your audience and write specifically for a reader. Remember to gather great questions and make bullet points for key words and ideas. Then, you are ready to write.

VARIATIONS

For Less Experienced Writers: While conferring with individuals, think together about possible questions a reader might ask, so as to broaden the range of ideas that each writer is incorporating while writing.

For More Experienced Writers: Challenge these writers to come up with open-ended questions that may have more than one right answer, forcing them to take a stance and generate support for their positions.

LINKS TO CD-ROM:
• Venus Flytrap
• Anticipating Reader Questions

Focus on "One"

WHEN TO USE IT: To help writers move beyond detached, generalized descriptions

FOCUS THE LEARNING

Nonfiction narratives are richly constructed descriptions that often focus on one single animal or subject. This helps the writing to take on a personal feel that evokes sensory imaging.

Model

Mentor books to support a focus on "one": *Bat Loves the Night* by Nicola Davies, *Walk with a Wolf* by Janni Howker, *Tigress* by Nick Dowson, *Voices of the Wild* by Jonathan London

STEP 1: Focus on an individual animal, and zoom in close with lots of detail.

Possible Think-Aloud: *One of the strategies we can use in nonfiction narratives is to zoom in close on an individual animal or subject and focus on "one." I am writing about geckos, so I could say, "Geckos can hang upside down. They have over a million hairs on each toe pad—enabling them to stick to slick surfaces." That kind of writing is fine, but it is very general. Watch as I zoom in and write with a focus on a single gecko—turning my writing into an informational narrative. "A banded gecko hangs upside down high in the lush foliage. . . ." Notice how the focus on "one" zooms in close and attends to details? Watch closely as I write sentence two: "His toe pads. . . ." Did you notice that when you focus on "one," you use pronouns such as "he," "she," "his," and "her"? With a focus on "one," you still insert details and important facts. That doesn't change. The difference is that nonfiction narrative zooms a reader in close and supports sensory imaging.*

A banded gecko hangs upside down high in the lush foliage of the rainforest, waiting patiently for an insect to come within reach. His toe pads, each covered in nearly one million hairs, provide sure footing on the slickest of surfaces. Suddenly, a stalk-eyed fly zooms in close. In an instant, the gecko curls up his toes and leaps. With the fly clutched in his mouth, he uses his tail like a rudder and drops to a safe landing on the ground.

Sample Modeled Writing

TURN &TALK *Analyze my writing. What do you notice about the focus on "one?" How does it affect you as a reader? If you wanted to try this type of writing, what should you remember to do?*

STEP 2: Add some action.

Possible Think-Aloud: *I am going to pause and visualize. I know that geckos eat mostly insects. To catch them, they have to lift up the tips of their toes to break the hold on whatever surface they are hanging from. Then, they leap to catch their prey using their tail like a rudder. I am visualizing my gecko hanging upside down from the branches of a tree, and in zooms a fly. The gecko leaps! Watch as I write: "Suddenly, a stalk-eyed fly zooms in close. In an instant, the gecko curls up his toes and leaps. With the fly clutched in his mouth, he uses his tail like a rudder and drops to a safe landing on the ground."*

TURN &TALK *Consider the advantage of adding a bit of action. Then, compare and contrast this focus on "one" with nonfiction writing that describes animals in general terms.*

Analyze

STEP 3: Reread and reflect.

Possible Think-Aloud: *To me, the secret to a focus on "one" is to do lots of visualizing. Get an image in your mind with lots of details and facts. See the action—like a movie in your mind. Then, zoom in close and help your reader connect to the one you are writing about. Let's reread my writing and consciously focus on visualizing—make that movie in your mind. Then, we'll evaluate and decide if more detail is needed.*

Sum It Up

Nonfiction writers can write in ways that are general but can be very specific as well. When we write about "one," we help our readers come in close and look very carefully. It is like focusing a camera and seeing a single animal in detail. As you begin writing today, spend a moment thinking about "one."

VARIATIONS

For Less Experienced Writers: Guide them in visualizing with attention to detail as a pre-writing support to focusing on "one."

For More Experienced Writers: Stretch the focus on "one" beyond animals with something like: "A tiny seed, softened by water, cracks open, and a slim green shoot reaches out. An aging tree, weakened by constant wind and lack of water. . . ."

Use Comparisons

WHEN TO USE IT: To help writers integrate comparisons into their writing

FOCUS THE LEARNING

When comparisons are included in nonfiction writing selections, a reader has support in making connections between prior knowledge and the information in the passage. These comparisons may appear as a comparison diagram, a descriptive passage, or a simile.

Model

STEP 1: Share comparisons from *Tigress* by Nick Dowson or Seymour Simon books such as *The Sun* or *The Heart*. It may also be helpful to print or use a projection device to display the comparison diagrams on the Resources CD-ROM.

Possible Think-Aloud: *In* Tigress *by Nick Dowson, there are wonderful comparisons that are designed to help a reader connect information about a tigress to things in the everyday world. He compares her nose to the size of a human fist, her eyes to bright yellow torches, her paws to the size of a plate. Those are comparisons that really connect for me. Hold your hands out as though you were holding onto a dinner plate. Isn't it amazing to "see" the enormous size of a tiger paw? I also notice that Nick Dowson uses similes such as this one: "Weighing only a few pounds, her babies drink rich mother's milk and fill up like fat, furry cushions."*

TURN &TALK *Put your heads together, and talk about that simile. The cubs are like fat, furry cushions. Describe what that comparison helps you to visualize.*

STEP 2: Model creating comparisons in writing.

Possible Think-Aloud: *I am going to write about the blue whale using comparisons to support my reader in understanding the tremendous size of this whale. Scientists believe that it is the largest animal to have ever lived on earth. It is larger than the*

Blue Whale

Size: bigger than the biggest dinosaur, as large as a Boeing passenger jet

Hearing: can hear another blue whale 1,000 miles away—about the distance between Washington, D.C., and New Orleans

Ear: the size of a pencil eraser

Tongue: weighs as much as fully grown elephant

Sample Modeled Writing

biggest dinosaur—as big as a Boeing passenger jet! Its tongue alone weighs as much as a full-grown elephant. To gather ideas for writing, I am going to list comparisons between the blue whale and things that are familiar to me. Watch as I write: "Size . . . jet."

> Did you know that a blue whale is bigger than the biggest dinosaur and as large as a Boeing passenger jet? Its tongue alone weighs as much as a fully grown elephant! Now that's a big whale! What may be more amazing is that the ear is only the size of a pencil eraser, but the blue whale can hear another blue whale up to 1,000 miles away! That is as far as from Washington, D.C., to New Orleans. Amazing.

Sample Modeled Writing

VARIATIONS

For Less Experienced Writers: Provide opportunities for these writers to analyze writing they have already completed and add comparisons.

For More Experienced Writers: Stretch these writers toward comparisons that add significant detail and sensory imaging such as those in *Tigress* by Nick Dowson or *Bat Loves the Night* by Nicola Davies.

TURN &TALK *Analyze these comparisons and use them to better understand the blue whale.*

Analyze

STEP 3: Use comparisons in a draft.

Possible Think-Aloud: *I am ready to reread the comparisons I have listed and begin to write. Watch as I use comparisons from the list in a draft. "Did you know that a blue whale is bigger than the biggest dinosaur and as large as a Boeing passenger jet?" Did you notice I included a simile, "as large as a Boeing?" I'll continue writing: "Its tongue alone weighs as much as a fully grown elephant! Now that's a big whale! What may be more amazing is that the ear is only the size of a pencil eraser, but the blue whale can hear another blue whale up to 1,000 miles away! That is as far as from Washington, D.C., to New Orleans. Amazing." Think together. Which comparisons would be logical to include as I continue this piece of writing?*

Sum It Up

Comparisons help readers connect what they already know to what they are learning, so it is important for nonfiction writers to use lots of comparisons. Look closely at your writing today, and insert at least one comparison. What will you write?

LINKS TO CD-ROM:
• Blue Whale Comparison Diagrams

Develop a Persuasive Text

WHEN TO USE IT: To make and support an argument

Argument or persuasion is a powerful structure in which writers learn to take a stance and support an argument.

Model

STEP 1: Introduce the features of persuasive text, and begin to write.

Possible Think-Aloud: *Persuasive texts allow nonfiction writers to take a position on a topic and then support their argument with details and facts. It is important to notice that persuasive writing has a very distinct structure. First, state the position or make a call to action. Next, offer supporting facts. Finally, restate your position. I am going to create a persuasive poster focused on saving energy by turning off lights. Watch as I write: "Leaving the room? Turn off the lights!" Notice that there is not a subject in these sentences. These are imperative statements in which it is understood that the subject is **you**—the reader. In a persuasive piece such as this, you get to sound really bossy. Since this is a poster, I will center the text in the middle of the page, rather than justifying to the left as we would normally do in a draft.*

TURN &TALK *I am ready to add some facts to support my argument. Identify some good reasons for turning off the lights.*

STEP 2: Insert supporting facts.

Possible Think-Aloud: *Saving energy is the primary reason for turning off lights, so I will focus on that first with "Conserve energy." This is really about the planet— and using our resources with care. Watch as I add, "Help the planet while you save money! It's easy and it's free."*

Leaving the room?

Turn off the lights!

Conserve energy.

Help the planet while you save money!

It's easy and it's free.

Flip That Switch—Today!

Sample Modeled Writing

TURN &TALK *Evaluate my facts. Are these the strongest supports I could offer for an argument to turn off lights? Consider other facts that would strengthen my persuasion.*

Analyze

STEP 3: Use repetition. Restate the call to action.

Possible Think-Aloud: *Now I am ready for the conclusion. The idea of the conclusion is to restate the position or the call to action. That means repetition is okay. Sometimes you can even repeat the very same words. I could repeat the first two lines and say, "Leaving the room? Turn off the lights!" But instead, I think I will get at the same idea with different words. How about "Flip That Switch— Today!" Think together about my conclusion. Is it strong enough? Does it make you want to turn off some lights?*

Sum It Up

Persuasive arguments are powerful nonfiction opportunities to call for action that will make the world better or create change to improve a situation. In a piece of persuasion, you need to state a position or create a call to action. Offer supporting facts and details, and use imperative, bossy language. Then, repeat the main idea by restating the call to action or using wording that gets your point across in a new way. The idea of persuasive text is to get a reader to see things **your** way.

VARIATIONS

For Less Experienced Writers: Provide an opportunity for partners to create persuasive posters so they can plan and draft together.

For More Experienced Writers: Stretch these writers into persuasive letters and essays that require them to use complete sentences and formal language.

LINKS TO CD-ROM:
- Persuasive Framework
- Mentor Text: *Reversing a Heavy Trend*
- Writing Samples

Creating a Biographical Poem

WHEN TO USE IT: To help writers see that ideas can be presented in many formats

FOCUS THE LEARNING

Nonfiction poetry comes in many formats and organizational patterns, offering writers a wide range of possibilities for communication about their learning. Nonfiction poems are **poems that teach**— bringing facts to life in new and unique ways.

Model

STEP 1: Begin drafting a biographical poem.

Possible Think-Aloud: *We have all read biographies that are written in narrative form. But a poem can be biographical, too. I am writing a poem about Martin Luther King, Jr., so I want my poem to emphasize his focus on peace and kindness. Watch as I begin with "Some kings rule with a clenched fist. This one stood on a throne of peace." Notice that I am using his last name as though Martin Luther King were royalty. "Some kings rule. . . ." I also reference a throne, but I don't mean a royal throne. I am using this as a symbol for the power of peace and the leadership that he displayed.* (Continue writing up to "lives were changed.")

TURN &TALK *Reread the portion of the biographical poem I have completed so far, and analyze it. Consider: Many poems rhyme. This one does not. What are the advantages and disadvantages of rhyming in a poem like this?*

STEP 2: Continue writing.

Possible Think-Aloud: *Because this is a biographical poem, I want to continue emphasizing the importance of Martin Luther King's life, but I also want to include a few factual details. We know that he was assassinated on April 4, 1968. Watch as I weave that detail into the poem. "We lost this King to a rush of hate. April 4, 1968." That is a significant fact because this act of violence ended the*

Martin Luther King, Jr.
Some kings rule with a clenched fist.
This one stood on a throne of peace.
He dared to dream—and lives were changed.
We lost this King to a rush of hate.
April 4, 1968.
His dream lives on.
This King stands tall.
And we remember.

Sample Modeled Writing

life of a man who was really making a difference in reaching for equal treatment for all people.

TURN &TALK *Consider the possibilities. Are there any other significant facts that should be incorporated into this biographical poem? We could use so many different ideas from Martin Luther King's life, so making a choice isn't easy.*

Analyze

STEP 3: Write a conclusion, reread, and reflect.

Possible Think-Aloud: *As is true of any type of writing, biographical poems need a conclusion that gives a reader a clear sense of the end. I am thinking about the fact that we now have a national holiday to celebrate Martin Luther King's birthday. That might make a good conclusion. I also think it would be interesting to focus on the idea that his dream didn't die. It lives on—and we remember him. Come in close and think with me as I write: "His dream lives on. This King stands tall. And we remember." Let's reread the entire poem and reflect together.*

Sum It Up

Biographical poems are a tribute to the life of a person. They don't need to contain complete sentences, and they don't need to rhyme. They do need to emphasize that person's contributions to the future or to a time in history. They do need to be factually accurate. Best of all, they are another way to express our ideas as nonfiction writers.

VARIATIONS

For Less Experienced Writers: Use the informational poems lesson on page 76 of this resource, and guide writers in coming up with descriptors for figures from history that they can then arrange as a list poem.

For More Experienced Writers: Introduce narrative nonfiction poems that tell a story. With a poetic format, these poems establish a situation, add action, and then bring it to resolution. See the Resources CD-ROM for examples.

LINKS TO CD–ROM: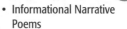
• Informational Narrative Poems

Organization

Giving Structure to Our Work

The internal structure of a piece of writing gives it stability just as the foundation of a home provides a solid base for the dwelling. Writing with strong organization begins with a clear purpose; then arguments, descriptions, and explanations flow logically with information organized in meaningful clusters. Transition words, inviting leads, and satisfying endings draw readers smoothly through the writing.

LESSON	3	4	5	RELATED LESSONS
1 Organizing a Description	●	●	●	*Research:* Lesson 8, Using a Research Notebook
2 Using a Timeline	●	●	●	*Planning:* Lesson 8, Using a Flowchart
3 Compare/Contrast		●	●	*Ideas:* Lesson 8, Using Comparisons
4 Main Idea Maintained Throughout	●			*Revising:* Lesson 4, Main Idea Maintained Throughout *Ideas:* Lesson 5, Focus on the Main Idea(s)
5 Using Headings to Group Related Information	●	●	●	*Drafting:* Lesson 1, Headings Keep Writing Organized
6 Create an Inviting Lead	●	●	●	*Drafting:* Lesson 8, Experimenting with Leads
7 Craft an Ending that Brings Closure	●	●		*Drafting:* Lesson 9, Creating a Conclusion
8 Paragraphs		●	●	*Editing:* Lesson 6, Paragraphs and Indentations
9 Using a Persuasive Framework		●	●	*Drafting:* Lesson 10, Drafting a Persuasion *Ideas:* Lesson 9, Develop a Persuasive Text
10 Utilize Transitions and Linking Statements		●	●	*Drafting:* Lesson 4, Infusing Transition Words and Phrases *Sentence Fluency:* Lesson 8, Smooth Transitions with Linking Words and Phrases

Organizing a Description

WHEN TO USE IT: When students need support in planning and organizing their writing

FOCUS THE LEARNING

FOCUS THE LEARNING

Graphic organizers provide a visual aid that can help facilitate writing. Once students collect and organize facts using a spider organizer, they can craft a draft that is clear and organized, since each arm of the organizer can be developed into a paragraph.

Model

STEP 1: Introduce the graphic organizer and your topic.

Possible Think-Aloud: *I want to show you a tool that writers sometimes use to help them organize their facts and plan for their writing. It's called a spider organizer. Today I'm working on a piece of writing that is meant to teach my reader about the three main types of clouds. I'm going to use this organizer to help me think about how to organize my writing. First, I'll write "Types of Clouds" on the circle in the middle, since that is the focus of my piece. One kind of cloud is called "stratus." I'll write that on one of the vertical lines. Now I can use the horizontal lines to jot down a few notes about stratus clouds.*

TURN &TALK *Partners, examine this type of organizer. How might it help me to organize the information this way?*

STEP 2: Demonstrate how you use the spider organizer to organize your facts and plan for your writing.

Possible Think-Aloud: *Now I'm ready to jot down some details that tell more about stratus clouds. This resource states that stratus clouds are usually lower than other kinds of clouds and that they can often cover the entire sky, although they generally don't produce much precipitation. Watch as I jot those facts down on my organizer. On the first line, I'll write, "low clouds." On the next line, I'll write, "cover entire sky." Finally, I'll write, "usually no precipitation" on the last line. Notice that I don't write complete sentences. When you use a spider organizer, you can use single words or phrases to record your thinking.*

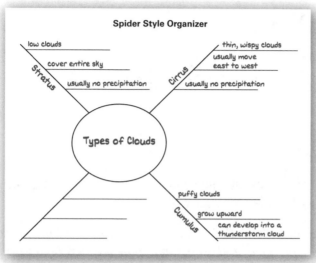

Sample Modeled Writing

TURN &TALK *Let's read what I have on my spider organizer so far. What might I add next? Do you think using this tool will help me as I begin to write? How might it help me?*

Analyze

STEP 3: Reread and reflect.

Possible Think-Aloud: *Next, I'll record some information about cirrus clouds. I'll write "Cirrus" on the vertical line and then jot down some important details about those kinds of clouds. As I researched, I discovered that these types of clouds are thin and wispy and usually mean that no precipitation is in store. Watch as I record those facts on the spider organizer.*

Sum It Up

Today we learned how a spider organizer can help you organize factual information in preparation to write. Once I've collected and organized my facts, I can develop each arm of my organizer into a complete paragraph. As you return to work today, try using a spider organizer like we did together and see if it helps you clarify your thinking as a writer.

VARIATIONS

For Less Experienced Writers: Less experienced writers may benefit from guided practice as they complete their own spider organizers. Consider coaching a small group of writers in creating an organizer about a common topic. Then, demonstrate how to use the organizer to create clear and cohesive paragraphs.

For More Experienced Writers: Demonstrate how you can use the spider organizer to plan for other types of nonfiction text structures. For example, show students how you can organize points of an argument for a persuasive selection or use the organizer to map out directions for a procedural piece of writing.

LINKS TO CD-ROM:
• Graphic Organizer: Spider Style Organizer

Using a Timeline

WHEN TO USE IT: When students are crafting a piece of writing that involves time order

FOCUS THE LEARNING

Students often become overwhelmed when sequencing dated events within a piece of writing. Our goal is to teach them how to organize these events using a timeline and then use it to help support them as they write.

Model

STEP 1: Demonstrate how you use the timeline to organize your thoughts and plan for your writing.

Possible Think-Aloud: *Writers, I am going to use a timeline to organize my facts and events in a logical order. I'm writing about the events that led up to the Civil War. Watch as I add the date 1820. In that year, Missouri wanted to become a state. Watch as I add that information on the timeline. Next, I'll add 1860 because Abraham Lincoln was elected as president, and he vowed that slavery would not extend to new territories or states. Did you notice that I didn't write complete sentences? When you record information on a timeline, you can simply write the date and words or phrases that capture your thinking.*

TURN &TALK *I'm ready to start writing using my timeline. Partners, think together. How might a timeline help me as I begin to write? How might it help me to organize the writing?*

STEP 2: Show students how you write about each item on your timeline.

Possible Think-Aloud: *Now I'm ready to begin writing. Watch as I use my timeline to help keep my writing organized. One trick I use is to write a paragraph about each item on the timeline. When I do that, my writing stays focused and organized. The first item on my timeline is "1820: Missouri applies for statehood." As I craft this*

Timeline

Missouri applies for statehood

Attack at Ft. Sumter

YEARS | 1820 | 1860 | 1861 | 1862 | 1863 | 1864

Abraham Lincoln elected president

Sample Modeled Writing

In 1820 tension between the North and the South flared. In that year, Missouri met the requirements for statehood and applied to be admitted to the union. However, Missouri allowed slavery, and if it were to be admitted as a state, it would upset the balance of free states and slave states.

Tensions flared again in 1860, when Abraham Lincoln was elected as the 16th president. He believed that the South was becoming too powerful, and he vowed that slavery would not be extended to any of the new territories or states. This enraged the South. South Carolina and six other states seceded from the Union. The conflict was heating up. . . .

Sample Modeled Writing

paragraph, I'll be sure to include the date along with some details that will give my reader more information about this event. I'll write, "In 1820 tension between the North and the South flared. . . ." (Continue drafting the first paragraph.)

TURN &TALK *Think together about my first paragraph. Is it organized and clear? Is there anything else I should add about this date and event?*

Analyze

STEP 3: Reread and reflect.

Possible Think-Aloud: *I'm ready to begin a new paragraph and tell about another event that led up to the Civil War. The next date and event on my timeline are 1860 when Lincoln was elected president. I don't want to start this paragraph the same way I started the last one, so I'll write, "Tensions flared again in 1860, when Abraham Lincoln was elected as the 16th president." (Continue writing.)*

Sum It Up

When you take the time to record some dates and events on a timeline, it will help you craft a cohesive and organized draft. As you begin writing today, try using a timeline and see if it helps you as a writer.

VARIATIONS

For Less Experienced Writers: Invite students to help you create a timeline about a shared event such as a field trip or a visit from a guest speaker. Then, coach partners as they use the timeline to craft a written text describing the events.

For More Experienced Writers: Gather published nonfiction selections that utilize timelines. Lead a discussion about why each author chose to include the timeline in the finished product. Challenge students to consider adding a timeline, complete with illustrations or photographs, to their published work.

LINKS TO CD-ROM:
• Graphic Organizer: Timeline

Compare/Contrast

WHEN TO USE IT: When students need support in planning and organizing a piece of writing that compares or contrasts

FOCUS THE LEARNING

Graphic organizers help students to visually arrange their ideas and plan for writing. This lesson shows students how a comparison chart can be one more tool to help them as they prepare to write.

Model

STEP 1: Introduce the comparison chart, and think aloud as you organize your thinking about the topic.

Possible Think-Aloud: *Today I am going to use a graphic organizer called a comparison chart. I can use this kind of organizer when I am writing about similarities and differences between two topics or ideas. I'm writing a piece that compares wolves and dogs. Watch as I use the comparison chart to help me organize my thinking. First, I need to think about how wolves and dogs are alike and how they are different. As I compare the teeth in both wolves and dogs, I'll write the attribute "Teeth," in the box on the left. Then, I'll record brief notes about that attribute in both wolves and dogs. Wolves and dogs both have 42 teeth, so I'll write "42 teeth" in both boxes. Notice how the chart makes the comparisons so clear.* (Complete comparison chart.)

Comparison Chart

	Topic 1 Wolves	Topic 2 Dogs
Attribute 1 Teeth	· 42 teeth · used to break bones and tear flesh of prey	· 42 teeth · used to chew smaller food
Attribute 2 Fur	· shed fur once a year to grow a winter coat	· shed fur throughout the year
Attribute 3 Communication		
Attribute 4		
Attribute 5		
Attribute 6		

TURN &TALK *Partners, think together. Identify the attributes of a comparison chart, and consider ways in which a chart such as this can help you create well-organized writing.*

STEP 2: Complete the comparison chart, and demonstrate how you use it to help you as you begin writing.

Sample Modeled Writing

Possible Think-Aloud: *Now I'm ready to use the comparison chart to fuel my writing. I need an introductory sentence that will alert my reader to the fact that I'm comparing dogs and wolves. I'll write, "There are many differences between wolves and dogs, but there are also many similarities." The first item on my chart is "Teeth," so I'll write about that first. I'll say, "Wolves and dogs both have a set of 42 teeth that are designed to eat meat. However, wolves . . . chew smaller, softer bits of food." Did you notice how I used the information I recorded on my chart as I began to write? Notice also that I am deliberately inserting words that highlight comparisons such as "similarities," "differences," "both," and "however." These linking words help comparison writing, too.*

TURN & TALK *Analyze the chart together, and create a sentence about fur that compares and contrasts wolves and dogs. Use the information in the chart, and be sure to include some of those helpful linking words to highlight the comparisons.*

Analyze

STEP 3: Reread and reflect.

Possible Think-Aloud: *I have used a comparison chart to organize my facts and make comparisons easier to see. I have also tried to insert words of comparison such as "however," "similar," "different," and "both." After you share the sentences you have created from the chart, we can double-check to be sure that this comparison writing is well organized and sounds interesting when we read it aloud.* (Insert additional sentences and a conclusion.) *Let's reread what I have written and see how it sounds. Get ready to analyze my comparison and evaluate its organization.*

Sum It Up

When I take the time to record some similarities and differences between my topics in a chart like this, it helps me to draft a piece of writing that is organized and a joy to read. Today as you begin writing, try using a comparison chart like we did together, and focus on writing comparisons that are organized and supported by linking words.

VARIATIONS

For Less Experienced Writers: Bring a small group of writers together, and continue modeling and providing guided practice with a comparison chart on a new topic. Then, confer and coach them as they use a comparison chart for their own topics.

For More Experienced Writers: Examine and analyze other kinds of graphic organizers, and discuss how they can be utilized to create writing that exhibits different kinds of nonfiction text structures. Challenge writers to try a variety of organizers, including a Venn diagram (on the Resources CD-ROM), and reflect on which ones were helpful.

LINKS TO CD-ROM:
• Comparison Chart
• Graphic Organizer: Venn Diagram

Main Idea Maintained Throughout

WHEN TO USE IT: To help writers stay focused as they craft their writing

FOCUS THE LEARNING

It is easy for the main idea to become muddled as a writer gathers more and more information on a topic. The goal of this lesson is to teach writers to stay focused and "on topic" as they craft each sentence.

Model

STEP 1: Think aloud as you construct a short piece with a clearly focused title.

Possible Think-Aloud: *I know that sometimes when I am writing, it's easy to get off track and start writing about something else. I'm going to start my section about how sea turtles lay their eggs. Watch me as I write, and think about staying focused on what I really want my writing to say. I'll start with the sentences, "The female loggerhead will travel thousands of miles . . . back flippers to dig a hole."*

TURN &TALK *Partners, think together. Have I stayed focused so far? Are my sentences all about how a sea turtle lays its eggs?*

STEP 2: Demonstrate how you are tempted to get off track but that you remember your main idea, think about your title, and work to stay focused.

Laying Eggs

The female loggerhead will travel thousands of miles to return to the same beach where she was hatched. There, she'll lay her own eggs. Once she finds a suitable location along the shore, she uses her front flippers to clear a spot in the sand and her back flippers to dig a hole. She carefully deposits the soft–shelled eggs into the hole. She covers the eggs with sand using her hind flippers. Inside their sandy nest, the eggs are kept moist and protected from hungry predators.

Sample Modeled Writing

Possible Think-Aloud: *When I write the word "hole," it reminds me of what I read about the baby turtles once they hatch. They wait until nightfall to dig out of the hole and head to the sea. I am tempted to start writing about that. However, I remember that I want this part of my writing to be all about how the turtle lays her eggs. I'm going to get right back on track and write more about that. I'll add, "She carefully deposits the soft-shelled eggs. . . ."*

TURN &TALK *My topic is "how sea turtles lay their eggs." Can you think of any other ideas that I could add to this section that would help me stick to my main idea?*

Analyze

STEP 3: Reread and reflect.

Possible Think-Aloud: *Let's reread my writing and think together. Have I stayed focused on the main idea of this section? Do all of my sentences tell about how a sea turtle lays her eggs? Is my writing clear and focused?*

Sum It Up

Writers, don't be surprised when you are writing and you become distracted. You can often be tempted to start writing about something else. It happens to all writers from time to time. When it happens, remember to stop and ask yourself, "What did I want this section of my writing to be about? Am I still on track?" Then, get right back to writing about your topic. Let's begin!

VARIATIONS

For Less Experienced Writers: Gather writers in a small group, and coach them as they use a graphic organizer to arrange facts about their topics into sections. Show them how this organizer can help them stay focused. Coach them as they begin to write. (See Resources CD-ROM.)

For More Experienced Writers: Challenge pairs to listen to their partner's writing. Have Partner A read to Partner B while Partner B tries to listen for any points where the writer has gone off track. Partner B can then coach Partner A in revising the piece. Have partners switch and repeat.

LINKS TO CD-ROM:
- Graphic Organizer: Main Idea and Details
- Writing Samples

Using Headings to Group Related Information

WHEN TO USE IT: To help writers organize their writing and more clearly understand an important text feature of nonfiction writing

FOCUS THE LEARNING

Headings serve as mini-titles that are spaced throughout a text to help keep each section clear and organized. Our goal is to teach students how to use headings to group related information about their topics.

Model

STEP 1: Display facts you have collected about a topic. Think aloud as you analyze the facts to group facts together under a single heading.

Possible Think-Aloud: *As readers of nonfiction, headings help give us a focus for reading. They tell us what to expect from a section of writing. As writers of nonfiction, headings can help us organize the facts we have collected about our topic. This helps our whole piece stay focused and organized! I have collected a variety of facts about wolves, and I'm ready to craft some headings. I notice that I have a few facts about why wolves howl. I can group those facts together under one heading. A heading can be represented with a word, a phrase, a declarative sentence, or a question. I could use the heading "Howling Wolves." Another idea for a heading could be "Wolves: Why They Howl." I may need to experiment with several headings before I find one that works for this section.*

TURN &TALK *Think together and identify other headings that might work for this section.*

STEP 2: Think aloud as you choose a heading and group related facts together.

Facts About Wolves	
· howl to get attention of pack	· howl to protect territory
· hunt in packs of 6–10	· howl because other wolves are howling
· eat deer, elk, moose	· can eat 20 lbs. in one sitting

Sample Modeled Writing

Heading: Why Do Wolves Howl?
· to get attention
· to protect territory
· because other wolves
   are howling

Sample Modeled Writing

Why Do Wolves Howl?
Scientists believe that wolves howl for a variety of reasons. A wolf may howl in order to get the attention of the other wolves in the pack. Wolves also howl when they are protecting their territory or simply because other wolves are howling.

Possible Think-Aloud: *I'll use a question for this heading, "Why Do Wolves Howl?" Now I can group my facts together and begin writing. First, I'll write the heading, "Why Do Wolves Howl?" Then, I'll write a sentence that introduces this section. I'll say, "Scientists believe that wolves howl for a variety of reasons." The first fact under this heading is "to get attention." I can now write about that. Watch as I write, "A wolf may howl in order to get the attention of other wolves in the pack."*

TURN &TALK *Partners, examine the other facts I have listed under this heading. How might I craft the next few sentences?*

Analyze

STEP 3: Reread and reflect.

Possible Think-Aloud: *Let's reread my writing so far. Is it clear and organized? How does the heading help my reader? I think I have a heading that works, and I'm pleased with what I've written so far. When I craft a heading and group my facts under that heading, it helps me stay focused and organized as I write.*

Sum It Up

When we construct a powerful heading, it is easy to remember the focus of our writing. Furthermore, these headings can tell a reader exactly what to expect from each section. Try to use headings to group related information together, and then use the headings to help you stay organized in your writing.

VARIATIONS

For Less Experienced Writers: As you confer with writers one-on-one, coach them in how to use sticky notes to add headings to previously written pieces. Then, guide them as they create headings for their current pieces of writing.

For More Experienced Writers: Provide a small group of writers with copies of a text that you have prepared by covering the headings with sticky notes. Challenge partners to read the text and craft headings for each section. Then, display the headings the author chose.

LINKS TO CD-ROM:
• Mentor Text: *Animal Architects*

Create an Inviting Lead

WHEN TO USE IT: When writers need a strong and engaging lead that will draw the reader in

FOCUS THE LEARNING

It takes time, thought, and focused attention to begin a piece of writing in a way that engages readers and makes them want to read on. In this lesson, we teach students how to take those extra moments to create an intriguing beginning.

Model

STEP 1: In advance of the lesson, create a chart displaying weak leads. Think aloud as you revise each lead to make it more inviting.

Possible Think-Aloud: *As you begin writing about your topic, it's important to think about how you will draw your reader in. You want to create a lead, or a beginning, that is interesting and will make your reader want to read more! Let's take a look at these beginnings and think about making them more inviting. First, let's look at lead 1 about falling out of a canoe. It is just okay. I think I'll start by speaking to my reader, "Sometimes something unexpected. . . ."*

TURN &TALK *Compare these two leads and discuss. Which one is stronger? Which one draws a reader in, like a magnet? What makes one lead better than the other?*

Column 1	Column 2
This is going to be a really cool story about a time I fell out of a canoe.	Sometimes something unexpected happens that you'll remember for the rest of your life. I had just such a moment.
Once my friend dropped a whole stack of dishes and broke every one of them. I'll tell you about it.	Smash! Shatter! Crash! I could tell from the sounds coming from the kitchen that something was amiss.

Sample Modeled Writing

STEP 2: Model how to make a lead about breaking dishes more inviting.

Possible Think-Aloud: *Let's try again. Lead 1 about the time my friend broke a stack of dishes is pretty ho-hum—not very exciting. I am going to think about the sounds you would hear if someone broke several dishes at once. I might* hear, "Smash! Shatter! Crash!" Now there's a great way to start a piece of writing—onomatopoeia! I'll write "Smash! Shatter! Crash! I could tell from the sounds. . . ." Sound words can make a lead really inviting.

TURN &TALK *Partners, think together. If you were to create a list of attributes of a strong lead, what would be on your list?*

Analyze

STEP 3: Reread and reflect.

Possible Think-Aloud: *I've shown you how writers can use onomatopoeia and questions to draw their readers in. What are some other ways we could start a piece of nonfiction writing?*

Sum It Up

Writers, today we were reminded that a strong and intriguing lead draws readers in like a magnet and makes them want to read more. We've talked about several ways that we can do that. Today try one of the strategies that we discussed. You may need to experiment with more than one lead before you find one that works best. I'll look forward to reading your leads!

VARIATIONS

For Less Experienced Writers: Provide additional guided practice by gathering a small group of writers and inviting them to work with you to revise several ho-hum leads. Add these revisions to an ongoing chart that you display in the classroom.

For More Experienced Writers: Invite students to notice strong leads in the books they are reading. Start a collection of "leads we love." For example, the first lines from *Caves* by Stephen Kramer are ones to be cherished: "Far below the earth's surface, water drips from the roof of a cave. The drops fall through the darkness into a large stone room no one has ever seen."

LINKS TO CD-ROM:
- Teacher Tool: Books with Strong Leads
- Mentor Text: *Africa's Diverse Landscape*

Craft an Ending that Brings Closure

WHEN TO USE IT: When the writing ends abruptly or when writers struggle with how to wrap up

FOCUS THE LEARNING

As writers, we need to recognize that the ending gives us one more chance to make a good impression on our reader. This lesson is designed to challenge students to take time to craft an ending that will bring closure and satisfaction.

Model

STEP 1: Display a short section of your writing. Pause before the ending to think aloud about how you can make it strong and satisfying.

Possible Think-Aloud: *As a writer, one of my important (and most difficult) jobs is to craft an ending that will wrap up my piece. Watch me as I think about an ending for my piece about making pizza. I've told the readers all I want to tell them, but I need to find a way to end. I could write, "The End," but I think I can do better than that. How about, "Once you've let the pizza cool slightly, slice it, serve it up, and enjoy!"*

TURN &TALK *What do you think of this ending? Does it bring about a sense of closure? Is it interesting? Can you think of another way to end this piece?*

STEP 2: Experiment with several endings, and decide which one is most satisfying.

First Draft:

Finally, pop your creation into a preheated oven and wait for the crust to brown and the cheese to bubble.

Second Draft:

Finally, pop your creation into a preheated oven and wait for the crust to brown and the cheese to bubble. Once you've let the pizza cool slightly, slice it, serve it up, and enjoy!

Sample Modeled Writing

Possible Think-Aloud: *Let's keep thinking about endings. Here is another one we could try: "There's nothing quite as delicious as a pizza that you made yourself."*

TURN &TALK *Evaluate this ending. How does it compare with my first try? Which one do you prefer?*

Analyze

STEP 3: Reread and reflect.

Possible Think-Aloud: *I have several fascinating nonfiction books here. Let's examine the endings.* (Read the ending from each one.) *As we read these endings, it helped me think about my writing. Let's reread my ending one more time and see if we can think of more ways to bring about a sense of closure.*

Sum It Up

Today we talked about the importance of a good ending. We know that in order to create a strong and satisfying ending, we must choose our words carefully. As you work on your own writing today, think about how you might wrap it up in a way that is interesting and powerful. Let's begin!

VARIATIONS

For Less Experienced Writers: Gather a small group of writers together. Provide partners with a short published text, but cover the ending sentences. Invite partners to work together to craft an ending for the piece. Ask partners to share their suggested ending with the group. Then, uncover the actual ending, and discuss the ending that the students chose.

For More Experienced Writers: Invite writers to offer up their pieces for a group revision exercise. Challenge the group to read the writing and suggest some other possible endings.

LINKS TO CD-ROM:
- Mentor Text: *Africa's Diverse Landscape*

Paragraphs

WHEN TO USE IT: When students are crafting several sentences about a single topic, or when writing seems to go on and on with no breaks

FOCUS THE LEARNING

In this lesson, we show students a simple way to plan, organize, and write clear and coherent paragraphs.

Model

STEP 1: Explain that writers can divide a blank paper into fourths and then list a fact in each box so that they can easily organize their writing into paragraphs by developing each fact.

Possible Think-Aloud: *When we write, it's important to visually organize our thoughts into paragraphs. This makes our writing easier for someone to read and understand. We've been collecting facts about the rainforests. Now I'm ready to begin organizing and writing my piece. I could write a little bit about each of the facts listed here. Watch me as I divide this blank paper into fourths and write one fact in each box. In the first box, I'll write, "Rainforests provide many of the foods that we enjoy each day."*

TURN &TALK *Writers, if you were going to write this paragraph, what would you include? Think about all you know about the food that can be found in rainforests. What facts could you add under this main idea?*

STEP 2: Model and think aloud as you write the first paragraph and begin writing the second paragraph.

Possible Think-Aloud: *Watch me as I think about the fact in the first box and write about it. Since I'm writing a paragraph, I'm going to indent a few spaces. That tells my reader that I've begun a new paragraph. (Write the first few sentences about food that comes from the rainforest.) Now I can move on to the second box. I know that rainforests help to stabilize the world's climate by absorbing carbon dioxide from the atmosphere. I'll indent again and write about that topic.*

Provide food	Help stabilize climate
Home to plants/animals	Interesting places to visit

Rainforests provide many of the foods that we enjoy each day. Bananas, rice, corn, and cocoa beans can all be found growing in the dense Amazon Rainforest. In fact, some scientists believe that over half of the food eaten today comes from the abundance of the rainforest.

Sample Modeled Writing

TURN &TALK *If you were going to craft this paragraph, what would you include? Remember that all the ideas in a paragraph should be about the same topic.*

Analyze

STEP 3: Reread and reflect.

Possible Think-Aloud: *Let's read the paragraphs that we have written so far. How did using a planning page with boxes for each paragraph help me as I began to write?*

Sum It Up

Today I showed you something that writers can do when they want to organize their writing into cohesive paragraphs. Now you know how to divide a paper into boxes to plan out your writing, and you know how to indent to show your reader that you are beginning a new paragraph. As you begin writing today, try this technique and think about how it helps you as you think about paragraphs.

VARIATIONS

For Less Experienced Writers: Teach writers the acronym T.I.P.S. (Time, Incident or Topic, Place, Speaker) to help them remember when to start a new paragraph. Challenge them to try utilizing paragraphs in other types of writing.

For More Experienced Writers: Provide partners with a short published text that you have typed without paragraphs. Show them the copy editor's symbol for adding a new paragraph. Challenge them to use the symbol whenever they think a new paragraph should begin. Then, compare their results with the actual published piece of writing.

LINKS TO CD-ROM:
• Reference Chart: T.I.P.S. When to Start a New Paragraph

Using a Persuasive Framework

WHEN TO USE IT: When students are crafting persuasive texts

FOCUS THE LEARNING

When students learn how to write a convincing persuasive piece, they increase their knowledge of the subject matter while also learning how to analyze, classify, synthesize, and verbalize. This lesson is designed to teach students how to use a persuasive framework when planning and organizing their arguments.

Model

In advance of the lesson, print copies of the planning page provided on the Resources CD-ROM. Then, create a version of the planning page to display for the lesson.

STEP 1: Using an article such as the one on the Resources CD-ROM, lead the students in a conversation about how the author organized his argument.

Possible Think-Aloud: *Writers, let's examine this article called "Reversing a Heavy Trend."* (After reading.) *Did you notice how this author organized her argument? You'll notice that in the first three paragraphs, she makes a case for her argument and states her position. Then, in the next section, "Small Changes," she calls her readers to action. She challenges readers to make small changes in what they eat and drink. She goes on to support her position with facts. For example, she says that limiting soft drinks can save thousands of calories.*

TURN &TALK *Think together. What other facts does this author use to support her position?*

STEP 2: Think aloud as you use a persuasive framework to plan for writing.

Possible Think-Aloud: *Writers, the author of this article organized her argument in a way that is compelling, didn't she? Today I want to show you how to use a framework to help you plan and organize your own persuasive pieces. Let's look at this chart I've created. This is a planning page I can use when organizing my thinking. I'm going to write a piece that is meant to convince my reader to save energy around the house. First, I'll make a case for my* position. *"When we work to save energy, it saves money and reduces the need to burn fossil fuels."* *Watch as I add that in the first section.*

Analyze

STEP 3: Reread and reflect.

Possible Think-Aloud: *Next, I'll jot down my call to action, or what I want my reader to do. I want my reader to look for ways to save energy around the house. I'll record that in the next section of my planning page.* (Complete framework.) *Let's analyze my planning page. Have I mapped out an argument that will be convincing and compelling? Is it organized and clear? Using this persuasive framework helped me to think about my argument. I think it will help me as I begin to write!*

Sum It Up

Today I showed you how to use a persuasive framework to organize and plan for your writing. As you begin writing your arguments today, try using the framework the way we used it together, and see if it helps you as a writer. If you take the time to map out your thinking, I know you can create clear, organized, and compelling arguments! Who is ready to begin?

Statement of Position: (Make a case for your cause.)

We all need to do our part to conserve natural gas, electricity, and gasoline. When we work to save energy, it saves money and reduces the need to burn fossil fuels. When we burn less fossil fuels, we lower the emissions of carbon dioxide. Carbon dioxide is one of the factors that contribute to global warming.

Call to Action: (Tell your reader what you want him or her to do.)

Look for ways to save energy around the house.

Support Your Position With Facts:
- Close curtains/blinds during winter (this keeps heat from leaving through the windows)
- Use copper-bottom pots and pans (copper heats faster than other metals)

Use Repetition: (Repeat your argument for the cause or the call to action.)

Recognize the Opposing View: ("Others might say," "Be aware that some people think . . . ," and so on.)

Conclusion: (Sum up the argument, and restate the call to action.)

Sample Modeled Writing

VARIATIONS

For Less Experienced Writers: Revisit Voice and Audience: Lesson 9, and scaffold these writers with more explicit instruction in using imperative language in their persuasive pieces.

For More Experienced Writers: Stretch these writers to infuse other features of strong persuasive text. These might include exaggeration, hypothetical situation ("imagine if, " "you may wonder, " "have you ever"), emotive language to make the reader feel an emotional connection, and connecting words that provide specific examples ("specifically," "for example," "in fact," "to illustrate").

LINKS TO CD-ROM:
- Mentor Text: *Reversing a Heavy Trend*
- Graphic Organizer: Persuasive Framework Planning Page
- Writing Samples

Utilize Transitions and Linking Statements

WHEN TO USE IT: To help students learn to include smooth transitions within a piece of writing

FOCUS THE LEARNING

Linking statements can serve two main functions. They can remind readers of the main points of the piece, and they can direct readers to the fact that they are being moved from one point to another point in the piece.

> In the event of an earthquake, you should remember three important things. Drop, cover, and hold on.
>
> The first thing you should do is drop onto your hands and knees. You want to be sure to drop before the earthquake knocks you down. When you are on your hands and knees, you're protected from falling while still retaining your ability to move if necessary.
>
> Dropping is just one of the three important things to remember during an earthquake. Another critical thing you need to do is cover. When you cover your head and neck (and your entire body if possible) with a sturdy table or desk, you reduce the chances that you will be injured by falling debris.

Sample Modeled Writing

Model

Provide students with a list of transition words and phrases like the one provided on the Resources CD-ROM.

STEP 1: Craft a short piece of writing, pausing to think aloud about including transitions and linking statements.

Possible Think-Aloud: *I'm working on a piece that is meant to teach my reader about how to stay safe during an earthquake. I want to highlight the three things you should do: drop, cover, and hold on. Each of these points is going to be a separate paragraph in my piece, so I'll need to think about how to add some links between the paragraphs. This will ensure that my writing is clear and organized for my reader. First, I'll write an introductory sentence. I'll write, "In the event of an earthquake, you should . . . cover, and hold on."*

TURN &TALK *Writers, if you were going to write the next paragraph that describes more about how and why you should drop during an earthquake, how would you begin the paragraph? How could you link this paragraph to your introductory sentence?*

STEP 2: Model and think aloud as you continue to write and add transitions and linking statements.

Possible Think-Aloud: *I want my reader to be clear that I'm going to talk about how and why we drop during an earthquake. I think a good way to link this paragraph to my introduction is to say, "The first thing you should do is drop onto your hands and knees." The phrase "The first thing" makes it clear that I'm going to talk only about dropping.* (Continue writing paragraph one.) *Now I'm ready to write about how to cover yourself during an earthquake. I need another linking statement, or transition, don't I?*

TURN &TALK *Think together. How can I link my next paragraph with the rest of what I've written?*

Analyze

STEP 3: Reread and reflect.

Possible Think-Aloud: *Watch as I write the first sentence in this paragraph. I am going to link it to what I have already written. "Dropping is just one of the three important things to remember during an earthquake. Another critical thing you need to do is cover." Now I can go on to tell more about how and why the reader should seek cover. Let's reread my writing so far. How did using linking statements and transitions make my writing more clear? I think my writing will be easy to follow now, don't you?*

Sum It Up

Today I showed you how to link the ideas in your paragraphs in such a way that your reader will be clear about the order and sequence of your piece. Today as you return to your writing, reread what you have written so far, and see if there are places where you could insert some linking statements. Your reader will be glad you did!

VARIATIONS

For Less Experienced Writers: Revisit Word Choice: Lesson 3, and scaffold with more explicit instruction on the inclusion of linking words and phrases.

For More Experienced Writers: Challenge writers to reread a completed piece of writing and underline the transitions and linking statements that they have used. Coach and confer if writers determine that they need to revise.

Word Choice

Seeking Precision and Excitement in Word Selection

Word choice is about the richness and precision that can be infused into communication. Word selection isn't a function of correctness but rather one of clarification and expansion of thinking. Carefully orchestrated word choice is the gateway to writing that features beautiful language and exquisite details.

LESSON	3	4	5	RELATED LESSONS
1 Use Descriptive Words and Phrases	●	●	●	*Revising:* Lesson 1, Revising to Add Precise Words
2 Target Powerful Action Verbs	●	●	●	*Ideas:* Lesson 2, Visualize Action—Then Write
3 Linking Words and Phrases	●	●	●	*Organization:* Lesson 10, Utilize Transitions and Linking Statements *Sentence Fluency:* Lesson 8, Smooth Transitions with Linking Words and Phrases
4 Use Concrete Words to Support Visualization	●	●	●	*Revising:* Lesson 6, Tuning Up Concrete Words and Sensory Images
5 Using Domain-Specific Vocabulary	●	●	●	*Text Features:* Lesson 4, Bold Words
6 Use Simile	●	●	●	*Word Choice:* Lesson 7, Use Metaphor *Word Choice:* Lesson 8, Select Words that Evoke Strong Imagery
7 Use Metaphor	●	●	●	*Word Choice:* Lesson 6, Use Simile *Word Choice:* Lesson 8, Select Words that Evoke Strong Imagery
8 Select Words that Evoke Strong Imagery	●	●	●	*Revising:* Lesson 6, Tuning Up Concrete Words and Sensory Images
9 Using Temporal Words or Phrases to Signal Event Order		●	●	*Organization:* Lesson 2, Using a Timeline
10 Compound Descriptors	●	●	●	*Word Choice:* Lesson 1, Use Descriptive Words and Phrases
11 Use Onomatopoeia	●	●	●	*Word Choice:* Lesson 8, Select Words that Evoke Strong Imagery
12 Use Persuasive Language	●	●	●	*Drafting:* Lesson 10, Drafting a Persuasion

Use Descriptive Words and Phrases

WHEN TO USE IT: To create rich descriptions in nonfiction writing

FOCUS THE LEARNING

Without rich and powerful descriptors, nonfiction writing can become flat, lifeless, and unappealing to a reader. It is important that we teach writers how to bring the subject to life through descriptive words and phrases.

Model

STEP 1: Demonstrate how you describe a subject with rich details and precise word choice.

Possible Think-Aloud: *I am examining this picture of an eagle's beak, and I want to describe it. I could say, "An eagle has a yellow beak." That's okay, but I think I could add some words that would help my reader get a clear picture of the beak. Listen to this description: "An eagle's beak is yellow in color and has a sharp hook at the tip. There is an external nostril on both sides of the beak."*

TURN & TALK *Consider my two descriptions: (1) "An eagle has a yellow beak." (2) "An eagle's yellow beak. . . ." Decide which description is better. Which one helps you create a clear picture in your mind? Why are great descriptions important in nonfiction writing?*

STEP 2: Model writing and emphasize including strong descriptors.

Possible Think-Aloud: *I want to focus on the words and phrases I am selecting for my writing. Watch as I write the phrase "dagger-like beak." That phrase really describes the hook, doesn't it? Now I need to choose some words that tell **what** the eagle does with this sharp hook. If I write that the hook is used to tear meat, my reader will know it is an important part of an eagle.*

An eagle's beak is yellow in color and has a sharp hook at the tip. This dagger–like beak is used to tear the meat of fish, snakes, and other birds. The upper part of the beak is sharp as a knife. It can slice through the tough skin of the eagle's prey.

©Digital Vision/Getty Images/HIP

Sample Modeled Writing

TURN &TALK *There are so many powerful words that would help me describe how the eagle uses the sharp upper part of the beak. I could say it cuts, slices, rips, or lacerates. Think together and identify the best describing word I could use here.*

Analyze

STEP 3: Reread and reflect.

Possible Think-Aloud: *Let's reread my writing and analyze this description. I need to be sure that the words and phrases I have selected give us a clear picture of the eagle's beak. As we reread, be thinking about my words and phrases. You may have an idea to help make this even better!*

Sum It Up

Nonfiction writers need to make careful choices so their words and phrases describe, giving a reader as much information as possible. One of the things we need to do is challenge ourselves to consider different words and then pick the ones that provide the best descriptions. As you begin writing today, reread a bit of what you have already written, and check your descriptions. Are you satisfied with the words and phrases you have chosen, or could you challenge yourself to do even better?

VARIATIONS

For Less Experienced Writers: Provide students with hands-on experiences with real objects. Consider using a classroom pet, real food items, or a real plant. As the students generate descriptive words and phrases, record their thinking on a chart so they have a rich cache of words and phrases to support their writing.

For More Experienced Writers: Invite students to read their writing to a partner without showing any illustrations. Then, challenge the partner to create an illustration based solely on the writing. Ask the partners to think together and evaluate the descriptive words and phrases to see if revisions might improve the writing.

LINKS TO CD-ROM:
• Eagle's Beak

Target Powerful Action Verbs

WHEN TO USE IT: To energize writing or improve precision in descriptions

FOCUS THE LEARNING

Writers of all ages need to learn that verbs are the engines of sentences. Carefully chosen verbs energize descriptions and enhance reader comprehension.

Model

STEP 1: Engage students in dramatizing various verbs, and then use each verb in a descriptive sentence.

Possible Think-Aloud: *Verbs serve as the engines of powerful sentences. They energize the writing and help make descriptions come to life. So it's important to choose precise verbs when we are crafting nonfiction. I have written four verbs on this chart. Let's start with "talk." Please talk with your neighbor. Now "whisper" with your neighbor. Let's try "chatter."*

TURN &TALK *When you compare "whisper" and "chatter" to "talk," which words are more precise? Which ones give us more specific information? Look at the other verbs on my chart, and identify the ones that you think are precise and powerful.*

STEP 2: Model writing as you think aloud about action verbs.

talked
whispered
yelled
chattered
squealed

looked
glanced
gazed
stared
peered

Huddled together, my mom and I _____ and tried to decide what to do next. Suddenly, we again heard a fluttering sound from inside the cave. We flipped on our flashlight and _____ into the dark opening of the cave.

Sample Modeled Writing

Possible Think-Aloud: *I am writing a narrative about a time when my mom and I discovered a bat cave when we were hiking. I am ready to put our thinking about verbs into action. I have a few words that describe how we might have talked: "talked," "whispered," "yelled," "chattered," and "squealed." Listen as I read the sentence and try each of these verbs in the blank. As I insert each verb, I need to keep visualizing what my mom and I actually did and think about the verb that best describes it.*

TURN &TALK *It's time to vote! With your partner, dramatize these ways to talk, and get ready to vote on the best verb.*

Analyze

STEP 3: Reread and reflect.

Possible Think-Aloud: *I adore the verb you selected, and I can really picture my mom and I chattering about what to do next. Let's try another sentence. Which verb would be the best choice for the sentence, "We flipped on our flashlight and. . . ?" Put your heads together, and choose a powerful action verb!*

Sum It Up

Remember that verbs are the powerful engines of sentences. As nonfiction writers, we need to think of a variety of options and include verbs that are powerful and precise. As you get ready to write today, think about the verbs that you can include that will make your writing sparkle.

VARIATIONS

For Less Experienced Writers: Work together to create a classroom resource of powerful verbs that could be posted in the room to support great verb choice. Students could gather verbs from their own writing or from nonfiction resources in the classroom. Once the chart is posted, encourage all writers to reference it as they are drafting.

For More Experienced Writers: Show more experienced writers how you analyze your verb choices. Demonstrate how you go back to your writing and examine the verbs. Challenge them to do the same with their own work. Then, guide them in identifying passive verbs that show no action and replacing them with powerful action-oriented selections.

LINKS TO CD-ROM:
• Teacher Tool: Powerful Verbs, Powerful Writing

Linking Words and Phrases

WHEN TO USE IT: To show a relationship between ideas and sentences

FOCUS THE LEARNING

Linking words and phrases can summarize, give reasons, give examples, or contrast ideas. Conscious infusing of linking words into nonfiction writing produces smoother-sounding language and provides clarity for the reader.

Model

STEP 1: Create a chart with linking words and phrases, and discuss it with the students. A sample chart can be found on the Resources CD-ROM. Demonstrate how you use words and phrases from the chart as you craft a short paragraph.

Possible Think-Aloud: *As nonfiction writers, we need to be able to create pieces of writing that are clear and easy to follow. Linking words can help you connect ideas and sentences so that your reader can follow your thoughts more easily. I have posted a chart that lists some linking words and phrases and shows how they can be used. I'm going to use this chart as I write about honeybees. My first sentence is "Honeybees survive in large groups."*

TURN &TALK *I want my next sentence to explain that honeybees are unique in the fact that they survive year after year, while most other kinds of bees don't. Think together. What word or phrase could I use in my next sentence?*

STEP 2: Continue writing and thinking aloud as you infuse linking words.

Honeybees survive in large groups. Unlike other kinds of bees, honeybee colonies are able to live on year after year. Since honeybees huddle together during the winter, they keep warm enough to survive even when the temperatures dip below freezing.

Sample Modeled Writing

Possible Think-Aloud: *I heard some great suggestions. Since I'm comparing honeybees to other kinds of bees, I think I should use a word from our chart that will show contrast. I'll write, "Unlike other kinds of bees, honey colonies are able to live on year after year." Did you notice how the word "unlike" provided a link between my first two sentences? When we use linking words, it provides unity between the sentences that make up a paragraph.*

TURN &TALK *I will want to give the reader a reason why honeybees are able to survive. Use the chart to select a word I could use to start the sentence about why honeybees can survive through the cold winter while other kinds of bees cannot.*

Analyze

STEP 3: Reread and reflect.

Possible Think-Aloud: *Some of you suggested using the word "since" to begin my next sentence. Let's try it. "Since honeybees huddle together during the winter. . . ." I think the word "since" will link the first part of that sentence with the last part. Now let's reread this paragraph. Determine if I chose the best words from the chart or if there are other words that might help my writing.*

Sum It Up

Words that link or connect sentences help to strengthen our writing. They serve as cues that help the reader interpret the ideas that you, as the writer, want them to understand. When we use linking words, it helps to clarify our ideas and to make our writing sound more natural when it is read. Today as you begin writing, try using some of the linking words and phrases from our chart. Let's begin!

VARIATIONS

For Less Experienced Writers: Prepare sentence strips with sentences such as "Bears can smell human food and garbage from miles away," "Many national parks provide bear-proof garbage cans for campers," and "The number of aggressive encounters with bears decreased after the installation of the special garbage cans." Then, work with writers to experiment with adding linking words to the sentences.

For More Experienced Writers: Linking words should not only hold together sentences within a paragraph, but also connect one paragraph to another. Show students how to utilize linking words to create smooth transitions between paragraphs. Then, coach and confer as they try using linking words in their own writing.

LINKS TO CD-ROM:
• Linking Words and Phrases

Use Concrete Words to Support Visualization

WHEN TO USE IT: When student writing fails to create vivid mental images

FOCUS THE LEARNING

Writers need to learn how to create vivid images in the minds of their readers. This lesson is designed to help students understand how utilizing all five senses can enhance a piece of nonfiction writing.

Model

STEP 1: Engage students in visualizing an event, and invite them to think of words that would describe it.

Possible Think-Aloud: *One of the ways authors create rich and vivid mental images for readers is by including concrete words that involve the five senses. I am writing about a time that my sister and I hiked to a huge waterfall. I want to focus my attention on choosing words and phrases that will help my reader feel as though he or she is right there with me.*

TURN &TALK *Close your eyes and think about what it would feel like to be standing near a huge waterfall. What sensory words come to mind? What do you imagine smelling, hearing, feeling, tasting, and seeing? As I listen to you share, I will record some of the words I hear on this chart.*

STEP 2: Create a modeled writing example that utilizes concrete words to create sensory images.

> When we arrived at the waterfall, we were mesmerized. We breathed deeply and smelled the <u>pungent</u> and <u>piney</u> smell of evergreens growing nearby. The <u>deafening</u> sound of rushing water made it difficult to hear each other speak, so we remained silent as we let the <u>wet spray cool</u> our bodies.

Sample Modeled Writing

Possible Think-Aloud: *I heard some fantastic images and words! Some of you imagined smelling the pine trees near a waterfall. I could describe that smell by using words such as "pungent" and "piney." Those words would definitely create a sensory image for my reader. Watch me as I write: "We breathed deeply and smelled the pungent and piney smell of evergreens growing nearby."*

TURN &TALK *Are there any other words on my chart that I could use to help my readers feel as though they are right there with us near the waterfall?*

Analyze

STEP 3: Reread and reflect.

Possible Think-Aloud: *I think I could use the phrase "deafening sound of rushing water" to describe what we heard as we stood near the waterfall. Watch as I write: "The deafening. . . ."* (Read the passage out loud.) *Analyze the words and phrases I have used so far to create sensory images. Determine if I chose the best words from my chart or if there are other words that might help my writing.*

Sum It Up

As writers, we need to be sure we think about the mental images we are helping our readers create in their minds. As you return to your writing today, focus on including concrete words that can help make your writing come to life. Who is ready to begin?

VARIATIONS

For Less Experienced Writers: Consider sharing a few brief but powerfully written poems that create sensory images. Invite students to categorize the words based on the five senses. Coach writers as they come up with other words that describe the senses. Then, post the list of words so that all students have access to the words.

For More Experienced Writers: Encourage writers to take time to visualize and verbally describe the setting in which their subject is placed. Encourage them to create a list of words that describe what they see, taste, hear, touch, and smell. Invite them to use the words from their list as they continue to draft.

LINKS TO CD-ROM:
- Teacher Tool: Words to Use When Describing What You See, Hear, Taste, Smell, and Touch
- Mentor Text: *The Last Living Symbol of the American West*

Using Domain-Specific Vocabulary

WHEN TO USE IT: When students are explaining or describing a topic that requires specific vocabulary

FOCUS THE LEARNING

Domain-specific words are words that are specific to a field of study or topic. These kinds of words are common throughout informational texts. Therefore, it's important for students to learn how to effectively use them in their writing.

Model

STEP 1: Create a chart listing domain-specific words that pertain to a topic of study. Think aloud as you use the list to plan for writing.

Possible Think-Aloud: *As nonfiction writers, we need to be able to create pieces of writing that are clear and accurate. We also want our writing to teach the reader more about our topic. We have been learning about geysers, and we've collected a list of words that are used when explaining or describing them. I'm going to write a short paragraph that is meant to teach readers about how a geyser is formed.*

TURN &TALK *Think together. What words from our chart might I include in this paragraph? How might they help readers learn more about my topic?*

STEP 2: Demonstrate how you infuse the words from the chart as you craft a short paragraph.

Geyser Words
eruption
geothermal energy
magma
spring
plumbing system
fissures
earth's crust

Geysers are formed when water travels through a **plumbing system** underground. This plumbing system contains **fissures**, or openings, in the **earth's crust**. The water, which comes near to **magma**, becomes extremely hot. The water rises back toward the surface and causes an **eruption**.

Sample Modeled Writing

Possible Think-Aloud: *Watch as I use the list of words to support me as I write. I know that water travels through a plumbing system underground, so I'll begin my paragraph with a sentence about that. I'll write, "Geysers are formed when water travels through a plumbing system underground." The words "plumbing system" are specific to this topic, so it is important that I include them. Now I want to tell about the openings near the earth's surface.*

TURN &TALK *Examine our list of words. What words might I include next? If this were your writing, what would your next sentence say?*

Analyze

STEP 3: Reread and reflect.

Possible Think-Aloud: *I heard some great suggestions. I think I'll include the words "fissures" and "earth's crust" as I continue to describe how geysers are formed. (Continue writing.) Now let's reread what I have written so far and think about how using these specific words strengthened the text.*

Sum It Up

Today we learned how to infuse words that are specific to our topic. This is incredibly important as we craft high-quality nonfiction texts. As you begin working on your writing today, see if you can include some domain-specific words that will help your reader learn more about your topic. I'll look forward to reading your work!

VARIATIONS

For Less Experienced Writers: Continue to use the list to create a common text with a small group of writers. Then, encourage students to create a list of domain-specific words that pertain to their own topics. Coach and confer as they begin to write independently.

For More Experienced Writers: Show students how nonfiction writers use **bold** words when including domain-specific vocabulary. Challenge them to utilize this nonfiction text feature when publishing their own texts.

LINKS TO CD-ROM:

- Mentor Text: *Animal Architects*

Use Simile

WHEN TO USE IT: When students are ready to experiment with another way to create sensory images and connections for a reader

FOCUS THE LEARNING

Good nonfiction writing includes words and phrases that create strong and vivid sensory images. One way authors do this is to include similes in their writing. The goal of this lesson is to help students understand how to include similes to bring their writing to life.

Model

STEP 1: Explain what a simile is and how similes can strengthen a piece of writing.

Possible Think-Aloud: *As I craft any piece of nonfiction, I want to focus on choosing words and phrases that will help make my readers feel like they are right in the middle of the action. One way I can do this is to use similes. A simile uses "like" or "as" to compare two things that are not alike. For example, instead of saying, "A cheetah runs fast," I could say, "A cheetah runs like the wind." A well-placed simile makes your writing more interesting.*

TURN &TALK *Think together. Have you seen similes used in other kinds of texts? Have you heard similes used as people talk? What does a simile do for the reader or listener?*

STEP 2: Think aloud about your topic and what simile you might include.

> Beekeepers need to be smart when they collect honey. Often they will use smoke to help them. The smoke is like a dinner bell that tells the bees it's time to chow down! It causes the bees to want to eat, and while they are busy, the beekeeper can open the hive and work without fear.

Sample Modeled Writing

Possible Think-Aloud: *I am writing a piece that describes how beekeepers collect honey. I want to explain how the beekeepers use smoke to make the bees want to eat. I'm thinking this might be a good place to insert a simile. A simile could help my readers make a powerful connection and visualize more clearly. I could say that the smoke is like a dinner bell. It tells the bees that it's time to eat. Watch as I include that.*

TURN &TALK *Partners, imagine that you are crafting this piece of writing. What other similes might you use to help the reader understand how the beekeeper uses the smoke?*

Analyze

STEP 3: Reread and reflect.

Possible Think-Aloud: *Let's reread this paragraph and think about how the simile impacts the writing. I like the way I compare the smoke to a dinner bell. I think it creates a mental image that helps teach my readers more about my topic.*

Sum It Up

Today I showed you how writers of nonfiction use similes to help their readers visualize and make connections between something they know and something new. Today, as you write, think about including some similes to boost your writing. Your reader will be glad you did!

VARIATIONS

For Less Experienced Writers: Using a book such as *My Best Friend Is as Sharp as a Pencil* by Hanoch Piven, ask partners to find all of the similes that the author included. Show students how similes often use the words "like" and "as." Then, coach and confer as they attempt to infuse similes in their own writing.

For More Experienced Writers: Challenge more experienced writers to come up with several similes that pertain to a specific topic that you are studying. Create a chart with a list of examples. Display the chart in the classroom so that students can reference it as they are writing.

LINKS TO CD-ROM:
• Teaching Chart: Similes

Use Metaphor

WHEN TO USE IT: When students are ready to experiment with another way to paint a picture for their readers

FOCUS THE LEARNING

Metaphors are short and powerful ways to make writing more interesting and lively. They also convey a great deal of information about a topic. When we teach writers to experiment with metaphors, we open up a world of possibility!

Model

STEP 1: Explain the benefits of using a metaphor, and showcase some examples.

Possible Think-Aloud: *With a simile, you use the words "like" and "as" to compare two things that are not alike. When you use a metaphor, you also compare two things that are not alike, but instead of saying something is like something else, you say that it is something else. For example, "The cat was a lightning bolt, fast and deadly." A well-placed metaphor helps the reader find similarities between a topic and the object to which it is being compared.*

TURN &TALK *Think about my example, "The cat was a lightning bolt, fast and deadly." Tell your partner what you visualize when you hear that sentence. What does the metaphor do for you, as a reader?*

STEP 2: Think aloud about your topic, and include a metaphor as you craft a short section.

A frog's tongue is a whip, striking its prey with deadly speed. Slurp! Dinner is served.

Sample Modeled Writing

Possible Think-Aloud: *I am working on a section of my writing describing how a frog captures its prey. I want to include a metaphor that will help my reader understand the quick and deadly action of the frog's tongue. The tongue's movement is so fast, it reminds me of a whip. I could say, "A frog's tongue is a whip, striking its prey with deadly speed." I think that would create a vivid image in the mind of my reader.*

TURN & TALK *Imagine that you are crafting this piece of writing. What other metaphors might you use to describe how a frog uses its tongue to catch its prey? Share your thinking with your partner.*

Analyze

STEP 3: Reread and reflect.

Possible Think-Aloud: *Let's reread what I have written so far and think about what the metaphor does for the piece. I like the way I compare the frog's tongue to a whip. I think it creates a mental image that helps my reader create a clear mental picture. It helps the reader understand that the frog's tongue is fast and deadly. A strong metaphor can make all the difference in the world!*

Sum It Up

Today I showed you how infusing a strong metaphor every now and then can help to add zest and interest to your writing. I hope that you'll experiment with metaphors today as you continue working on your own pieces of writing. Be ready to share any metaphors that you try!

VARIATIONS

For Less Experienced Writers: Using a book such as *My Mouth Is a Volcano* by Julia Cook, ask partners to find all the metaphors that the author included. Ask students to describe the true meaning behind the metaphors. What does each mean? Then, coach and confer as students experiment with metaphors in their own writing.

For More Experienced Writers: Challenge more experienced writers to come up with several metaphors that could be used with a current topic of study in social studies or science. Create a chart with a list of examples. Display the chart in the classroom so that students can reference the examples as they are writing.

Select Words that Evoke Strong Imagery

WHEN TO USE IT: To help writers broaden the range of words they use to describe their subjects

FOCUS THE LEARNING

When we are careful about the words we use when crafting nonfiction, we can emphasize the object we are describing and help our reader create a powerful visual image. This lesson teaches students how to slip in words that evoke imagery in the mind of the reader in a natural and effective way.

Model

STEP 1: Explain how to select words that evoke strong imagery and how this can boost a piece of writing.

Possible Think-Aloud: *When we carefully select words that are clear and descriptive, we emphasize the object we are describing and help our reader create a rich visual image. If I were to say, "The flowers danced in the gentle breeze," it would create a certain mental image. I could have said, "The flowers swayed," but the word "danced" paints a more vivid picture.*

TURN &TALK *Analyze my example, "The flowers danced in the gentle breeze." Tell your partner what you visualize when you hear that sentence. What does the word "danced" do for the sentence?*

STEP 2: Think aloud about your topic and the words you choose as you craft a short section of writing.

> The thunder <u>clapped angrily</u> in the distance as I began to walk faster. I desperately wanted to make it back to the cabin before the storm reached me with all its fury. But before I knew it, the storm <u>attacked</u>, dumping rain and hail on my tired body.

Sample Modeled Writing

Possible Think-Aloud: *I am writing about the time I got caught in a storm while I was hiking. I'm ready to describe the thunder I heard, and I think I can use some words that would evoke imagery. I remember that the thunder sounded like a clap and that it was really loud, like a person might sound when he or she is very angry. I could say that the thunder clapped angrily. Watch as I write: "The thunder clapped angrily in the distance as I began to walk faster."*

TURN &TALK *Partners, what other ways could I describe the thunder?*

Analyze

STEP 3: Reread and reflect.

Possible Think-Aloud: *Now I'm ready to tell about the moment it started raining and hailing. I felt like I was being attacked! That's it! I can describe the storm as "attacking" me. That word would create a vivid mental image for my readers, wouldn't it? I'll write, "But before I knew it, the storm attacked . . . ." Let's reread this paragraph together and think about how I included these words that evoke strong imagery.*

TURN &TALK *What do you think of the words I chose? Can you think of other ways I could have described the thunder and the storm?*

Sum It Up

When we carefully select the words we use, we enhance and invigorate a piece of nonfiction writing. Today as you return to your own writing, look for places where you might infuse words that evoke strong imagery. Then, reread the piece and see if they add some liveliness and interest. Let's begin!

VARIATIONS

For Less Experienced Writers: With the students, create a list of nouns such as "tree," "leaf," "zebra," and "house." Then, create a list of verbs such as "whispered," "laughed," and "smiled." Invite partners to craft sentences using the words from the lists. For example, "The leaf danced in the wind before it landed on the park bench."

For More Experienced Writers: Provide pairs of students with copies of the poem "The Train" by Emily Dickinson. Challenge them to highlight examples of words that evoke strong imagery throughout the poem. Discuss the possible reasons why Dickinson used these words, and talk about the effects they had on the text.

LINKS TO CD-ROM: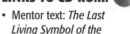
- Mentor text: *The Last Living Symbol of the American West*

Using Temporal Words or Phrases to Signal Event Order

WHEN TO USE IT: When the writing lacks clear order and sequence

FOCUS THE LEARNING

In this lesson, we show writers how to include temporal words or phrases that will create a clear sense of order and sequence for readers.

Model

STEP 1: Create a chart with temporal words and phrases that highlight order or sequence. A sample chart can be found on the Resources CD-ROM.

Possible Think-Aloud: *One of the ways writers help their readers understand the order of events is by including words or phrases that show the passage of time and signal a change in time. I have posted a chart that lists temporal words and phrases that we often use when we talk.*

TURN &TALK *Think back to yesterday when we had a fire drill. If you were going to tell someone about it, what would you say? Use as many of the words from our chart as you can.*

STEP 2: Show students how you use temporal words and phrases from the chart as you craft your writing.

> <u>Not long after</u> I lifted the binoculars to my eyes and scanned the water, I saw a burst of water and gasped as the whale leaped out of the water. <u>For a minute</u>, I couldn't breathe or move. I was in awe of the immense power and beauty of what I saw.

Sample Modeled Writing

Possible Think-Aloud: *As authors, we can also use these temporal words and phrases when we write. I'm writing about a time I saw a whale breaching. "I lifted the binoculars to my eyes and scanned the water. I saw a burst of water and gasped as the whale leaped out of the water." I think I could combine these two sentences and add a phrase to tie it together. "<u>Not long after</u> I lifted the binoculars to my eyes and scanned the water, I saw a burst. . . ."*

TURN &TALK *Partners, think together. What other words or phrases could I use with these sentences to signal the passage of time and help my reader know when these things happened?*

Analyze

STEP 3: Reread and reflect.

Possible Think-Aloud: *I'm ready to write my next sentence. I remember that I was so mesmerized by what I saw that I hardly breathed or moved. Perhaps I can include another phrase from our chart that will make the order and sequence crystal clear for my reader. I will use the phrase "for a minute" to begin this sentence.*

Sum It Up

Writers use temporal words and phrases to show order or sequence. These are important to include when you are writing directions, an explanation of the life cycle of an animal, or a piece of writing about an important event from your own life. As you write today, reference the chart of temporal words and phrases. And challenge yourself to experiment with others!

VARIATIONS

For Less Experienced Writers: Bring a small group of writers together, and show them how to use the Planning Sheet for Sequencing Events (found on the Resources CD-ROM) to plan for writing. Then, confer with and coach them as they use the organizer and the chart of temporal words for their own topics.

For More Experienced Writers: Stretch more experienced writers by challenging them to examine how authors like Cynthia Rylant use more complex words and phrases to show sequence. For example, in *The Relatives Came*, she writes: "<u>Finally, after a long time</u>, the relatives loaded up their ice chest and headed back to Virginia <u>at four in the morning</u>."

LINKS TO CD-ROM: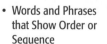
• Words and Phrases that Show Order or Sequence
• Planning Sheet for Sequencing Events

Compound Descriptors

WHEN TO USE IT: To increase precision and add variety to descriptions

FOCUS THE LEARNING

When descriptors are linked by a hyphen and used to modify a noun, the result is richly structured internal punctuation and increased precision in descriptions. Compound descriptors might include structures such as "sharp-toothed," "fast-flying," "hawk-like," and "thin-skinned."

Model

STEP 1: Generate a list of compound descriptors to tell about yourself.

Possible Think-Aloud: *I can use compound descriptors when I want to describe something in a way that is unique or very precise. Watch as I create some compound descriptors to describe myself. I love to climb mountains, so I can create a compound that says "mountain-climbing." Notice I use a hyphen, and the second word has an -ing ending—"climbing." When we create descriptive compounds, they need to end in -ing or -ed. I have green eyes, so I can write "green-eyed." Notice that I utilized a hyphen and that the second word ends in either -ing or -ed.*

TURN &TALK *Use some compound descriptors to describe yourself to your partner.*

STEP 2: Think aloud about your topic, and infuse compound descriptors into your writing.

> The arctic fox is a furry-footed, short-eared omnivore that makes itself at home in the frigid Arctic temperatures. Deep inside a cozy burrow, the arctic fox stays warm during the long winter nights. However, during a blizzard, this highly skilled mammal may dig into the snow to create a warm shelter from the storm.

Sample Modeled Writing

Possible Think-Aloud: *We have been learning about arctic foxes, and I am working on a piece of writing that describes them. I can use compound descriptors to show what I know about these creatures. I know that arctic foxes have furry feet and short ears, so I'll write, "The arctic fox is a furry-footed, short-eared omnivore that makes itself at home in the frigid Arctic temperatures." "Furry-footed" and "short-eared" are very precise descriptors for arctic foxes, aren't they?*

TURN &TALK Think together. What else do we know about arctic foxes? What compound descriptors can you and your partner think of to describe this animal?

Analyze

STEP 3: Reread and reflect.

Possible Think-Aloud: *Next, I want to describe how the arctic fox can dig into the snow during a blizzard to create a shelter from the storm. This time, I'll use the compound descriptor "highly skilled." I'll write, "However, during a blizzard, this highly skilled mammal may dig into the snow to create a warm shelter from the storm." Did you notice that I didn't use a hyphen this time? We don't use a hyphen between an -ly word and the next word. That is important in nonfiction writing. Evaluate my writing. Think together and check each compound descriptor that I used. Check to make sure that I included a hyphen and that the second word ends in -ing or -ed. And check to make sure that when I used an -ly word, I didn't use a hyphen.*

Sum It Up

As nonfiction writers, we need to describe our subjects very precisely. We need to give our readers information that is so clear that it is easy to form a mental picture. Compound descriptors are helpful tools that can make our nonfiction writing really powerful. Remember, to create a compound descriptor, we need to use two words that describe something, link them together with a hyphen (unless the first word ends in *-ly*), and make sure the second word ends in *-ing* or *-ed*.

VARIATIONS

For Less Experienced Writers: Provide additional practice in a small-group setting as you invite students to build compound descriptors about familiar subjects. Then, coach and confer as writers use them in their own writing.

For More Experienced Writers: Stretch more experienced writers by challenging them to analyze previously completed pieces of their writing and insert compound descriptors.

LINKS TO CD-ROM:
- Teacher Tool: Compound Descriptors
- Mentor Text: *Penguins: Belly-sliding, Fast-swimming, Birds!*

Use Onomatopoeia

WHEN TO USE IT: To add focused attention on sounds related to the topic or the setting

FOCUS THE LEARNING

When writers include onomatopoeia, words that sound like what they mean, writing sparkles with auditory images. Our goal is to encourage our students to experiment with the kind of lively language play that creates powerful images for the reader.

Model

STEP 1: Remind students of the sounds they can hear in their environment, and discuss how you can use those words in your writing.

Possible Think-Aloud: *Have you ever listened to popcorn popping? I can write those sounds, can't I? Watch: "Pop, pop, poppety, pop!" What about high-heeled shoes on the pavement? I can write that sound, too. "Click, clack, click, clack." When writers use words that sound like what they mean, they are using onomatopoeia. When nonfiction writers include onomatopoeia, their writing better captures the interest of their readers. I'm writing a piece about bees, and I'm thinking I could include onomatopoeia to help create some auditory images for my reader.*

TURN &TALK *Think together. What sounds could I include in this piece? Where would be the best place to include these sounds?*

STEP 2: Model how to write using onomatopoeia.

Buzz . . . Buzz . . . Buzz . . . Have you ever wondered why bees buzz? Most of the time when you hear bees buzzing, you are hearing the sound of their wings vibrating rapidly as they fly. Other times, you might be hearing a bee shake in a certain way to get the pollen off of a flower. The shaking can make a buzzing sound.

Sample Modeled Writing

Possible Think-Aloud: *I heard many of you say that I could add onomatopoeia right at the beginning of this section. I agree! An obvious sound to include would be "buzz, buzz," right? Watch as I add that to the beginning of this section. When I do that, I will tell my reader exactly what bees sound like.*

Analyze

STEP 3: Reread and reflect.

Possible Think-Aloud: *Let's reread my piece again. What do you think of it now? How did the sound words help improve my writing? Are there any other places I could add onomatopoeia?*

Sum It Up

When nonfiction writers include words that sound like the sounds associated with them, their writing is more interesting and appealing and readers are better able to visualize what is being said. As you return to your writing today, think of places where you could slip in a sound word or two to make your writing more exciting!

VARIATIONS

For Less Experienced Writers: Show students how to create a poem using onomatopoeia. Choose a topic such as an animal or a large piece of machinery. Brainstorm a list of sound words associated with the animal or machinery, and then, together, experiment with page layout to create a poem.

For More Experienced Writers: With students, brainstorm a list of onomatopoeic words, and then challenge them to find examples in poems. For example, you might display a short excerpt from Edgar Allan Poe's poem "The Bells." Once students have identified examples, lead a discussion about how these words add to the poem and the writer's message.

LINKS TO CD-ROM:

- Planning Page: Onomatopoeia
- Mentor Text: *Penguins: Belly-sliding, Fast-swimming, Birds!*

Use Persuasive Language

WHEN TO USE IT: To help writers identify the unique language features of persuasion

FOCUS THE LEARNING

Persuasive texts are identified by a call to action that includes imperative statements and bossy language. A strong persuasive text also uses repetition to restate the call to action in the conclusion.

Model

STEP 1: Point out the linguistic features of a persuasive text.

Possible Think-Aloud: *In a persuasive text, writers need to use imperative sentences that clearly urge readers to take action. This means that you speak directly to your readers and tell them what they should do. Watch as I write an example: "Start recycling today!" Did you notice that there is no subject in that sentence? It is an imperative sentence, so it is understood that the subject is "you." When you write a persuasive piece, it is important to make careful word choices that will convince a reader to take action. The opening sentence of a persuasive poster such as this one is a call to action—an imperative statement that tells a reader to take action on an important topic.*

TURN &TALK *Think together. Create an imperative sentence in which "you" is understood that we could add to this persuasive poster about recycling.*

STEP 2: Model the creation of additional imperative sentences and a restatement of the call to action.

Start recycling today!

Reduce our carbon footprint.

Save natural resources.

Don't wait—Start recycling today!

Sample Modeled Writing

Possible Think-Aloud: *Here are two more imperative sentences that we can use to support our persuasive argument: "Reduce . . . resources." With careful word choices, this is making a convincing argument for this persuasive poster. Now I am ready to write a conclusion. In the conclusion of a persuasive piece, you want to use repetition to restate the call to action. Watch as I open with "Don't wait—" Notice that, again, the subject of the sentence is understood to be "you" because this is an imperative statement. Now comes the repetition: "Start recycling today!"*

Analyze

STEP 3: Reread and reflect.

Possible Think-Aloud: *Join me in rereading my persuasive poster about recycling. As we reread, take special notice of the imperative sentences, the bossy tone, and the repetition of the call to action. Careful word choices are essential in persuasive writing.*

Sum It Up

You know that persuasive texts need to have a call to action that uses imperative statements and bossy language. This means that the subject of the sentences is understood to be the reader. Persuasive texts, such as this poster, also include repetition—especially in the conclusion that restates the call to action.

VARIATIONS

For Less Experienced Writers: Have partners work together to create persuasive posters based on a list of the linguistic features identified in this lesson. As they work together, help them make careful word choices as they orally rehearse imperative sentences with inferred subjects.

For More Experienced Writers: Experiment with repetitive word choice by adding repetition in the middle of a persuasive piece as well as in the conclusion. Then, transfer understanding of word choice on persuasion to writing persuasive letters, persuasive essays, and so on.

LINKS TO CD-ROM:

- Self-Assessment Persuasive Language
- Mentor Text: *Reversing a Heavy Trend*
- Writing Samples

Sentence Fluency

Creating Sentences that Flow Smoothly

Sentence fluency is best tested with the ear. Pieces that have sentence fluency are easy to read aloud, with a rhythm and flow that draw us along. To achieve sentence fluency, writers must weave a tapestry of sentences that are of varying lengths and styles while offering variety in sentence beginnings. Interesting sentence structures can significantly enhance sentence fluency.

LESSON	3	4	5	RELATED LESSONS
1 Sentences Are of Varying Lengths	●	●	●	*Sentence Structure:* Lesson 1, Two-Word Sentences
2 Rereading to Check Sentence Fluency	●	●	●	*Revising:* Lesson 5, Revising for Sentence Fluency
3 Using a Variety of Sentence Beginnings	●	●	●	*Sentence Structure:* Lesson 4, Opening Element *Sentence Fluency:* Lessons 4 and 5
4 Varying Sentence Beginnings with Prepositional Phrases	●	●	●	*Sentence Fluency:* Lesson 3, Using a Variety of Sentence Beginnings
5 Vary Sentence Beginnings with Adverbs and Adverb Phrases	●	●	●	*Sentence Fluency:* Lesson 3, Using a Variety of Sentence Beginnings
6 Two-Word Sentences	●	●	●	*Sentence Fluency:* Lesson 1, Sentences Are of Varying Lengths
7 Using a Dash		●	●	*Punctuation and Capitalization:* Lesson 5, Using a Dash
8 Smooth Transitions with Linking Words and Phrases		●	●	*Drafting:* Lesson 4, Infusing Transition Words and Phrases
9 Use the Rule of Three		●	●	*Punctuation and Capitalization:* Lesson 1, Commas: Separating Phrases in a Series

Sentences Are of Varying Lengths

WHEN TO USE IT: When student writing contains sentences that are mostly short and choppy or long and rambling

FOCUS THE LEARNING

A high-quality piece of writing contains a variety of sentence lengths organized in such a way that the writing flows smoothly and naturally when it is read. This lesson is designed to help students examine their writing and revise, if necessary.

Model

STEP 1: Display a short section of writing like the one provided below, and think aloud about the variety of sentence lengths using the Varying Sentence Length Checklist from the Resources CD-ROM.

Possible Think-Aloud: *When I am writing, I want to make sure that there is variety in the length of my sentences. If all of my sentences are short, my writing can sound choppy. However, I don't want my sentences to go on forever, either. Watch as I use this sentence length checklist to analyze the paragraph I have on display. I will count the number of words in each sentence to be sure that there is some variety in length. Sentence one, "Whoosh!" is just one word.*

TURN &TALK *Analyze the other sentences in this paragraph. Have I utilized short sentences, long sentences, and medium-length sentences?*

STEP 2: Finish using the Varying Sentence Length Checklist to check your paragraph.

> Whoosh! When moist, warm air from the Gulf of Mexico meets the cool, dry air from Canada, it creates instability in the atmosphere. This can lead to thunderstorms. Sometimes these thunderstorms produce powerful and dangerous tornadoes.

Sample Modeled Writing

Possible Think-Aloud: *I'm feeling good about the sentence fluency in this paragraph. I have one short sentence, one medium-length sentence, and two fairly long sentences. Now I'll read this section aloud. One of the best ways to check for sentence fluency is to read your writing out loud and see how it sounds. Our writing should sound smooth and natural when we read it out loud, just like speaking.*

TURN &TALK *What did you notice about the fluency of my writing? Did it sound smooth when I read it aloud? Were the sentences of varying lengths? How did that impact the fluency?*

Analyze

STEP 3: Reread and reflect.

Possible Think-Aloud: *Let's look at my checklist. Notice that I used both long and short sentences. I have some sentences that are medium in length as well. So far, I think I'm on track! I have a variety of sentence lengths that will help my writing sound natural when it is read aloud. Let's all read it aloud one more time and see how it sounds to the ear.*

Sum It Up

Today we learned one way to do a check on our writing to see if it flows smoothly. When we count the number of words in each sentence, we may find that all of our sentences are short or that all of our sentences are long. That would lead us to revise. As you return to your own pieces of writing, try using the Varying Sentence Length Checklist and see what you discover. Let's begin!

VARIATIONS

For Less Experienced Writers: Provide students with a simple sentence, such as "The caterpillar crawls up the mulberry leaf." Then, ask partners to try improving sentence fluency by adding an introductory element followed by a comma. For example, the revised sentence might be, "As the sun rises, the caterpillar crawls up the mulberry leaf." Then, coach and confer as writers try it with their own writing.

For More Experienced Writers: Challenge partners to revise a piece that is short and choppy or long and rambling. Demonstrate how to combine short sentences to add flavor and variety or how to correct run-on sentences to add order and structure.

LINKS TO CD-ROM:
- Varying Sentence Length Checklist

Rereading to Check Sentence Fluency

WHEN TO USE IT: To help writers move beyond short, choppy sentences

FOCUS THE LEARNING

Strong (or weak) sentence fluency becomes apparent when a piece of writing is read aloud. When we help students develop an expectation that they need to reread with an ear for sentence fluency, their writing develops a natural flow and rhythm.

Model

STEP 1: Display a piece of writing, and think aloud as you reread it to listen for fluency in the sentences.

Possible Think-Aloud: *Writers, when I think I am finished with a piece of writing, I have an important job to do. I need to focus on how my writing might sound to a reader or a listener. It should sound natural and be pleasant to read aloud. It is also important that the sentences are of different lengths and that each sentence begins with a different word.* (Read the writing.) *The first few sentences are quite choppy when I read them aloud.*

TURN &TALK *Analyze my writing. What can I do to help this paragraph have a more natural flow?*

STEP 2: Model how to improve sentence fluency.

First Draft:

Freshwater is found in rivers. It is found in lakes. It is found in underground sources. It is also found in glaciers. It is limited, so we have to use it wisely.

Second Draft:

The amount of freshwater that is found in rivers, lakes, underground sources, and glaciers is limited. Therefore, it's important that we use water wisely and not waste it.

Sample Modeled Writing

Possible Think-Aloud: *I am going to add some sentence fluency to this paragraph. I can do that by combining the first three sentences into one sentence. Watch me as I write, "The amount of freshwater that is found in rivers, lakes, underground sources, and glaciers is limited." Do you see how I included the sources of freshwater along with the idea that freshwater is limited? By doing this, I think my piece will have a more natural, fluent sound.*

TURN &TALK *With your partner, read my first sentence out loud, and determine if my sentence fluency is improving. Consider other ways in which I might enhance the fluency of each of my sentences.*

Analyze

STEP 3: Reread and reflect.

Possible Think-Aloud: *Wow! When I combined those sentences, it made a big difference in the fluency of my writing. Let's look at the last sentence. Transition or linking words such as "therefore" can enhance sentence fluency, too. Watch as I insert "therefore" to begin the sentence and conclude by encouraging my reader to use water wisely. "Therefore" plus a comma causes my reader to take a breath. That is another way to improve sentence fluency and signal my reader that the writing is about to conclude. Now let's read my revised paragraph and analyze it for sentence fluency.*

Sum It Up

Today we learned that the best way to see if a piece of writing is fluent is to read it out loud and pay close attention to how it sounds to our ears. Fluent writing needs to have sentences that vary in length and sentence beginnings that use different words. As you return to your writing today, take some time to read it out loud, focusing on its flow and rhythm.

VARIATIONS

For Less Experienced Writers: Share several short pieces of writing like the ones provided on the Resources CD-ROM. Some should showcase strong sentence fluency; some should be weak in sentence fluency. Read the pieces together and discuss: *"Which ones do you prefer? Why? What makes this piece more fluent than this one?"*

For More Experienced Writers: Collect or write a short piece of writing that is weak in sentence fluency. Together, revise the piece by combining sentences and changing sentence beginnings. Then, coach and confer with writers as they revise their own pieces of writing.

LINKS TO CD-ROM:
• Writing Samples: Strong and Weak Sentence Fluency

Using a Variety of Sentence Beginnings

WHEN TO USE IT: When sentence beginnings are dull and repetitive

FOCUS THE LEARNING

Often students are so engaged with crafting text that is factual that they don't realize that they are using a limited number of words to begin most sentences. We want to draw attention to this challenge and offer a range of options that will help them add variety to their sentences.

Model

Craft part of the modeled writing, and display it on a chart or whiteboard before launching the lesson.

STEP 1: Think aloud as you continue crafting a piece of writing, and consider how to keep your sentence beginnings varied.

Possible Think-Aloud: *Writers, one challenge we have in crafting any piece of writing is making sure that our sentences don't all start the same way. I'm working on a piece about blue herons, and I want to show you what I'm thinking as I begin each sentence. (Read piece up to "sharp bill.") I want to add, "Once the sun sets," but when I stop and think, I realize that I just used the word "once" to start the last sentence. I need to choose another way to begin the next sentence.*

TURN &TALK *Partners, put your heads together, and see if you have some ideas for me. How could I start my next sentence using different words?*

STEP 2: Continue writing and thinking about varying your sentence beginnings.

> The great blue heron stands silently along the shore of the river, scanning the water for a tasty fish. Once it spots its prey, it lunges forward and stabs the creature with its sharp bill. When the sun sets, it will return to the mudflat in hopes of finding a few voles for dinner. Voles make up much of the heron's diet in the cold winter months.

Sample Modeled Writing

Possible Think-Aloud: *I heard some fabulous ideas. Some of you suggested that I try using a phrase that focuses on time. I like that idea! I'll begin my next sentence with "When the sun sets. . . ." Next, I want to add, "When it's winter, herons eat a lot of voles." But if I used the word "when," it would begin just the way my last sentence did. I'll start with the word "voles" instead.*

TURN & TALK What are you learning about varying sentence beginnings? Help each other remember what we should think about when we are crafting our sentences.

Analyze

STEP 3: Reread and reflect.

Possible Think-Aloud: *Let's reread my piece and see how it sounds. It is important to check the sentence beginnings and be sure that I am using a variety of words. I like the way my sentences sound, and I think my reader will, too!*

Sum It Up

Today I showed you how I think about each sentence before I write it. I think about opening words I've used for the last few sentences, and I take some time to consider other words I can use to spice up my writing. As you continue to write your own pieces today, challenge yourself to think about each sentence beginning. Consider analyzing a few paragraphs using the Sentence Beginnings Checklist on the Resources CD-ROM.

VARIATIONS

For Less Experienced Writers: Display a sentence, such as "The grizzly bear is the most dangerous animal in the forest." Ask partners to reword the sentence by using different words to begin: "The most dangerous animal in the forest is the grizzly bear." Challenge them to reword it.

For More Experienced Writers: Provide writers with several short, simple sentences. Challenge them to combine the sentences to create compound and complex sentences. For example, you might provide them with: "Komodo dragons are carnivores. They eat only meat. They eat live prey. They also are scavengers. They eat the carcasses of dead animals." How might these sentences be combined?

LINKS TO CD-ROM:
• Sentence Beginnings Checklist

Varying Sentence Beginnings with Prepositional Phrases

WHEN TO USE IT: When students are ready to experiment with phrases to begin sentences

FOCUS THE LEARNING

When we use prepositional phrases, our writing comes to life and sentence fluency improves. The goal of this lesson is to teach writers how to use prepositional phrases as another exciting way to begin their sentences.

Model

In advance of the lesson, construct a Personal Sentence Planning Chart like the one provided below.

STEP 1: Think aloud as you use the Personal Sentence Planning Chart to begin writing.

Possible Think-Aloud: *We've been collecting information about sloths. Today I want to show you how we can use this information along with a Personal Sentence Planning Chart to help us start our sentences in a rich and interesting way. I am writing about how much sleep sloths need. I want to say, "Sloths sleep up to 20 hours a day." I see on my chart that we listed "deep in the rainforest." If I begin my sentence with that phrase, I think it will help to strengthen the sentence fluency of my writing.*

TURN &TALK *What do you think of that prepositional phrase? Does it help you visualize? Say the sentence aloud, and evaluate its fluency. Is there any other phrase from our chart that we could use?*

STEP 2: Model a sentence beginning with a prepositional phrase.

Personal Sentence Planning Chart

Author _____ Date _____

Topic _____

Prepositional Phrases (where)	Adjectives (describing words)	Verbs (action words)
deep in the rainforest		
in the tropical forest		
in Central America		
high in the trees		
in the tropical regions of South America		
on a tree branch		

Starting sentences with phrases helped my writing because
_____
_____

When planning interesting sentences, I want to be sure to
_____
_____

Sample Modeled Writing

Deep in the rainforest, sloths sleep up to twenty hours a day. Even when they are awake, sloths barely move. In fact, they move so infrequently that algae sometimes grow on their fur.

Possible Think-Aloud: *I like the phrase "deep in the rainforest."*
I think I'll use it to begin this section of my writing. Watch as I
write: "Deep in the rainforest, sloths sleep up to 20 hours a day."
That gives my writing some fluency! Now I can go on to tell my
reader more.

TURN
&TALK *Examine the chart and create a sentence that begins with a*
prepositional phrase. Give me a thumbs up when you and
your partner are ready to share.

Analyze

STEP 3: Reread and reflect.

Possible Think-Aloud: *Let's reread what I have written so far. What do*
you think? I think we added a lot of richness, detail, and variety by
using a prepositional phrase to begin one of the sentences.

Sum It Up

Writers, today I showed you how to begin a sentence in a fresh
and exciting way. You've been working on your own topic chart.
Challenge yourself today to use the chart to craft a sentence or
two that start with a prepositional phrase. Be ready to share your
sentence with your partner.

VARIATIONS

**For Less Experienced
Writers:** Invite writers
to have some fun with
the topic chart. Ask
students to choose three
adjectives, one verb,
and one prepositional
phrase. Then, ask them
to write the sentence
they have created.
For example, "Slow,
sluggish, two-toed sloths
sleep on the branch."

**For More Experienced
Writers:** Challenge
writers to be on the
lookout for prepo-
sitional phrases in their
reading selections. Ask
them to record these
phrases in their reading
log and share their
collection during the
next lesson.

LINKS TO CD-ROM:
• Personal Sentence
  Planning Chart
• Teacher Tool:
  Prepositions

Vary Sentence Beginnings with Adverbs and Adverb Phrases

WHEN TO USE IT: When students are ready to experiment with another powerful way to begin sentences

FOCUS THE LEARNING

When we use adverbs and adverb phrases to start our sentences, we give our readers more information while at the same time strengthening the fluency of the writing. The goal of this lesson is to help students see the power (and fun) in using these kinds of sentence openers.

Model

In advance of the lesson, prepare a chart with adverb and adverb phrases as per the Resources CD-ROM.

STEP 1: Explain how adverbs and adverb phrases help the reader, and then display an anchor chart with adverb and adverb phrases. (See Resources CD-ROM.)

Possible Think-Aloud: *Writers, I created a chart to guide us as we think about starting our sentences with adverbs and adverb phrases. Today I want to show you how using adverbs and adverb phrases can provide more information about our topic while also improving our sentence fluency. Adverbs and adverb phrases tell our readers when, where, how, and to what extent. For example, if I say, "Phil worked **extremely hard**," the word "extremely" is an adverb that explains to what extent.*

TURN &TALK *Partners, examine our chart. Can you think of any other adverb or adverb phrase that we could add?*

STEP 2: Model writing a few sentences using an adverb or adverb phrase to begin.

> At the stroke of midnight, my friend and I crept out of the tent and made our way to the creek. Quickly, we looked back to see if we were being followed. Carefully, we unwrapped the package and placed it on the rocky shore.

Sample Modeled Writing

Possible Think-Aloud: *I'm going to begin writing about the time that my friend and I devoured some chocolates. Watch as I write the first sentence, using an adverb phrase to begin. An adverb or adverb phrase is always separated from the rest of the sentence with a comma.* (Write first sentence.) *For my next two sentences, I am going to begin with a single adverb. You might notice that adverbs often end in -ly. They are also followed by a comma.*

TURN &TALK *I'm going to underline each adverb or adverb phrase that I used. Examine them and tell your partner which one spoke to you most. Was it the phrase, or was it one of the single-word adverbs?*

Analyze

STEP 3: Reread and reflect.

Possible Think-Aloud: *Did any of you have the same reaction? Did any of you have different reactions? It's important to remember that authors and readers have different thoughts and reactions, and that's okay! Let's read my writing once again and think about how the adverbs and adverb phrases gave the writing more richness.*

Sum It Up

Writers, today I showed you how I can use adverbs and adverb phrases to vary my sentence beginnings. We noticed that these powerful words and phrases help our readers create a clear mental image as they read our writing. Today as you begin drafting, challenge yourself to use the chart and experiment with infusing adverbs and adverb phrases. Let's begin!

VARIATIONS

For Less Experienced Writers: Provide partners with cookbooks, and invite them to browse the recipes to look for adverbs. (For example, *"Rapidly* boil the spaghetti for 10–12 minutes." *"Slowly* simmer the tomato sauce.") Ask students to share the adverbs that they found, and add them to an ongoing chart in the classroom.

For More Experienced Writers: Show writers how adverbs can also be used to make an adjective stronger or weaker. Provide partners with a simple adjective such as "hot." Then, have them add adverbs such as "very," "extremely," "increasingly," "rather," and "so" to create two-word phrases. Finally, ask students to rank the phrases in order of heat.

LINKS TO CD-ROM:
- Teacher Tool: Adverbs and Adverb Phrases

Two-Word Sentences

WHEN TO USE IT: To add variety to writing by stripping sentences down to core components

FOCUS THE LEARNING

The knowledge that a sentence has an underlying structure that can be broken down into two words can help students create writing that is varied, fluent, and controlled. The object of this lesson is to help students understand what a sentence is and how using a two-word sentence can help to add variety and richness to writing.

Model

STEP 1: Think aloud as you craft a piece of writing, and consider how to infuse short powerful sentences amid longer sentences.

Possible Think-Aloud: *Writers, we've been talking about improving sentence fluency by varying the length of our sentences. We want our writing to contain short, long, and medium-length sentences so it is a joy to read aloud. Today I want to show you how you can insert two-word sentences into your writing. I'm writing about how I love to sit on my deck in the morning. I'll begin by writing, "On weekends, I love to get up early . . . stretched before me." Two-word sentences are sentences that have only a subject and a verb—no extra words! They look simple, but they can add a lot of punch. Watch as I write: "Night fades."*

TURN &TALK *With your partner, read what I have written so far. How did inserting a two-word sentence impact the writing?*

STEP 2: Continue writing and think aloud as you craft some two-word sentences.

> On weekends, I love to get up early, grab a cup of coffee, and head out to my deck. The air is fresh and clean, and the whole day is stretched before me. Night fades. Dawn breaks. All is still and quiet. After a few moments of breathing in the silence and the sweet air, I am ready to start my day.

Sample Modeled Writing

Possible Think-Aloud: *I'm ready to tell my reader how the dawn breaks as I'm enjoying my coffee. I could say, "The dawn breaks," but I think I could add another two-word sentence here. I think it would sound better if I said, "Dawn breaks." Watch as I write that.*

Analyze

STEP 3: Reread and reflect.

Possible Think-Aloud: *I'll finish this paragraph by writing about how still and quiet it is in the morning and how I spend some time breathing in the silence and the sweet air.* (Continue writing.) *Let's reread this paragraph and analyze the sentence fluency. I like the way this paragraph sounds, and I think my reader will, too. Have you noticed that I used strong verbs in these short sentences? Most two-word sentences contain a powerful verb—it gives them a punch!*

Sum It Up

Today I showed you how I include two-word sentences every now and then when I'm writing. It helps to spice up the writing and make it sound more interesting. As you continue to write your own pieces today, challenge yourselves to think about each sentence you are crafting, and try to add some short and powerful sentences. Then, reread to see how the sentences sound when they are read together.

VARIATIONS

For Less Experienced Writers: Provide more explicit instruction on the difference between a sentence and a fragment. For example: "Frogs leap" is a sentence, while "or not" is a fragment. To solidify the learning, ask students, *"Who or what did something? What did they do?"* If students have no answer, it is a fragment.

For More Experienced Writers: Challenge students to collect two-word sentences from their reading. Post the collection on a wall chart. Guide students as they notice how rare these sentences are, and lead a discussion about why that is the case.

LINKS TO CD-ROM:
• Teacher Tool: Two-Word Sentences

Using a Dash

WHEN TO USE IT: When students are ready to experiment with another tool to improve sentence fluency

FOCUS THE LEARNING

A dash can draw attention to extra information in a dramatic fashion, or it can serve to showcase an interruption in speech. In short, the dash calls attention to what follows it. This lesson is designed to teach students that they can use a dash much like a comma but for different purposes. Like other writing tools, we need to give students an opportunity to see how an expert—you!—uses a dash in your own writing.

Model

STEP 1: Think aloud as you begin crafting a piece of writing, and consider how to use dashes to define a word.

Possible Think-Aloud: *Writers, today I want to show you another way to make your sentences fluent and interesting—using a dash! A dash works somewhat like parentheses or commas, but we use them where we want a more dramatic effect. I'm working on a section of my piece about fingerprints. I'll begin by saying, "For centuries scholars had hypothesized that people's finger-prints differed from person to person." I want to interrupt the sentence after the word "fingerprints" so that I can define what a fingerprint is.*

TURN &TALK *Think together. If you were going to define what a fingerprint is, how would you do it?*

STEP 2: Continue writing and think aloud as you insert dashes.

> For centuries scholars had hypothesized that people's fingerprints—the patterns of looped and branching ridges on our fingertips—differed from person to person. However, it wasn't until the 19th century that the British scientist Francis Galton proved that fact. Galton also proved that fingerprints remain unchanged—even throughout a person's lifetime!

Sample Modeled Writing

Possible Think-Aloud: *I'm going to interrupt this sentence to tell my reader what a fingerprint is. I could use a comma, but I'm going to use a dash instead. After the dash, I'll write, "the patterns of looped and branching ridges on our fingertips." Now I'll add another dash and finish my original sentence. Do you notice the way the dash interrupter acts just like the interrupter you create with a comma?* (See lesson on using an interrupter in Sentence Structure, page 282.) *What is special is that a dash causes a reader to pause for a bit longer and really pay attention to what comes next.*

Analyze

STEP 3: Reread and reflect.

Possible Think-Aloud: *I'm ready to try using another dash. I want to say that Galton proved that a person's fingerprints remain unchanged even as he or she ages. Watch as I use a dash to give emphasis to this fact. I'll write, "Galton also proved that fingerprints remain unchanged—even throughout a person's lifetime!" This time I used the dash to emphasize a part of my sentence. Let's reread this section and think about what the dashes do for the writing.*

Sum It Up

Today I showed you how you can use a dash much like you use a comma. You can use it to interrupt a sentence or to add emphasis to a sentence. As you return to your writing today, have fun experimenting with ways to add a dash to your writing. Keep in mind that you won't want to overdo it, but a well-placed dash can add liveliness and fluency to your writing.

VARIATIONS

For Less Experienced Writers: Using a nonfiction book like *She Loved Baseball: The Effa Manley Story* by Audrey Vernick, lead a discussion about how the author utilizes the dash in her writing. For example: "So many people—not just baseball fans—were proud and hopeful about change and equality in baseball and bold new music—jazz—blared and folks stepped out in strange new shoes called sneakers." Then, coach and confer as writers attempt to use the dash in their own writing.

For More Experienced Writers: Show students how dashes can be utilized as an opener to a sentence, an interrupter to the sentence, and as a closer to a sentence. Then, challenge students to find examples of these in the books they are reading during independent reading time.

LINKS TO CD-ROM:

• Mentor Text: *Africa's Diverse Landscape*

Smooth Transitions with Linking Words and Phrases

WHEN TO USE IT: To add fluency and structure to a piece of nonfiction writing

FOCUS THE LEARNING

Smooth transitions are invaluable because they clarify the content by showing relationships between ideas. When we infuse linking words and phrases into nonfiction writing, we produce smoother-sounding language, and we provide a structure that makes our writing easier to read and understand.

Model

STEP 1: Create a chart with linking words and phrases, and discuss it with the students. A sample chart can be found on the Resources CD-ROM. Demonstrate how you use words and phrases from the chart as you craft a short paragraph.

Possible Think-Aloud: *As nonfiction writers, we need to be able to create pieces of writing that are fluent and organized. Linking words and phrases can help you accomplish both goals! Linking words and phrases connect ideas and sentences so that there is a clear and easy flow to your writing. I have posted a chart that lists some linking words and phrases and how they can be used. I'm going to use this chart as I write about the Supreme Court Building. Right away, I want to tell my reader when the building was designed. I can use a linking phrase that shows time. I'll write, "In 1932, . . . Building."*

TURN &TALK *I want my next sentence to explain that Taft chose Cass Gilbert to design the building because he had designed other capital buildings. Use the chart and think together. What word or phrase could I use to link my next sentence?*

STEP 2: Continue writing and think aloud as you insert linking words and phrases.

In 1932, Chief Justice William Howard Taft asked Cass Gilbert to design the U.S. Supreme Court Building. Since Gilbert had designed the capital buildings for states such as Minnesota and Arkansas, Taft thought he would be a good choice. Gilbert proved to be an excellent choice. Before long, Gilbert had designed a beautiful and stately building to match the other buildings in the capital city.

Sample Modeled Writing

Possible Think-Aloud: *Since I'm giving reasons why Taft chose Gilbert, I think I should use a word from our chart that will give reasons. I'll write, "Since Gilbert had designed the capital buildings for states such as Minnesota and Arkansas, Taft thought he would be a good choice." Did you notice how the word "since" provided a link between the ideas in my sentence? When we use linking words and phrases, they provide a unity between the ideas that make up our sentences. They can also connect the sentences that make up a paragraph.*

TURN &TALK *I will want to tell the reader that Gilbert designed the building right away. Use the chart to select a word I would use to start my last sentence.*

Analyze

STEP 3: Reread and reflect.

Possible Think-Aloud: *Some of you suggested using the phrase "before long" to begin my next sentence. Let's try it. "Before long, Gilbert had designed a beautiful and stately building. . . ." I think the phrase "before long" will link the first part of that sentence to the last part. Now let's reread this paragraph. Determine if I chose the best words from the chart or if there are other words that might help my writing.*

Sum It Up

Words and phrases that connect sentences help to enhance the fluency of our writing. They also serve as cues that help the reader interpret the ideas that you, as the writer, want them to understand. When we use linking words and phrases, it helps to clarify our ideas and helps our writing sound more natural when it is read. Today as you begin writing, try using some of the linking words and phrases from our chart.

Use the Rule of Three

WHEN TO USE IT: When writing is choppy or loaded with short sentences

FOCUS THE LEARNING

Writers can improve sentence fluency and descriptions by organizing descriptions in sets of three. This is often called the "rule of three." If we teach writers to create complex sentences that combine three descriptors, the writing becomes richer, and nonfiction communication is enhanced.

Model

STEP 1: Use a projection device to display three short sentences. If you don't have access to a projection device, use a pocket chart to display the sentences.

Possible Think-Aloud: *I am working on this section of my writing about turtles. As I read these sentences aloud, I notice that my writing sounds pretty choppy. When we use all short sentences like these, the sentence fluency is fairly weak. Today I want to show you what I can do to turn these short sentences into one longer and more fluent sentence.*

TURN &TALK *Imagine for a moment that this is your writing. Tell your partner what you would do to make this section more fluent.*

STEP 2: Think aloud as you apply the "rule of three" to your writing.

First Draft:

The turtle quickly flattens himself to the ground.
He pulls his legs and head into the safety of his shell.
He waits for the hungry eagle to pass.

Second Draft:

The turtle quickly flattens himself to the ground, pulls his legs and head into the safety of his shell, and then waits for the hungry eagle to pass.

Sample Modeled Writing

Possible Think-Aloud: *Watch as I use something that's called the "rule of three" to improve the fluency of this section. First, I need to focus on the verbs in each sentence. The verbs in these sentences are "flattens," "pulls," and "waits." The trick is to put them all in one sentence! Watch as I take out the word "he" from sentence two and sentence three. Now I'm going to turn the period at the end of sentences one and two into commas. Finally, I'll add the phrase "and then" after the last comma.*

TURN &TALK *Analyze my new "rule of three" sentence. What is your opinion of the new sentence? How did the "rule of three" improve the fluency of this part of my writing?*

Analyze

STEP 3: Reread and reflect.

Possible Think-Aloud: *Listen as I reread my new sentence.* (After reading.) *Combining these three short sentences into one longer sentence makes my writing more interesting and fluent.*

Sum It Up

The "rule of three" helped me create a rich and fluent sentence with three actions. By writing one sentence that contains three verbs, I have a richer description of what a turtle does to avoid becoming an eagle's lunch! I wouldn't want to do this to all of my sentences, but every now and then, it's helpful to combine sentences this way. Who thinks they can try this today?

VARIATIONS

For Less Experienced Writers: Help writers notice the use of transitional words and phrases after the last comma. Consider creating an anchor chart of the most common transitional words and phrases that are used when combining sentences.

For More Experienced Writers: Stretch these writers to revisit a previously completed piece of writing and use the "rule of three" to revise for sentence fluency.

Voice and Audience

Bringing Personality to the Page— Thinking About Our Readers

Nonfiction writing can represent a range of voices from quiet and objective to energetic and enthusiastic. When a nonfiction writer integrates voice into his or her work, there is a sense that a real person with feelings and emotions is speaking to you. A strong voice makes it clear that the author cares about the message and has consciously thought about you—the reader.

LESSON	3	4	5	RELATED LESSONS
1 Match Voice to Audience		●	●	*Planning:* Lesson 1, Selecting a Format for Writing
2 Show Engagement with the Topic	●	●	●	*Ideas:* Lesson 3, Jaw-Dropping Details Add Interest
3 Open with a Question	●	●		*Ideas:* Lesson 6, Anticipating the Questions of Your Reader *Sentence Fluency:* Lesson 3, Using a Variety of Sentence Beginnings
4 Speak Directly to Your Reader		●	●	*Voice and Audience:* Lesson 1, Match Voice to Audience
5 Surprise Your Reader		●	●	
6 Pick an Enticing Title	●	●	●	*Text Features:* Lesson 1, Powerful Titles
7 Shift Point of View or Perspective		●	●	
8 Add Humor		●	●	
9 Target Voice in Persuasive Writing	●	●	●	*Drafting:* Lesson 10, Drafting a Persuasion
10 Use a Repeating Refrain			●	
11 Help Readers Infer		●	●	
12 At the End, Reveal Your Thoughts, Feelings, and Opinions	●	●	●	*Organization:* Lesson 7, Craft an Ending that Brings Closure

Match Voice to Audience

WHEN TO USE IT: When writers have not chosen an appropriate tone for the purpose and audience

FOCUS THE LEARNING

Audience and purpose should determine the voice and tone of a piece of writing. For example, if you are writing a note to a friend thanking her for a birthday present, you don't want to sound like an angry person. Likewise, if you are writing a research paper on the effects of pollution on our ocean waters, you wouldn't want to sound as casual as you do when you're talking to a good friend. The goal of this lesson is to teach writers how to choose a voice that matches their purpose and audience.

Model

STEP 1: Think aloud as your craft a brief email to a friend.

Possible Think-Aloud: *We've been talking about the importance of infusing voice into our writing. Voice, or tone, tells the reader something about a nonfiction writer's personality through his or her writing. Today I want to show you how your voice shifts in response to the audience that will read your writing. I'm going to craft two emails. The first one is to my dear friend, Mary. Sometimes, I start an email with "Dear" and then the person's name. But Mary is a close friend. I can start with something more casual, like "Hi Mary."* (Continue writing email.)

TURN &TALK *Think about the way you speak with your friends. Is this the same way you would speak with your teacher, your coach, the principal, or a police officer? How does your tone change when you speak to different people in your life?*

STEP 2: Craft the second email.

Possible Think-Aloud: *The second email I'm writing is to our principal, asking her to consider installing a vending machine in our foyer. It wouldn't work to start this email with, "Hi!" I need to show Ms. Miller respect, so I want my voice and my words to sound more formal. I'll start with "Dear Ms. Miller." I'm going to use a more formal voice for this email. Watch as I include more formal terms such as "please consider," "furthermore," and "respectfully request your consideration." These terms are used to create a formal tone and show respect to a reader.*

First email:

Hi Mary,

I'm planning on seeing a movie tomorrow night. Are you free? It would be totally fun, and I'd even spring for the popcorn! Let me know if you want to join me.

Later,
Kelly

Second email:

Dear Ms. Miller,

I am writing to ask you to please consider installing a healthy-options vending machine in the foyer by the fifth-grade hall. There are several companies that offer healthy choices for vending machines, and it is my belief that students would benefit from the ability to occasionally purchase a snack during the school day. Furthermore, we could use the money earned by the vending machine to update some of the computers in our lab. I respectfully request your consideration of this proposal.

Sincerely,
Mrs. Boswell

Sample Modeled Writing

VARIATIONS

For Less Experienced Writers: Provide more guided practice with additional modeled texts. Examples may include an invitation, a thank-you note, and a letter to the governor of your state.

For More Experienced Writers: Consider bringing in real letters from history such as the Bixby letter written to Widow Lydia Bixby from Abraham Lincoln in 1864. Provide partners with a piece of writing that is written with a casual voice. Challenge them to revise the piece to include a more formal voice.

Analyze

STEP 3: Reread and reflect.

Possible Think-Aloud: *Let's read both emails again. I want to double-check the voice in each. I need to be sure that my letter to the principal utilizes a more formal and respectful voice than the email to my friend, Mary. With the email to my friend, I can use a voice that is more relaxed and casual.*

Sum It Up

Today I showed you how my voice and tone shift based on the audience for my writing. It's important to think about the kind of voice that is appropriate for each kind of writing and each audience. As you begin writing today, take some time to think about your potential audience and purpose, and then consider the kind of voice that would be best for your piece.

Show Engagement with the Topic

WHEN TO USE IT: When the writing sounds like the author lacks passion for or interest in the topic

FOCUS THE LEARNING

When we show students how to pick a topic that interests them and then show them how to showcase that interest, their engagement with the topic shines through. This enhances the voice in their writing. We need to encourage students to put forth a conscious effort to let their personal interest in their topics come through.

Model

STEP 1: Think aloud as you discuss the importance of showing engagement with a topic, and then choose a topic about which to write.

Possible Think-Aloud: *To craft an engaging piece of writing, you have to care about your topic. If you're not interested in or engaged with your topic, your audience probably won't be interested either. As writers, we don't end our writing with "I really care about this topic. I do. Sincerely, The Author." We need to show engagement with our topics in such a way that the reader will simply know that we care. We've been learning about rocks and minerals, and I found it interesting that gold is really soft. Since gold is a topic that I find interesting, I'm going to write about it.*

TURN &TALK *What are some topics that interest you? Tell your partner about some of the rocks and minerals that make you curious. What topic would you enjoy learning more about?*

STEP 2: Begin crafting a short piece of writing, thinking aloud as you consciously show engagement with the topic.

> Most people know that gold is one of the most valuable minerals, but did you know that gold is also incredibly soft? In fact, it is so soft that you could roll an ounce of it into a hair-thin wire that could stretch 50 feet long! Gold is a mineral that is known for this and other unique properties such as its weight. The biggest pure-gold nugget was found in Australia in 1869. It weighed a whopping 156 pounds!

Sample Modeled Writing

Possible Think-Aloud: *The first tip to remember when showing engagement with a topic is to pick a topic that interests you. When you do that, it's easier to let your voice shine through. Now that I've chosen my topic, I think I'll start my piece about gold with a question. That is a great way to add voice and show that I am engaged with my topic—that I find it interesting. I'll write, "Most people know that gold is one of the most valuable minerals, but did you know that gold is also incredibly soft?"*

Analyze

STEP 3: Reread and reflect.

Possible Think-Aloud: *I'll continue writing by telling my reader more about gold. I learned that gold is so soft that just an ounce of it can be rolled into a thin wire 50 feet long. I'll add that here. Did you notice how I used an exclamation point after the word "long"? That is another way to show that I am passionate about my topic. Now I'll tell my reader how gold is the heaviest of all minerals, and then I'll insert an interesting fact about the largest gold nugget ever discovered. Let's reread my writing so far and see what we think. Does my writing showcase my interest and engagement in the topic?*

Sum It Up

Writers, today we learned how to show engagement with our topics. We learned that this often starts with choosing a topic that we are interested in and curious about. As you begin to write today, ask yourself if you've chosen a topic that interests you. Once you begin writing, pause to ask yourself if that interest and engagement are coming through in your work.

VARIATIONS

For Less Experienced Writers: Collect excerpts from books by several nonfiction authors with whom the students are familiar (examples: Steve Jenkins, Seymour Simon, Gail Gibbons, Aliki, and Nicola Davies). As you read the excerpts aloud, challenge students to identify the author. Ask: "How did you identify the author? Could you hear the author's voice and engagement come through?"

For More Experienced Writers: Invite students to examine and analyze a book like *Living Color* by Steve Jenkins (or any other nonfiction book that contains a strong voice). Together, make a list of the characteristics of writing with a strong voice. The list might include statements such as "It shows the writer's personality," "The words come to life," and "It sounds different from other authors' works."

Open with a Question

WHEN TO USE IT: To add variety and boost voice

FOCUS THE LEARNING

We, as humans, are naturally curious about the world around us. When we teach students to harness that curiosity by infusing their writing with questions, their voices come through loud and clear.

Model

STEP 1: Display a copy of *Global Warming* by Seymour Simon or *Birds* by Nicola Davies. Guide a conversation about how these authors use questions to enhance voice and draw in their readers.

Possible Think-Aloud: *Let's examine what Seymour Simon does in the opening pages of* Global Warming. *As I read the first few paragraphs, pay attention to the questions he asks and think about why he asks them.* ["Why is the climate changing? Could Earth be getting warmer by itself? Are people doing things that make the climate warmer? What will be the impact of global warming? Can we do anything about it?"—p. 5] (After reading.) *Wow! He asks the reader four questions right in a row! After I read these questions, I'm curious to know more, and I'm hoping that he'll answer these questions throughout the book.*

TURN &TALK *Think together. What do these questions do for you as a reader? Why do you think Seymour Simon chose to include them in the opening pages of this book?*

STEP 2: Think aloud as you begin a piece of writing with a question.

Have you ever started to plant a vegetable garden and given up because it looked too daunting? Growing and harvesting your own produce can save you money, but it can seem overwhelming when you first begin. Breaking the job into smaller and more manageable chunks is essential to starting your own garden. Here's how to do it.

Sample Modeled Writing

Possible Think-Aloud: *Asking a question is a good way to draw readers into your piece. You can also hint that you have an answer to the question and invite the reader to continue reading. I'm starting a piece that is meant to teach my reader how to plant and maintain a vegetable garden. I want to open with a question. I think I'll write, "Have you ever started to plant a vegetable garden . . . overwhelming when you first begin." I think this question will draw my reader in while drawing attention to a common dilemma that gardeners face.*

Analyze

STEP 3: Reread and reflect.

Possible Think-Aloud: *Now I'm ready to hint that I have some answers to this question. I want my piece to outline how to make gardening more manageable by breaking it into smaller chunks. I'll write, "Breaking the job into smaller . . . how to do it." Let's reread my opening paragraph. How does it sound? Did asking a question boost the voice in my piece so far? I think the question not only adds voice but sets the stage for the rest of my writing.*

Sum It Up

Today I showed you how a well-placed question can enhance the author's voice in a piece of writing. A good question draws the reader in and makes him or her curious to know more about the topic. As you return to your writing today, experiment with using a question to introduce your topics or to begin a new paragraph. I look forward to reading your work!

VARIATIONS

For Less Experienced Writers: Show students how authors use a question-answer format to craft nonfiction. Consider analyzing books like *Meet the Meerkat* by Darrin Lunde or *Do Whales Have Belly Buttons?* by Melvin Berger. Then, encourage students to try the same type of question and answer format with their own writing.

For More Experienced Writers: Show students how authors like Steve Jenkins use a repeated stem to connect information on a page. For example, in his book *What Do You Do with a Tail Like This?* he uses questions such as "What do you do with eyes like these? What do you do with a mouth like this?" Coach and confer as writers use a question to focus and organize each section of their writing.

Speak Directly to Your Reader

WHEN TO USE IT: To add voice and connection between the author and the reader

FOCUS THE LEARNING

When writers speak directly to their readers and invite them to "imagine themselves in the action," writing becomes much more personal, and readers find it easier to consider the content.

Model

STEP 1: Model talking directly to a reader.

Possible Think-Aloud: *When I create writing in which I talk directly to readers, I don't just describe the subject. I try to make my readers feel like they are right there in the action. When I start writing, I will need to change my sentences to say things like, "Imagine that you are. . . ." Notice that I am telling readers to put themselves in the middle of the subject, scene, or action I am describing. That is part of the fun when you are speaking directly to a reader.*

TURN &TALK *Listen as I read my first four sentences, and try to think like a reader.* (Read the first four sentences.) *Describe the mental image you are getting. How does it make you feel when I talk directly to you and tell you to imagine that you are a slave? In your mind, do you see yourself working from sunup to sundown?*

STEP 2: Continue writing and speaking directly to your readers.

Imagine that you are a slave working the tobacco fields in Virginia. Everything you have and everything you are belong to your master. You work from sunup to sundown six days a week. You sleep in a small wooden cabin on an old hay mattress.

You hear whispers of freedom when others talk about escape and a railroad without tracks. "The Underground Railroad," some call it. But freedom means a hard and perilous journey. Do you have the courage?

Sample Modeled Writing

Possible Think-Aloud: *I am ready to speak to my reader again. This time, I want to focus on the Underground Railroad. I know that slaves heard about the Underground Railroad from other slaves. I could say, "You hear whispers of freedom when others talk about escape and a railroad without tracks." I like the way that sounds, and I think my reader will, too. The journey along the Underground Railroad was hard and dangerous, so slaves would have to decide if they wanted to try it. I think I'll end this section with a question. Watch as I write, "But freedom means. . . . Do you have the courage?"*

Analyze

STEP 3: Reread and reflect.

Possible Think-Aloud: *Analyze the section about the Underground Railroad. How did I do at talking to my readers? Is there anything else I could do to make it clear that I am not talking to the world but just to the people who are reading my writing? When I spoke directly to my readers, I invited them into the action.*

Sum It Up

Writers can add voice to their writing by talking directly to their readers and inviting them into the action on the page. In this kind of writing, you get to be a bit bossy and say things like, "You dive into the frigid waters of the Antarctic with your penguin brothers and sisters all around." or "Run! The bald eagle is diving directly at us!" These statements all speak directly to a reader and are one more way that you can create variety and add voice to your work.

VARIATIONS

For Less Experienced Writers: Give these writers additional experience in speaking directly to their readers by showing students how an author can strengthen his or her voice by shifting a piece's point of view. Consider using *Heartland* or *Sierra* by Diane Siebert as a mentor text.

For More Experienced Writers: Stretch more experienced writers by challenging them to create a chart of questions and statements that speak directly to readers. Questions and stems you might consider include "Did you know? Are you aware? I have a surprise for you. A tiger's nose is huge, bigger than your fist. If you were close enough, you could. . . ."

Surprise Your Reader

WHEN TO USE IT: When writing is flat and lifeless or when writers are showing a lack of audience awareness

FOCUS THE LEARNING

Every reader understands the importance of voice. Voice separates writing that is read from writing that is not read. Many of us, as readers, have abandoned a text because it's simply not interesting or surprising in any way. It's important that we model how to craft nonfiction with a reader in mind.

Model

In advance of the lesson, create a chart with facts about your topic.

STEP 1: Challenge students to think about how the element of surprise strengthens a piece of writing.

Possible Think-Aloud: *Have you ever read a book that wasn't very exciting or surprising? When I read a book like that, I usually don't finish it. I abandon it for something that is more fun and interesting to read. I know that one of my jobs as a writer is to stop from time to time and ask, "Would my reader enjoy this?" "Have I included some information that might surprise him or her?" I want the words that I write to come to life for my readers and keep them interested and engaged.*

TURN & TALK *Take a moment to think about a book that you have read that was interesting or surprising. What did the author do to keep you, as a reader, engaged?*

FACTS ABOUT
DASYPELTIS SNAKES
· forked tongues
· keen sense of smell
· live in Africa
· non-venomous
· swallow eggs whole
· can break eggs inside body
· vary in size

Gulp! Did you know that some snakes can swallow enormous eggs whole? One such snake is called Dasypeltis. These non-venomous snakes are equipped with extremely flexible jaws and necks that allow them to eat eggs much larger than their head. Once the egg is swallowed, bony protrusions on its spine break the egg, allowing the snake to squeeze the liquid out of the inside of the egg.

Sample Modeled Writing

STEP 2: Think aloud as you craft a short piece of writing, and consider what fact or facts would surprise the reader.

Possible Think-Aloud: *I'm preparing to write a piece about the Dasypeltis snake. As I begin to write, I'm thinking about my readers. What would be surprising to them? I've collected several facts on this chart. As I read them, I'm thinking that a reader might be surprised to know that these amazing snakes can swallow eggs much larger than their heads. That surprised me! Watch as I write, "Gulp! Did you know . . . eggs whole?" Using a question while surprising my readers is one way to add voice to my writing.*

TURN &TALK *Identify other facts that might surprise readers or capture their interest.*

Analyze

STEP 3: Reread and reflect.

Possible Think-Aloud: *Many of you suggested that I tell more about how the Dasypeltis breaks eggs inside its body. I can write about that next. I'll write, "Once the egg is swallowed, bony protrusions on its spine break the egg, allowing the snake to squeeze the liquid out of the inside of the egg." I think this sentence will continue to surprise my readers! Not many people know that snakes can crack eggs like that! Let's read my piece so far. I think I've done a good job of using the facts that I collected to create some element of surprise for my readers.*

Sum It Up

We all want our writing to be read and enjoyed by our readers. When you take the time to think about your potential readers, it helps you create a piece of writing that is interesting, surprising, and fun to read. Today as you begin writing, think about how you might add some surprise and interest to your pieces.

VARIATIONS

For Less Experienced Writers: Guide students as you examine how an author like Steve Jenkins uses surprise throughout his many books (for example, *What Do You Do When Something Wants to Eat You?* and *Never Smile at a Monkey: And 17 Other Important Things to Remember*). Then, coach and confer as writers attempt to add surprise to their own drafts.

For More Experienced Writers: As students read independently, challenge them to look for the use of surprise to enhance voice. Gather students in a small group, and invite them to share what they have discovered.

Pick an Enticing Title

WHEN TO USE IT: When students are omitting titles or when the titles they choose are lackluster

FOCUS THE LEARNING

It has been said that you never get a second chance to make a first impression. The title is the author's chance to set the tone and entice readers to read the piece. The best titles are often selected after writing is complete, so help your writers learn a bit of patience by crafting their titles after drafting.

Model

STEP 1: Display a short piece of writing. Explain the importance of choosing a good title.

Possible Think-Aloud: *I have been working on my piece about animal tracks, and I think I am finished. Now all that is left is the title. I want to write a title that is clear, concise, and interesting. Watch as I think of a few titles and then choose the one that I think will work the best for this piece. One title could be "Animal Tracks: Everything You Need to Know." But my piece really doesn't address **everything** there is to know about tracks. Another idea for a title might be "Tracks All Around," or I could try "You Can Be a Track Detective."*

TURN &TALK *Partners, put your heads together and think. If you were the author of this piece, what title would you write? What title would tell my readers what my piece is about while making them curious to know more?*

STEP 2: Think aloud as you choose a title for the piece.

If you look carefully, you can find animal tracks just about anywhere in nature. Soft sand, mud, snow, and dust are all good places to look for tracks. As you scour the landscape, remember that some tracks are not easy to see. There may be no tracks or only a part of a track where an animal stepped on hard ground, plants, or rocks.

Sample Modeled Writing

Possible Think-Aloud: *I know that I want my title to be short, snappy, interesting, and clear. My piece is mostly about how to find and analyze animal tracks. I want to include something in my title about that. I have decided that my title will be "You Can Be a Track Detective." I think it might be fun to speak directly to my readers, and we all like to think we can be detectives! I'm glad I didn't try to create a title until the writing was finished. I never would have thought of this title before I did my research and writing.*

TURN &TALK *Are there any other titles that I should consider?*

Analyze

STEP 3: Reread and reflect.

Possible Think-Aloud: *Let's reread my title and my piece of writing. Did I choose a title that works for this piece of writing? Is the title short and snappy? Does it make my readers curious to read more? I'm happy with the title I chose, and I think my readers will like it, too.*

Sum It Up

Today we talked about the importance of choosing an enticing title. We know that readers often decide whether they want to read a piece after reading the title, so we want to choose our titles carefully. As you work on your own writing today, take some time to come up with a few titles that might work. Then, choose one that you think will interest your reader the most. Let's get to work!

VARIATIONS

For Less Experienced Writers: Collect a few short nonfiction books with strong titles. Read the books and have partners brainstorm some possible titles. Then, reveal each author's choice. Examples might include *Gulls . . . Gulls . . . Gulls . . .* by Gail Gibbons, *Never Smile at a Monkey* by Steve Jenkins, and *How to Clean a Hippopotamus* by Robin Page.

For More Experienced Writers: Challenge writers to collect strong titles from books they are reading during independent reading time. Encourage them to bring their lists to the writing workshop to share with the group. Collect strong titles on a chart and discuss what makes the titles work.

LINKS TO CD ROM:
• An Enticing Title

Shift Point of View or Perspective

WHEN TO USE IT: To help writers understand that shifting the point of view can bring an artistic and highly personal tone to their nonfiction writing

FOCUS THE LEARNING

Visualization is a well-known support for deep comprehension. When students visualize themselves taking on the characteristics of an animal, a bird, a river, or a slowly shifting glacier, they must engage in sensory imaging. They must also consider more deeply the essence of the topic, describing from within rather than from outside a subject.

Model

STEP 1: Think aloud and demonstrate how you create a mental image, shift point of view, and write from within the topic.

Possible Think-Aloud: *If I were a hurricane, I would swirl and churn above the warm ocean waters. I would gather heat and energy as I made contact with the seawater. When I finally came onto land, I would cause heavy rain, strong winds, and large waves. Did you notice that as I think out loud, my point of view is from the perspective of the hurricane? That kind of thinking is quite different from writing,* "A hurricane swirls and churns above the warm ocean waters. It gathers heat and energy as it makes contact with seawater."

TURN &TALK *Use the stem, "If I were a hurricane . . . ." Tell your partner what you would do if you were a hurricane. Visualize the swirling and churning that take place as a hurricane forms and the fierce storm it produces when it reaches land.*

STEP 2: Think aloud as you model how to write from within your topic.

> I am a hurricane. I swirl and churn over the open ocean as my winds spiral inward and upward. I gather heat and energy as I make contact with the warm tropical ocean waters. As seawater evaporates and joins me, my power increases. My center is calm and fair, but when I hit land, I dump heavy rain and bring strong winds and large waves that can wreak havoc. I am a hurricane.

Sample Modeled Writing

Possible Think-Aloud: *When we shift our point of view and visualize ourselves as being the subject of our writing, it helps us write great descriptions. Because I am writing as though I were a hurricane, I want to start with, "I am a hurricane." In my research, I discovered that the winds inside a hurricane spin inward and upward. I think I'll write, "I am a hurricane. I swirl and churn over the open ocean as my winds spiral inward and upward." Notice that I am selecting words that make it sound like the hurricane is doing the writing.*

TURN & TALK *What else can hurricanes do? What else do we know about these powerful storms? Use "I am" and think of more that we could write about hurricanes.*

Analyze

STEP 3: Reread and reflect.

Possible Think-Aloud: *As I reread this piece of writing, close your eyes and visualize. Make a movie in your head, and "see" the hurricane as it forms and churns.* (After reading.) *That visualization helped me to realize that I left out some important information about how hurricanes increase in power. I need to add that, so I will write, "As seawater evaporates and joins me, my power increases."* Wonder together: *Are we helping the reader understand what it would be like to be a hurricane? Have we included enough facts and descriptions of a hurricane?*

Sum It Up

Nonfiction writers can write about their subjects as though they are observing from far away, or they can think about what it would be like to be the subject and write in a much more personal way. Writers need to be able to do both kinds of writing, so as we confer this week, let's plan to talk about shifting point of view and writing, "I am. . . ."

VARIATIONS

For Less Experienced Writers: It is especially helpful to select topics for which these writers have personal experience. A few topics to consider are: "I am the rain." "I am a river." "I am a caterpillar wriggling from my egg." "I am a snake slithering through the grass."

For More Experienced Writers: Begin by creating a list of facts and understandings that would be good to include in the writing. Then, guide writers in shifting to the "I am" point of view by using mentor books by Diane Siebert such as *Heartland* and *Sierra*.

Add Humor

WHEN TO USE IT: To help students add whimsy and voice to their writing

FOCUS THE LEARNING

Our students are natural humorists. The trick is to help them add the element of humor to a piece of nonfiction writing. Once they learn how to infuse a little whimsy, they will realize that their writing sparkles with voice, and readers will enjoy reading their work.

Model

STEP 1: Think aloud as you decide to include a surprising and humorous fact.

Possible Think-Aloud: *Today I want to show you how you can spice up your writing by adding a sentence or two that are funny or whimsical. As I've been researching butterflies, I've discovered something unusual. Butterflies have taste buds on their feet! I surely can't taste my food with my feet; that fact is both interesting and humorous. I'm going to think about how I can add that fact and use a little humor to spice it up. First, I'll use a question to introduce the interesting fact. I'll write, "Did you know that butterflies taste with their feet? It's true!"*

TURN &TALK *Think together. Why do you think I've chosen to include humor in my nonfiction writing? What does humor do for the piece? Is it always appropriate to include humor in nonfiction writing?*

STEP 2: Add to your piece of writing as you think aloud.

Did you know that butterflies taste with their feet? It's true! The feet, or tarsi, of a butterfly are made up of taste buds that allow it to taste things in its environment. In other words, the unfortunate butterfly has to taste whatever it lands on! So the next time you see a butterfly floating by, just be glad that your feet are located as far as possible from your organ of taste.

Sample Modeled Writing

Possible Think-Aloud: *Now that I've introduced the interesting fact about butterflies, I want to tell my readers more about it. I think I'll write, "The feet, or tarsi, of a butterfly are made up of taste buds that allow it to taste things in its environment." Now I'm ready to add a little humor. I can do this by reminding my reader that this fact means that the butterfly "tastes" everything it lands on. I'll write, "In other words . . . it lands on!" This line definitely needs an exclamation point.*

TURN & TALK *I need one more line for this section, and I want it to be funny. What could I add to wrap it all up in a way that is humorous?*

Analyze

STEP 3: Reread and reflect.

Possible Think-Aloud: *I think I'll finish this section by adding, "So the next time you see a butterfly floating by, just be glad that your feet are located as far as possible from your organ of taste." Let's reread my piece and see if adding some humor helped to boost the voice in my writing. Humor is a helpful tool for creating voice. I'm glad I took the time to add a little whimsy.*

Sum It Up

Today we talked about how to add voice by including humor and funny facts. When you are researching your topics, be on the lookout for facts that might be funny or interesting to your reader. Then, challenge yourself to add those to your pieces.

VARIATIONS

For Less Experienced Writers: As students are reading independently, encourage them to look for the author's use of humor. Gather students in a small group, and encourage them to share what they have discovered.

For More Experienced Writers: Show students how to use a listing technique when making humorous connections. For example, if you're writing a piece about how paleontologists have a challenging job, you might compare working in the field to working in a garbage dump. Show students how you create two lists: One is for paleontologist-related things, and another list is for dump-related things. Then, look for similarities between the two.

Target Voice in Persuasive Writing

WHEN TO USE IT: When students are crafting persuasive texts

FOCUS THE LEARNING

In persuasive writing imperative, or bossy, language is often used to direct the reader to take action. This lesson is designed to challenge students to experiment with this kind of language to enhance the voice of their pieces.

Model

STEP 1: Display a persuasive poster like the one provided on the Resources CD-ROM. Draw attention to the imperative language used by the author of the poster.

Possible Think-Aloud: *Writers, to craft a compelling persuasive piece that contains a strong voice, we need to use something called "imperative language." That means we need to use language that sounds a bit bossy as we speak directly to our readers. Let's look at this poster that is meant to persuade people to wash their hands. Do you notice how the author is speaking directly to the reader? He says, "Wash your hands!" and then tells the reader how to do it correctly.*

TURN &TALK *Partners, think together. Do you think this kind of voice is effective? Why do you think the author uses this kind of voice with this kind of writing?*

STEP 2: Think aloud as you model how to use imperative language.

Climate change impacts all of us. It can affect our world's supply of food and threaten the stability of many countries. We can all pitch in and be part of the solution!

Take Action!
· Use sturdy reusable bags when grocery shopping.
· Buy energy-saving fluorescent lightbulbs instead of regular incandescent ones.
· Turn off electric appliances when they are not being used.
· Walk, bike, or use public transportation.

It's important that all of us do our part to slow down rapid climate change, so start making these small changes today!

Sample Modeled Writing

Possible Think-Aloud: *As I draft my piece about climate change, I am going to focus on speaking directly to my readers. When I do that, I'm going to include language that sounds a little bossy because I'm going to tell my readers to do something. I'll begin by telling my readers a bit about climate change and its impact on all of us. "Climate change impacts all of us. It can affect . . . many countries." Now I'll speak directly to my readers. I'll say, "We can all pitch in and be part of the solution." Next, I'll use a bulleted list to tell my readers what to do.*

TURN &TALK *Partners, think together. What mental picture do you see when you read this section? In your mind, can you see yourself doing the things I have listed?*

Analyze

STEP 3: Reread and reflect.

Possible Think-Aloud: *Did you notice the first words of the items on my list? I used words like "use," "buy," and "walk." These words sound a bit bossy because I'm telling my readers to do something. These kinds of words are called imperative words. They are often included in written arguments or persuasive texts. Now I've completed my list, and I am ready to speak to my reader again. This time, I'm going to challenge my reader to make these changes today. I will write, "It's important that all . . . changes today!"*

Sum It Up

When nonfiction writers use an imperative, or "bossy," voice in their persuasive texts, readers sit up and take notice! As you return to your writing today, see if you can infuse some imperative language and see how it boosts the voice in your pieces.

VARIATIONS

For Less Experienced Writers: Coach pairs of students as they create persuasive posters with imperative, or bossy, language. Partners might create a poster reminding students to recycle, wear appropriate winter clothes, wash hands often during flu season, and so on.

An example:
It's Time to Recycle
It's responsible.
It's needed.
We need to save the earth.
Start recycling today!

For More Experienced Writers: Challenge students to look for other reading selections where the authors use an imperative voice to speak directly to the reader. Some books to consider are *Should There Be Zoos?* by Tony Stead, *The Perfect Pet* by Margie Palantini, *Earrings!* by Judith Viorst, and *My Brother Dan's Delicious* by Steven L. Layne.

LINKS TO CD-ROM: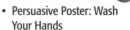
• Persuasive Poster: Wash Your Hands

Use a Repeating Refrain

WHEN TO USE IT: When students are ready to experiment with another way to add variety and enhance voice

FOCUS THE LEARNING

A repeated refrain is a good technique to try if you want to emphasize a certain thought in order to make it stick in the minds of your readers. When we read books that utilize a repeated refrain, we find ourselves thinking about the topic long after we have finished reading. This lesson is designed to teach students how to experiment with this voice-enhancing technique.

Model

STEP 1: Display a copy of *When I Was Young in the Mountains* by Cynthia Rylant or *If You're Not from the Prairie* by David Bouchard. Guide a conversation about how these authors use a repeated refrain to strengthen their voice and make a connection to the audience.

Possible Think-Aloud: *Sometimes authors of nonfiction utilize a repeated refrain as they write. It can strengthen the voice of a piece and keeps the reader interested. Let's examine the repeated refrain that Cynthia Rylant uses throughout her book* When I Was Young in the Mountains. *As I read this book, pay attention to the repeated refrain, and think about why she might have chosen to include it.*

TURN &TALK (After reading.) *Think together. What does the repeated refrain "When I was young in the mountains" do for you, as a reader? Why do you think Cynthia Rylant chose to include this refrain in her book?*

STEP 2: Think aloud as you use a repeated refrain in your own writing.

Possible Think-Aloud: *Using a repeated refrain is another way to enhance the voice of your piece and connect with your audience. I'm writing a piece about young emperor penguins. I'm going to experiment with using a repeated refrain. I need to think of a refrain that would work for me to repeat. How about, "When you are a young emperor penguin . . . ?" I'll try that. (Craft first paragraph.) I'm ready to start my next paragraph, where I'll describe how the young penguin meets his mother. I'll begin this paragraph with the same refrain, "When you are a young emperor penguin. . . ." (Finish drafting three paragraphs.)*

When you are a young emperor penguin, you hatch at a breeding site far from the icy sea. When you emerge, you'll meet your father. He'll place you under his warm brooding pouch to protect you from the frigid landscape. Your first meal will be a white, milky substance that is extracted from a special gland in your father's esophagus.

When you are a young emperor penguin, you'll meet your mother after she returns from feeding. She will be able to find you and your father by listening for the distinct song that your father sings.

When you are a young emperor penguin, your parents will care for you and make sure that you stay off the ice. They will feed you regurgitated food until you are old enough to hunt on your own.

Sample Modeled Writing

TURN &TALK *What do you think of this refrain? Can you think of any other repeated refrain I could try?*

Analyze

STEP 3: Reread and reflect.

Possible Think-Aloud: *Let's reread these paragraphs and see how they sound. Did using a repeated refrain work? How did it enhance my writing? I like the way I utilized this refrain, and I think my reader will, too. It not only helps a reader know what to expect but also asks the reader to put himself right in the middle of the action.*

Sum It Up

As we continue to grow and develop as writers, one thing we can do is to try new ways of adding voice and connecting to our audience. It's fun to try using a repeated refrain! Just remember, it's important not to overuse this technique. Just like Cynthia Rylant, we can try using the refrain every other page or so. Who's ready to give this a try?

VARIATIONS

For Less Experienced Writers: Together with the students, create a chart of possible refrains related to a common unit of study. For example, if the class is studying landforms, some stems might include "If you live in a canyon . . . ," "If you reside in the mountains . . . ," "If you were raised on a plateau . . . ," and so on. Then, show students how using a multiple-page format enhances the repetition.

For More Experienced Writers: Provide an opportunity for these writers to re-evaluate a piece of work they have already completed and consider places where they could insert a repeated refrain.

Help Readers Infer

WHEN TO USE IT: To add variety and enhance voice

FOCUS THE LEARNING

As readers, we are constantly making inferences. A skilled author will give us just enough hints to help us "read between the lines." As nonfiction writers, we can utilize this technique as well.

Model

STEP 1: Explain that sometimes writers give just enough information to help the reader infer, without telling the reader everything explicitly.

Possible Think-Aloud: *When we write, we don't always need to tell our readers everything. Sometimes it's fun to give readers some hints to help them make inferences. I'm writing about the time my sisters and I played with my dad's lawn mower—when we knew it was off-limits—and we broke it. I'm going to describe what happened when my dad returned home that evening. I could say, "When my dad came home, he was furious and we got in big trouble." That's okay, but I think I could craft something that would help my readers infer.*

TURN &TALK *Think together. What kinds of sentences could I write that would give my readers some hints about what happened without telling them directly?*

STEP 2: Think aloud as you write a short section, demonstrating how you help your readers infer.

> When my dad came home, we could hear Mom explaining the events of the day. My sisters and I waited downstairs, huddled together. Soon we heard my dad's voice from the top of the stairs. "Girls," he called. "Come upstairs this instant!" Every muscle in my body tightened, and I clenched my teeth together. Slowly and silently, we clutched hands and climbed the stairs.

Sample Modeled Writing

Possible Think-Aloud: *I think I'll begin by describing how my sisters and I could hear my mom explaining the events of the day to my dad. I remember that we were huddled together downstairs, just waiting for our judgment. I'll write, "When my dad came home . . . huddled together." The phrase "huddled together" helps my reader infer that we were pretty scared! Next, I'll describe how I felt when we heard my dad call us to come upstairs. "Soon we heard my dad's voice . . . I clenched my teeth together."*

TURN &TALK *What do you, as the reader, infer about my dad from reading those sentences?*

Analyze

STEP 3: Reread and reflect.

Possible Think-Aloud: *Let's reread this section of my writing and see how I did at helping my readers infer.* (After rereading.) *I'm pleased with what I wrote. My readers can tell that my dad was not a meek or mild person. I communicated the respect and fear that my dad inspired in my sisters and me. I think my readers will also be able to infer that my sisters and I were going to be in big trouble!*

Sum It Up

Today I showed you how you can add little hints to help your audience "read between the lines." It's important to remember that we don't always have to tell our readers everything. We can add some powerful words and phrases that will help them infer. As you return to your writing today, try experimenting with leaving some hints for your readers.

VARIATIONS

For Less Experienced Writers: Less experienced writers may need more support in understanding how readers make inferences before they can infuse their writing with inferences. Consider providing students with several examples of texts that require inferences and then guiding a discussion about the inferences that can be made.

For More Experienced Writers: Challenge these writers to look for examples of inferences in the books they are reading during independent reading time. Invite them to share these examples with the rest of the class.

At the End, Reveal Your Thoughts, Feelings, and Opinions

WHEN TO USE IT: To showcase thoughts, feelings, and opinions of the author

FOCUS THE LEARNING

Although most nonfiction writing tasks require us to be unbiased providers of information, there are times when a well-placed opinion or personal thought can add power to a piece of writing.

Model

STEP 1: Display a short piece of unfinished writing. Think aloud about how to include your thoughts, feelings, or opinions.

Possible Think-Aloud: *We've been talking about how to add voice to our writing. One way to do that is to share your thoughts, feelings, or opinions at the end of your piece. These give your writing voice. I've written a short piece about wolves. I'm ready to add some of my own thoughts, feelings, and opinions at the end. Let's read my piece so far and think about what I could add.*

TURN &TALK *Think together. What could I add next that would reveal my thoughts, feelings, or opinions about the debate about wolves?*

STEP 2: Think aloud as you end the section of writing with your own thoughts, feelings, and opinions.

> Throughout history, wolves have been admired as gods or denounced as devils. Today there is a heated and emotional debate raging concerning wolf control. Ranchers and farmers worry that wolves will destroy their livestock. Some people think that wolves should be destroyed. On the other hand, some wolf conservationists believe that wolves should never be killed. As with most issues that cause fierce debate, I believe the answer may lie somewhere in the middle of these positions. In order to save these magnificent animals, a few problem wolves might need to be destroyed.

Sample Modeled Writing

Possible Think-Aloud: *As I listened to your conversations, I heard some good ideas. I want to let my reader know that, in my opinion, we should develop a solution that lies somewhere in the middle of both positions. I think I'll say, "As with most issues that cause fierce debate, I believe the answer may lie somewhere in the middle of these positions." I also want to tell the reader that I think wolves are magnificent, so I could add the word "magnificent" before the word "animals." To say that wolves are magnificent is an opinion. That word shows what I think.*

TURN &TALK *Would you describe a wolf as magnificent? If not, what words would express your thoughts, feelings, and opinions about wolves?*

Analyze

STEP 3: Reread and reflect.

Possible Think-Aloud: *Let's reread my whole piece together. Did I add some thoughts, feelings, or opinions at the end? Do you think this improved my writing? I think that by adding those last two sentences, I strengthened my voice in the piece.*

Sum It Up

Today we learned how to add some spice to our writing by ending with our thoughts, feelings, and opinions. If you've chosen a topic that you really care about, you'll have a lot of thoughts, feelings, and opinions. The end of your piece is a great place to make those clear to your readers. When you go back to your writing today, challenge yourself to add some of your thoughts, feelings, and opinions at the end.

VARIATIONS

For Less Experienced Writers: Some less experienced writers may need more explicit instruction on the difference between **fact** and **opinion**. Provide guided practice by giving partners several facts and several opinions written on strips. Challenge them to sort the sentences.

For More Experienced Writers: Challenge students to support their opinions with specific facts, details, and reasons. Explain that if you really believe in something, you need to prove to your reader that you are right. Model how to do this using a common text.

LINKS TO CD-ROM:
Self-Assessment for Voice

Sentence Structure

A Tapestry of Pattern and Possibility

As with all expressions of language, sentences come in many forms and formats. When learning about sentence structure, it is helpful to teach writers the basic sentence elements and patterns so they can vary sentences in terms of both length and style of internal organization.

The basic sentence structures include:
- Simple sentence
- Compound sentence
- Complex sentence
- Introductory element followed by a comma
- Appositive, an interrupter, in the middle of a sentence
- Closing element at the end of the sentence set off by a comma

Two-Word Sentences

WHEN TO USE IT: When writers are confused about the elements of a sentence

FOCUS THE LEARNING

Two-word sentences such as "Horses trot," "Birds chirp," or "Babies cry" represent the essential framework of a sentence. When writers integrate these brief but powerful structures into their writing, sentence fluency is greatly enhanced, and understanding of sentence structure is elevated.

Model

Have writers bring a writer's notebook or clipboard to this lesson.

STEP 1: Learn to create and utilize two-word sentences.

Possible Think-Aloud: *Writers, we know that every sentence must have a subject and a predicate—or a noun and a verb. But did you know that a sentence can be as short as two words? Watch as I write "Horses trot," "Birds chirp," and "Babies cry." While I certainly wouldn't want all my sentences to be this short, it is important to understand that these are complete sentences—and that two-word sentences can be used in a variety of ways when we create nonfiction writing selections.*

TURN &TALK *Writers, put your heads together, and create as many two-word sentences as you can.*

STEP 2: Model how to integrate two-word sentences into a connected piece of writing.

First Draft:

Winds swirl. Lightning cracks. Skies darken. A super cell, characterized by its constantly rotating upward drafts, is a highly dangerous storm system that lasts for hours and may travel hundreds of miles.

Second Draft:

A super cell, characterized by its constantly rotating upward drafts, is a highly dangerous storm system that lasts for hours and may travel hundreds of miles. Winds swirl. Lightning cracks. Skies darken. Alarms begin to shriek.

Sample Modeled Writing

Possible Think-Aloud: *Now that you understand the structure of a two-word sentence, watch closely as I use two-word sentences to create a lead that stimulates visual imagery and brings a reader into the setting. "Lightning cracks. Skies darken." Did you notice that each of my two-word sentences has a subject and a verb? That is how I know they are complete sentences. But more importantly, a small number of two-word sentences can really capture the attention of a reader. Notice also that I follow the two-word sentences with a longer, more complex sentence to create balance and sentence fluency.*

TURN &TALK Analyze the impact of the two-word sentences on this piece about super-cell thunderstorms. Do the two-word sentences strengthen content understanding? Add sentence fluency? Make it seem more dramatic? What are your observations?

Analyze

STEP 3: Reread and reflect.

Possible Think-Aloud: *As I reread this, I am wondering how it would sound if I placed the two-word sentences in a different portion of the piece. Watch as I rewrite this and place them after the complex sentence. Two-word sentences can fit anywhere in the text. You just have to experiment a bit to find the best placement. Put your heads together, and analyze these two versions. Which one is better? What are the strengths of each?*

Sum It Up

Two-word sentences include the most basic building blocks of a sentence—a subject and a verb. They tell who or what did something. They also tell what was done. When two-word sentences are used in balance with longer, more complex sentences, they add dramatic affect and bolster nonfiction writing.

VARIATIONS

For Less Experienced Writers: Guide these writers in finding two-word sentences within longer sentences and in inserting two-word sentences into writing that they have already constructed.

For More Experienced Writers: Explore two-word sentence poems in which numerous two-word sentences on a given topic are developed and then linked together into a poetic format. An example:

Summer
Days lengthen.
Flowers bloom.
Heat builds.
Fans cool.
Smiles abound.
Summer

LINKS TO CD-ROM: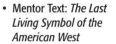
• Mentor Text: *The Last Living Symbol of the American West*

Write Complete Sentences

WHEN TO USE IT: When writers appear to be confused about complete sentences and fragments

FOCUS THE LEARNING

Writers in the intermediate grades often create writing that is filled with run-ons and unintentional fragments. It is very helpful to create and post a poster with two key questions: "Who or what did something?" "What did they do?"

Model

STEP 1: Test sentences with two key questions: "Who or what did something?" "What did they do?"

Possible Think-Aloud: *Writers, I have a poster that lists two critically important questions that we need to consider as writers. For each and every sentence, we need to ask if the sentence answers: "Who or what did something?" "What did they do?" I will place this poster next to the easel, so while I write today, I can actively challenge myself to focus on these questions. My first sentence is, "The giant . . . waters." Listen closely as I ask the two questions. "Who or what did something?" The devil ray. "What did he do?" Glide. I can confirm this is a complete sentence. Watch as I write the next line: "Flapping . . . wings."*

TURN &TALK *Challenge that line with the two critical questions. Decide if this is a complete sentence.*

STEP 2: Continue modeling and thinking aloud.

> The giant devil ray glides slowly and gracefully through warm ocean waters. Flapping great triangular wings, his powerful body propels him along the surface.

Sample Modeled Writing

Possible Think-Aloud: *Our two critical questions proved that "Flapping great triangular wings" is not a sentence—that is a fragment because it is not complete. I need to revise and tell who or what. Watch as I change the period to a comma and write "his powerful body . . . ." Next, I want to explain that devil rays have soft flaps that look like flippers on each side of the head. These "horns" sweep fish and small animals into the mouth.*

TURN &TALK *Put your heads together, and draft a complete sentence about the horns. Be sure to test it with our critical questions.*

Analyze

STEP 3: Reread and reflect.

Possible Think-Aloud: *I am going to reread this piece about the devil ray and analyze each sentence to be sure that there are no fragments. I will use the poster with the two critical questions as a visual reminder of the core components that I need to find.*

Sum It Up

When we write fragments or incomplete sentences, readers can be confused and learn too little about the subject. Remember, the secret is to focus on the two critical questions: "Who or what did something?" "What did they do?"

VARIATIONS

For Less Experienced Writers: Provide experience with the Two-Word Sentence lesson on page 274 to help writers establish a clear understanding of sentence structure. Then, assist them in finding two-word sentences within longer, more complex sentences and asking the two critical questions: "Who or what did something?" "What did they do?"

For More Experienced Writers: Guide these writers in analyzing sentences with passive verbs such as those found in many textbooks, and help them to identify complete sentences even when there is no action involved.

Compound Sentences

WHEN TO USE IT: When writers are creating short, stilted sentences that need to be lengthened

FOCUS THE LEARNING

Compound sentences are formed when two simple sentences are linked together with a conjunction such as "and," "for," "but," "yet," "nor," or "so."

Model

You will need a pocket chart and sentence strips. Students will need clipboards or a writer's notebook.

STEP 1: Display short sentences such as those in the modeled writing, First Draft, in a pocket chart. Model combining the sentences to create a compound sentence.

Possible Think-Aloud: *One way to add variety to writing is to balance short, medium, and longer sentences. Compound sentences are longer sentences that are constructed by joining two simple sentences with a comma and a conjunction. I will write conjunctions on a chart for reference. I have two short sentences in this chart—both focused on baby deer. I'll turn the period in the first sentence into a comma. Now I need a conjunction that links shaky legs to walking. Watch as I insert "so." The new compound sentence*

First Draft:

Newborn fawns have shaky legs. Walking is challenging until their legs become stronger. Most does hide their babies in tall grass. Many are found by predators and do not survive. Surprisingly, deer populations in the United States remain strong. Their numbers continue to increase in almost all regions.

Second Draft:

Newborn fawns have shaky legs, so walking is challenging until their legs become stronger. Most does hide their babies in tall grass, yet many are found by predators and do not survive. Surprisingly, deer populations in the United States remain strong, and their numbers continue to increase in almost all regions.

Sample Modeled Writing

now reads, "*Newborn fawns have shaky legs, so walking is. . . .*"
Next, I need to change the capital "W" on "Walking" to lowercase.
Now we have a compound sentence.

TURN &TALK *Read the sentence together, and analyze how it sounds. Then, test out different conjunctions to join these sentences. Identify the one that you think sounds best.*

STEP 2: Think aloud as you combine two shorter sentences with a conjunction to form one compound sentence.

Possible Think-Aloud: *The next two sentences are "Most does . . . grass" and "Many are . . . survive." I will change the period at the end of the first sentence to a comma. I'll make the capital letter of the first word in the second sentence lowercase. Then, I'll select and insert a conjunction to tie the sentences together. The conjunction "yet" supports the idea that even though does hide their babies, predators still find them.*

TURN &TALK *Analyze the conjunction I selected. Is there another one that would be a better or more appealing selection? Why?*

Analyze

STEP 3: Reread and reflect.

Possible Think-Aloud: *Now it's your turn to turn these two independent sentences into a compound sentence. Get your clipboards or your writer's notebooks and think together. Write a terrific compound sentence that merges these two sentences into a longer single sentence.*

Sum It Up

Compound sentences can make our writing seem more sophisticated. To combine two short sentences, however, you need a conjunction. Take a minute to create a place in your writer's notebooks where you can list the conjunctions and have them at your fingertips whenever you need them.

VARIATIONS

For Less Experienced Writers: Confer with individuals and coach them in selecting shorter sentences that could be combined.

For More Experienced Writers: Show experienced writers that compound sentences can be blended with shorter sentences to create sentence fluency.

LINKS TO CD-ROM:
• Combining Sentences

Opening Element

WHEN TO USE IT: To add complexity to sentence structure and precision to details

FOCUS THE LEARNING

Introductory elements launch writers into effective use of complex sentence structures and add sophistication to their work.

Model

STEP 1: Show students how to launch a sentence with a phrase focused on a detail.

Possible Think-Aloud: *As I write about frog eggs and the jelly-like spawn that nurtures them, I am going to focus on using a sentence structure called an opening element. With an opening element, you focus on a detail to bring your readers into the setting, and then you move to the main sentence. That means that the opening element is not a sentence by itself. It is a phrase that tells where or when or adds a detail. Watch closely as I write: "Nestled in a sun-warmed ball of jelly." That is my opening element. You see there is no subject. It focuses on the situation and draws attention to something nestled in jelly. Now I will add a comma and move to the main sentence: "clusters of frog eggs float at the surface of the pond." I am drawing a line under "clusters" because that is the subject of the sentence. Notice that the use of an opening element moves the subject to the middle of the sentence. That is a terrific sentence structure that makes writing very interesting to read.*

TURN &TALK *Analyze my opening element and the main sentence. What do you notice? What should you remember if you want to try this sentence structure?*

STEP 2: Continue modeling.

> Nestled in a sun-warmed ball of jelly, clusters of frog eggs float at the surface of the pond. Within this nurturing environment, tadpoles soon hatch— well fed by the nutrients that surround them.

Sample Modeled Writing

Possible Think-Aloud: *I am going to put an opening element on my next sentence as well. I want to focus the opening element on the nurturing environment that the spawn creates so I will begin with "Within this nurturing environment." You all know the test for a sentence: "Who or what did something?" "What did they do?" Test my opening element to see if it is a sentence. An opening element should not be a sentence. It is a phrase that tells more about where or when or adds a detail. Now I am ready for the rest of the sentence. I insert a comma and write, "tadpoles . . . them."*

TURN &TALK *Opening elements are not sentences. They are an introduction that comes before the sentence to add details about time, place, or action. Think together. What do you need to remember when using this sentence structure and crafting sentences with opening elements?*

Analyze

STEP 3: Reread and reflect.

Possible Think-Aloud: *Let's go back and reread these sentences. Watch as I cover the opening element for the first sentence. Notice that "clusters of eggs float . . . pond" is a complete sentence. The opening element has no effect on that. Also, remember that with an opening element, the subject of the sentence is shifted to the middle of the sentence, creating a very interesting sentence structure.* (Continue rereading and analyzing.)

Sum It Up

Opening elements are a powerful way to create interesting sentence structures that are rich in detail and add sentence fluency to your writing. With an opening element, the trick is to remember to focus on a detail such as time, location, or action. Then, add a comma and launch the main sentence.

VARIATIONS

For Less Experienced Writers: Scaffold these writers by providing a list of prepositions such as the one on the Resources CD-ROM and having them build opening elements from prepositions. Once they understand how to do that, you might expand to other types of opening elements.

For More Experienced Writers: Guide these writers in experimenting with opening elements that open with an adverbial phrase using starter words such as "just," "as," "because," "when," "after," "until," "before," or "if." Example: "As the first shimmers of morning begin to appear, birds start their hunt for seeds and nourishment."

LINKS TO CD-ROM: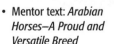

• Mentor text: *Arabian Horses—A Proud and Versatile Breed*

Appositive: An Interrupter that Renames or Explains

WHEN TO USE IT: To promote varied sentence structures and increase clarity

FOCUS THE LEARNING

An appositive, or an interrupter, is a noun or a noun phrase that renames or clarifies. This is a structure very commonly seen in nonfiction resources and a powerful sentence type that all students need to control.

Model

STEP 1: Display a sentence in a pocket chart, and show how you can add an appositive—an interrupter.

Possible Think-Aloud: *I placed a sentence in the pocket chart: "The Portuguese Man-of-War delivers a sting that is nearly as powerful as the bite of a cobra." Watch as I add an exciting element that changes the structure of this sentence. It's called an appositive, or interrupter. I will cut the sentence after "Man-of-War" and insert a comma. Then, I will add "a colony of venom-filled sea polyps" and add a second comma.* (Appositives are framed in front and back by commas.) *Let's read the sentence together.*

TURN &TALK *Analyze the impact of adding the appositive, or interrupter. What are the benefits of this type of sentence structure?*

STEP 2: Model an additional sentence and insertion of an appositive.

> ### Portuguese Man-of-War
>
> The Portuguese Man-of-War, a colony of venom-filled sea polyps, delivers a sting that is nearly as powerful as the bite of a cobra. Long tentacles, as much as 165 feet long, hang down from a balloon-like float. The Portuguese Man-of-War, a floating killer, is a danger to many forms of sea life and man as well.

Sample Modeled Writing

Possible Think-Aloud: *Many of you noticed that the appositive, or interrupter, adds information about the subject of the sentence. It is a noun phrase that can rename the subject or add information. In my first example, the appositive renamed the subject, calling it a "colony of venom-filled sea polyps." Watch as I try another one. In the next sentence, the subject is "long tentacles," so the interrupter needs to come next. Again, I will use my scissors and cut the sentence, adding a comma after "tentacles." Now I can add information about the tentacles. Notice that this time I will add information and say "as much as 165 feet long." Because appositives, or interrupters, need to be framed by commas, I add another comma, and we have a new sentence structure!*

TURN &TALK *Identify and list the steps in creating an appositive, or interrupter. What do you need to remember if you are going to integrate this sentence structure into your writing?*

Analyze

STEP 3: Reread and reflect.

Possible Think-Aloud: *I need one more sentence to conclude this writing. This time I won't start with a simple sentence. I am going to create the entire sentence from scratch. I will write, "The Portuguese Man-of-War." That is the subject, so I will insert a comma and think of a way to rename or add detail. How about "floating killer"? Now I add a comma, and I need an ending. I am thinking of "The Portuguese Man-of-War, a floating killer, is a danger to. . . ." Put your heads together. How should I finish this?*

Sum It Up

Appositives, or interrupters, are fun to add, and they make nonfiction writing look very sophisticated. This is a sentence structure that gives us an opportunity to interrupt a sentence after the subject and either rename the subject or add information that will clarify. We need to remember that it is framed by commas on both ends. As you begin writing today, watch for opportunities to insert an appositive, or an interrupter.

VARIATIONS

For Less Experienced Writers: Use writers' names in sentences in a pocket chart, and have them insert an interrupter about themselves. For example, "Olana, a dancer, loves to perform."

For More Experienced Writers: Experiment with more complex interrupters that include details. Examples: "Abraham Lincoln, a multifaceted political leader and lawyer, offered wisdom that lives on today." "Helio's desk, a nightmare of papers, books, and debris, needs to be removed."

Inserting a Closer

WHEN TO USE IT: To offer another sentence structure

Model

STEP 1: Model the insertion of a closer into a sentence.

Possible Think-Aloud: *A strategy for adding interest and variety to sentences is the use of a closer. Just like its name implies, a closer is inserted after a sentence is complete. Its purpose is to add information. Watch as I write a sentence, "Gorillas are known to be loving parents." That is a perfectly good sentence. Now watch as I change the period to a comma and insert a closer: "spending large amounts of time nurturing and playing with their young." My simple sentence just became rich and filled with interest. Lots of details were added. Notice also that I started the closer with an -ing form of a verb, which is a great way to launch a closer.*

TURN &TALK *Review the steps I followed to design and insert a closer with that sentence. Consider the benefits of infusing sentences with closers into your nonfiction writing.*

STEP 2: Continue demonstrating and thinking aloud.

Gorillas are known to be loving parents, spending large amounts of time nurturing and playing with their young. They are gentle and playful, unless they need to protect themselves or their babies.

Sample Modeled Writing

Possible Think-Aloud: *Watch as I create another sentence with a closer. The base sentence is "They are gentle and playful." It is important that I check and make sure that the base sentence is really a sentence. It has to tell who or what did something and what they did. Now I am ready for the closer. Notice that I change the period to a comma and add "unless. . . ."*

TURN &TALK Put your heads together, and finish this closer. Unless what? What would cause a gorilla to stop being gentle and playful?

Analyze

STEP 3: Reread and reflect.

Possible Think-Aloud: *Let's try the second sentence another way. Instead of starting the closer with "unless," what if I used an -ing word? "They are gentle and playful, cuddling, feeding, and playing with their babies for hours." Put your heads together, and compare the two closers. What are the advantages of each? (After writers confer.) I know I can't put a closer in every sentence—that would not be good writing—but I do think these closers are fun to create.*

Sum It Up

Closers are a great way to add variety to sentence structures. They add detail, create sentence fluency, and make writing sound sophisticated. You just need to be sure that the base sentence is complete with a subject and a verb and then use a comma instead of a period, and you are ready to insert a closer.

VARIATIONS

For Less Experienced Writers: Use a pocket chart, and guide writers in coming up with a variety of closers for one or two sentences, modeling the flexibility of this sentence structure.

For More Experienced Writers: Help these writers gain more flexibility by showing them how the same words can be changed within a sentence to shift from an opening element with a comma to a closer. An example: "I finished scrubbing the kitchen, wishing I were lounging on the beach." "Wishing I were lounging on the beach, I finished scrubbing the kitchen."

Text Features

Enhancing Our Messages and Supporting Navigation

Nonfiction text features are helpful adaptations that enhance readability of complex texts and improve the organization of nonfiction selections. Nonfiction text features include navigational tools such as a table of contents, headings, a glossary, page numbers, numbered steps, and an index. They may include attention-directing features such as boldface words, bullets, text boxes, and callouts. Visual organizers of information such as diagrams with labels, charts, graphs, tables, and photographs are text features that are of essential importance to reading and should be featured in most forms of nonfiction writing.

LESSON	3	4	5	RELATED LESSONS
1 Powerful Titles	●	●	●	*Punctuation and Capitalization:* Lesson 6, Capitalize Headings and Titles
2 Effective Headings	●	●	●	*Organization:* Lesson 5, Using Headings to Group Related Information *Punctuation and Capitalization:* Lesson 6, Capitalize Headings and Titles
3 Using Photographs	●	●	●	*Presenting:* Lesson 2, Inserting Illustrations and Visuals
4 Bold Words	●	●	●	*Word Choice:* Lesson 5, Using Domain-Specific Vocabulary
5 Cutaway Diagram with Labels		●	●	*Presenting:* Lesson 2, Inserting Illustrations and Visuals
6 Table of Contents	●	●	●	*Presenting:* Lesson 3, Infusing Text Features
7 Chart/Table/Graph	●	●	●	*Research:* Lesson 6, Represent Facts Visually
8 Citing Sources		●	●	*Research:* Lesson 9, Keep a List of Sources
9 Add Captions to Visuals		●	●	*Presenting:* Lesson 3, Infusing Text Features
10 Bulleted List	●	●		*Presenting:* Lesson 3, Infusing Text Features
11 Text Boxes		●	●	*Presenting:* Lesson 1, Experimenting with Page Layout

Powerful Titles

WHEN TO USE IT: When titles are too general

FOCUS THE LEARNING

Learners are reminded of the importance of titles every time they select a book for independent reading or join the class at the rug for a read-aloud. They know that the title either captures their interest or doesn't. As writers, they need to learn to create several titles before choosing the one that will be most likely to capture the interest of a reader. This lesson is designed to help writers move beyond lifeless labels and create specific titles that add interest and voice to their work.

Model

STEP 1: Display an array of nonfiction selections that are all on the same topic. Guide a conversation about titles. Which ones are powerful? Which ones could be improved?

Possible Think-Aloud: *I have three books on volcanoes. Their titles are* Volcanoes, Volcano Wakes Up, *and* Volcanoes! Mountains of Fire. *As I look at these books, they all appeal to me. They have terrific photographs on the covers that make me want to look more closely. However, the titles* Volcano Wakes Up *and* Volcanoes! Mountains of Fire *cause me to wonder and want to learn more. What happens when a volcano wakes up? Mountains of fire? That sounds cool!*

TURN &TALK *Look at these titles and think together. What are your opinions of these titles? Which ones would you most want to read? Which titles are the best and why?* (After discussing, repeat the process of considering titles and discussing with one more group of books.)

STEP 2: Create a T-chart (general and specific), and then think aloud about the components of an interesting title.

General	Specific
Bats	Night Hunters
	The Truth About Bats
	Amazing Bats
	Bats: Creatures of the Night

Sample Modeled Writing

Possible Think-Aloud: *It's interesting that we all preferred titles like* Volcano Wakes Up. *That title is really specific, and it makes us want to read the book. As writers, we need to remember that readers like a title that tells something specific about the topic. General titles like* Volcanoes *are not as appealing. Let's create interesting titles of our own. I have written the topic "Bats," on a chart. I want to create some titles that are specific and interesting, so I need to think about what makes bats special. They hunt at night, and they are often misunderstood. What would you think of the title* Night Hunters? *How about* The Truth About Bats?

TURN &TALK   *Think together. Let's make a great list of bat titles.*

Analyze

STEP 3: Reread and reflect.

Possible Think-Aloud: *Have you noticed that it helps to create several titles and then select the one that you think will be the most interesting to a reader? One of the tricks I use when I write is to keep a list of possible titles handy while I am researching and writing. Then, every time I get a great idea for a title, I can add it to the list. When I am finished writing, I have a menu of possible titles so I can be sure that my title won't just be good—it will be great!*

Sum It Up

Titles are important. They help readers decide if they want to read a book. The title is like a sign advertising your writing, so you need titles that are interesting and specific. When creating a terrific title, remember: Be specific. Make the reader wonder. Surprise the reader a bit. As you get ready to write, take a minute to examine some of your titles and see if you can find any that could be improved.

VARIATIONS

For Less Experienced Writers: Cover the titles of leveled books at the "just right" level for these writers. Sticky notes that are doubled will ensure that your students cannot see what is underneath. Then, have partners come up with several possible titles for each book before uncovering the title selected by the author and deciding which titles are better!

For More Experienced Writers: Challenge these writers to come up with bold titles that utilize humor, alliteration, or onomatopoeia. Then, have them present their titles to a partner to vote on the best and most interesting selection.

LINKS TO CD-ROM:
• Teaching Chart: Thinking about Titles

Effective Headings

WHEN TO USE IT: To help writers organize their writing and give readers a focus for reading

FOCUS THE LEARNING

Writers of nonfiction use headings as mini-titles that are spaced throughout the selection to keep the sections organized. This lesson is designed to help students learn how to create headings that represent the main idea of each section and pique reader interest.

Model

STEP 1: Using a nonfiction book or an article such as the one on the Resources CD-ROM, lead the students in a conversation about the headings.

Possible Think-Aloud: *Writers, let's examine the headings in this article about Africa's landscapes. Sometimes the author used just two words, like "Looking Ahead." On the first page, she used the phrase "A Long History Short." And on this page, she used three nouns, "Sun, Rain and Soil." Headings can be formatted as a word, a phrase, a declarative sentence, or a question. The important thing is that the heading represents a main idea and tells the reader what each section is going to be about.*

TURN &TALK *Analyze the headings this author crafted. Which ones work? Which could be improved?*

STEP 2: Display a section of modeled writing, and think aloud as you choose an effective heading.

Perils Along the Way

The journey along the Oregon Trail could prove dangerous and deadly. Many of the settlers who set out on the trail died before they reached the Willamette Valley. Some of the dangers the pioneers faced included river crossings, lightning and hail, and cholera. Some settlers perished under the heavy load-bearing wheels of their horse-drawn wagons.

Sample Modeled Writing

Possible Think-Aloud: *I'm ready to craft a heading for this section of my writing. It is mostly about the dangers that the pioneers faced along the Oregon Trail. My first idea is "Danger All Around." Perhaps a better heading would be "Perils Along the Way." That might give the reader an idea about this section. I know that sometimes headings are questions. I could write "Will They Make It?" Notice how the first letter in each word is capitalized. Headings are like titles, and they need capital letters.*

TURN &TALK *Are there other headings I could use for this passage?*

Analyze

STEP 3: Reread and reflect.

Possible Think-Aloud: *I think I'll use "Perils Along the Way" as a heading for this section. It is descriptive and interesting, and I think it tells the reader what to expect from this section of text. It really helped to think of several different headings before choosing the one that I thought would work best. Now let's look at another section of my piece. This section describes how settlers crossed the rivers along the way. My heading could be "Decision Time," "River Crossings," or "Sink or Float." I think I'll choose "Decision Time," since settlers had a few options for crossing the rivers they encountered.*

Sum It Up

Headings tell a reader what to expect from a section of writing. They can be a complete sentence, a phrase, a question, or even a single word. As writers, we need to think about the headings we include and take the time to make sure they are clear and effective. Headings make our writing easier for others to read. Today as you begin writing, challenge yourself to insert powerful headings throughout the text.

VARIATIONS

For Less Experienced Writers: Show writers how to use headings as they plan for a piece of writing. This will help them remember the focus for each section.

For More Experienced Writers: Provide a nonfiction book in which you have covered the headings with sticky notes. Invite partners to work together to craft headings for each of the sections. Then, have them compare their headings with the ones the author created.

LINKS TO CD-ROM:
• Mentor Text: *Africa's Diverse Landscape*

Using Photographs

WHEN TO USE IT: When written information can be enhanced by including a photograph

A picture is worth a thousand words! This lesson is designed to help students know when and how to include a photograph that will enhance their writing.

Model

STEP 1: Craft a piece of writing, and think aloud as you consider adding photographs.

Possible Think-Aloud: *Writers, as I craft this procedural text on how to make chocolate chip pancakes, I am thinking that I could add a couple of photographs to make the writing come to life. I know that when I browse through cookbooks, I'm always drawn to the photographs. So I think a couple of photographs would really boost this procedure.*

TURN &TALK *I've written the steps required for making chocolate chip pancakes. Now I want to add some photographs. Think together. Where do you think I should add a photograph? Where would it provide the most support to my reader?*

STEP 2: Demonstrate how you include photographs in your writing.

How to Make Chocolate Chip Pancakes

1. Choose your favorite kind of pancake mix.

2. Combine the pancake mix with water, as directed on the package.

3. Heat a griddle to medium–high heat.

4. Using a 1/4 c. measuring cup, pour the batter onto the griddle.

5. Place several chocolate chips on the pancake as it cooks.

6. When the pancakes bubble, use a spatula to flip them over.

7. When they are golden brown on both sides, place them on a plate and enjoy!

Sample Modeled Writing

Possible Think-Aloud: *Watch me as I reread my steps and decide where to place a photograph. I think my reader would benefit from a photograph after Step 5. That way, the reader can visualize what I am describing. I found a few photographs on the Internet that I think would work. The website I found them on clearly states that the photographs may be used without seeking permission, so I am free to use them in my own work. I'll choose this one that shows the chocolate chips on the pancake as it cooks. I think this visual will add some pizzazz to my procedure!*

TURN &TALK *Think together. Do you think I should include a caption with this photograph? If so, what would make a good caption for this image?*

Analyze

STEP 3: Reread and reflect.

Possible Think-Aloud: *I think it would make sense to include one more photograph. My reader will probably want to see what the pancakes will look like when they are finished. I'll add this photograph at the end of my procedure. I think this adds some interest to my piece of writing, and I think my reader will enjoy the photographs. Photographs can provide valuable information to a reader!*

Sum It Up

Today I showed you how I include photographs in my writing. When I choose powerful images and think about the right placement for them, my writing becomes more interesting and informative. Today as you continue writing, consider adding some photographs to make your pieces sparkle!

VARIATIONS

For Less Experienced Writers: With a small group of writers, craft a common piece of writing. Together, decide which photographs to include and where to include them. Then, coach and confer as students craft an individual piece of writing.

For More Experienced Writers: Show students how to use a digital camera to capture their own images. Coach them as they download the photos and add them to their writing.

Bold Words

WHEN TO USE IT: When students are crafting pieces that use domain-specific vocabulary

FOCUS THE LEARNING

When writers learn how to choose important words and make them bold, it gives them a sense of power and helps them see that their writing can teach a reader.

Model

STEP 1: Select a nonfiction book to examine how the author utilized words in bold print, or print the page from the Resources CD-ROM.

Possible Think-Aloud: *As we have been reading in our nonfiction books, we've noticed that some authors write a few words in bold. Boldface serves as a signal that a word is important and that we, as readers, should pay close attention to it. Let's look at a section from this book. Which words did the author decide were important? Which words are in boldface?*

TURN &TALK *Put your heads together, and talk about why the author might have chosen these words to write in boldface. Were there other words he could have chosen?*

STEP 2: Display a piece of writing. Demonstrate how you choose a few words to make bold.

> As pressure in the **magma** builds, it must escape. The magma forces its way up **fissures**, or narrow cracks in the earth's crust. Once it erupts through the surface, it is no longer called magma. It is called **lava**.

Sample Modeled Writing

Possible Think-Aloud: *I want to show you how to include bold words in your own writing. In this piece about volcanoes, there are some words that I could make bold. The word "magma" is an important word. I can go over it with a black fine-tip marker or type it using a bold command. Notice how the dark print makes the word stand out for a reader. I think I'll make the word "fissures" bold, too.*

TURN &TALK *Think about the bold words. What do they help you understand about volcanoes?*

Analyze

STEP 3: Reread and reflect.

Possible Think-Aloud: *Let's look at my piece again. I am feeling good about the bold words that I selected. These are words that are important to remember. I also notice that when I add some words in boldface, my writing looks more and more like a polished, published piece of nonfiction. Think together. If you were going to teach someone about using boldface words, what would you say? What would you want them to know?*

Sum It Up

Today we learned how to include boldface words in our writing. We learned that boldface words alert the reader that the words are important, and we learned how to carefully choose the words that we want our reader to pay special attention to. As you begin writing today, challenge yourself to choose two or three words that are important and make those words bold.

VARIATIONS

For Less Experienced Writers: Type out a short section from a published text, but do not denote which words were written in bold. Read the piece together, and challenge students to predict which word(s) the author chose to write in bold. Then, compare the predictions with the actual text.

For More Experienced Writers: Show writers how they can use the bold words they have included in their writing to create a glossary of terms or an index for their books.

LINKS TO CD-ROM:
• Weathering and Erosion

Cutaway Diagram with Labels

WHEN TO USE IT: When students are ready to try adding another nonfiction text feature to their writing

FOCUS THE LEARNING

Cutaway diagrams, like traditional diagrams, are pictorial representations of information. Unlike traditional diagrams, a cutaway shows the hidden parts of a subject by removing or "cutting away" part of its surface. When students learn to include this text feature in their writing, they strengthen the writing and teach the reader more.

Model

STEP 1: Use a nonfiction book or the cutaway diagram on the Resources CD-ROM to display a cutaway. Discuss how authors use factual information to create the cutaway.

Possible Think-Aloud: *Today I want to show you another text feature that nonfiction authors use to improve their writing. Writers can create a cutaway diagram as a way to show key features of something that is often hidden. Let's examine this cutaway diagram of a snake. I notice how the skin of the snake has been "peeled away" to reveal the skeleton and the lungs. I also notice that there are lines or arrows linking parts of the diagram to labels that tell the reader what each item is.*

TURN &TALK *Partners, think together. How does a cutaway diagram help the reader? Why do you think the author would decide to use a diagram like this?*

STEP 2: Display a short piece of writing. Demonstrate how you can create a cutaway diagram with labels from the information you have written.

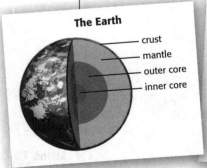

The Earth
- crust
- mantle
- outer core
- inner core

Sample Modeled Writing

Layers of the Earth

The first layer of the earth is called the crust. The crust, or the lithosphere, is the thinnest layer compared to the other three layers. Most earthquakes occur in this layer of the earth.

The next layer is called the mantle. It is the largest layer of the earth. Volcanic magma can be found deep in this layer.

Possible Think-Aloud: *I have begun writing about the layers of the earth, and I think that this might be a good place to insert a cutaway diagram with labels. Watch me as I carefully draw a picture of what the earth might look like if someone cut away a section of it. Now I'll label the layers by drawing a line from the layer to the word that tells what that layer is called.* (Complete the cutaway.)

TURN &TALK *What other information about the earth's layers should be included in my cutaway?*

Analyze

STEP 3: Reread and reflect.

Possible Think-Aloud: *I want to add a title to my diagram now. That will make it clear and informative. Let's reread this section and look at my cutaway diagram. Do you think the diagram will help my reader understand more about the layers of the earth? Is my cutaway clear and accurate? I think my reader will enjoy the cutaway diagram I made. The paragraph and the diagram work together.*

Sum It Up

Today we learned that adding a cutaway diagram with labels can boost your writing and make it more informative and interesting. We saw how a published author used a cutaway to teach the reader something new. As you begin work on your pieces today, challenge yourself to create a cutaway diagram with labels.

VARIATIONS

For Less Experienced Writers: Show students how to start a section of writing by creating a cutaway diagram to plan for writing. Demonstrate how you use each label of the diagram to create a new paragraph.

For More Experienced Writers: Give partners a different cutaway diagram. Challenge pairs to craft a paragraph based on the information in the diagram. Encourage them to share their paragraphs with the rest of the group.

LINKS TO CD-ROM:
- Visual: Earthworm Cutaway
- Visual: Volcano Cross-Section

Table of Contents

WHEN TO USE IT: When students have written a piece made up of several pages on a topic and the writing can easily be categorized into sections

FOCUS THE LEARNING

When we teach our students how to craft an effective table of contents in their nonfiction texts, they learn the importance of this text feature as both a writer and a reader.

Model

STEP 1: Select a nonfiction book, and examine the table of contents, discussing how it supports the reader.

Possible Think-Aloud: *Let's look at this book. When I open up to the first page, I don't see a paragraph about the topic. The first thing I see is the table of contents. As I scroll down, I see all of the sections that the author has included in his book. Now I know that if I want to read about how we can protect whales, I can turn to page 14. Using the table of contents helps me locate information quickly.*

TURN &TALK *Read and examine this piece I wrote about glaciers. If you were going to create the table of contents, how would you begin?*

STEP 2: Display a finished piece of nonfiction writing that has several sections, and demonstrate how to create a table of contents.

Table of Contents

Glaciers: Rivers of Ice...2

The Glacial Age 6

Motion and Change...10

Glaciers and the Changing Climate.............13

Sample Modeled Writing

Possible Think-Aloud: *Watch me as I create a table of contents for my piece about glaciers. In the first few pages, I have a section called "Glaciers: Rivers of Ice." That section begins on page 2, so I'll write the name of that section and then make little dots that lead to the page number over here. My next section addresses "The Glacial Age," so I'll add that section to my table of contents next.* (Complete this table of contents.)

TURN &TALK *What have you noticed about the table of contents so far? What are its features? What should you think about if you are going to create a table of contents for your writing?*

Analyze

STEP 3: Reread and reflect.

Possible Think-Aloud: *Let's look at my table of contents. It looks simple and organized, and I think it will help my reader find specific information in my writing. Making the table of contents was fun and easy! I used the headings for each section, a row of tiny dots, and page numbers.*

Sum It Up

When we are writing nonfiction texts, it's a good idea to add a table of contents. That way, our readers will be able to locate important information quickly. As you get to work on your nonfiction writing today, challenge yourself to create your own table of contents.

VARIATIONS

For Less Experienced Writers: Show writers how to use the headings in a text to create a table of contents. Provide partners with a copy of a nonfiction book with the table of contents covered. Challenge partners to use the headings to create a table of contents. Uncover the actual table of contents and have them compare.

For More Experienced Writers: Using a reference book or textbook, invite partners to create a table of contents for an individual chapter.

Chart/Table/Graph

WHEN TO USE IT: When writing includes information that can be represented graphically

There are times when words don't provide information as well as a well-placed graphic. As nonfiction authors, students need to learn how to include visually appealing and appropriate charts and tables in their writing.

Model

Before the lesson, poll your students about their favorite pizza toppings.

STEP 1: Demonstrate how you use data from your survey to create a bar graph.

Possible Think-Aloud: *I have created a graph on this chart paper and labeled it "Favorite Pizza Toppings of Students." This will give us a visual way to compare which pizza toppings are the favorites for our classroom. Notice I have written numbers going up the left side. Now watch as I write different kinds of pizza toppings across the bottom. I will write "pepperoni," "sausage," "cheese," and "pineapple." We learned that 10 people like pepperoni best, so watch as I count up to 10 in the column above "pepperoni" and quickly color the column in. That is the first bar in our bar graph.*

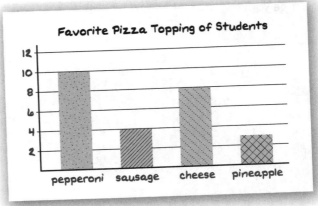

Sample Modeled Writing

TURN &TALK *I am getting ready to color in the column in the bar graph for sausage. Do you think this column will be shorter or taller than the column for pepperoni? Why?*

STEP 2: Model adding columns to the graph.

Possible Think-Aloud: *Watch as I add the second column to my bar graph. We learned that four people like sausage best, so watch as I count up to four on the left and then shade in the column for sausage. Notice that I am making the sausage column a different style because that helps me to compare.* (Continue creating the bar graph.)

TURN &TALK *Look at the bar graph we are creating, and summarize the information using words.*

Analyze

STEP 3: Reread and reflect.

Possible Think-Aloud: *Bar graphs such as this one make it easy to compare information. These are helpful tools to use in nonfiction writing. Watch as I create sentences to go with our bar graph. "The students in Mrs. Boswell's class have been polled, and we discovered that 10 people prefer pepperoni on their pizza."*

Sum It Up

Today we learned how to add a bar graph to our writing. I think you'll have a lot of fun creating your own. Today as you return to your own pieces of writing, think about how you could add a chart, table, or graph to boost your writing. Let's begin!

VARIATIONS

For Less Experienced Writers: Gather writers in a small group, and have them work together to use data to create another bar graph. Examples might include precipitation in different regions of the United States, types of weather experienced during the month, or goods exported by the United States each year.

For More Experienced Writers: Demonstrate how to create a variety of graphs and charts, including pie graphs, Venn diagrams, and line graphs. Challenge writers to experiment with several different types.

Citing Sources

WHEN TO USE IT: When students are using multiple sources to gather information about a topic

FOCUS THE LEARNING

It's important for students to learn how to give credit for the information they gather. This lesson shows writers how to cite sources by listing the author's name and the title of the book.

Model

STEP 1: Select a nonfiction book, and examine how the author cites sources or references. Consider using a book like *Saving the Baghdad Zoo* by Kelly Milner Halls and Major William Sumner, which displays "source notes" in the back. Lead a discussion about how the authors gathered information and cited the sources.

Possible Think-Aloud: *Writers, let's examine this book. Do you notice how the authors listed their sources in the back of the book? As they researched and wrote this book, they were careful to cite the sources they used. By citing their sources, they are telling the reader that they used more than one resource, which gives the writing more credibility. They are also giving credit to the sources from which they gleaned information.*

TURN &TALK *Think together. Can you think of any other reasons that an author might cite his or her sources?*

STEP 2: Display a finished piece of nonfiction writing and a list of resources you used as you researched and wrote a modeled writing piece. Demonstrate how to use the list to create a list of sources.

Resources

Glaciers by Larry Brimmer

Living Ice: Understanding Glaciers and Glaciation by Robert Sharp

Glaciers: Ice on the Move by Sally Walker

Glaciers and Glaciation by Douglas Benn

Glaciers by Michael Hambrey

Sources

Benn, Douglas. Glaciers and Glaciation.

Brimmer, Larry. Glaciers.

Hambrey, Michael. Glaciers.

Sharp, Robert. Living Ice: Understanding Glaciers and Glaciation.

Walker, Sally. Glaciers: Ice on the Move.

Sample Modeled Writing

Possible Think-Aloud: *When I researched about glaciers, I used my research notebook to record the sources that I used. I can use that list to create a list of sources that can be included in my finished piece. First, I need to list the authors in alphabetical order by their last names. The first author, then, is Douglas Benn. Notice that I write his last name first, followed by a comma. Then, I place a period, and I leave two spaces. Now I'll write the title of the book. I underline it and end it with a period.* (Complete the list of sources.)

TURN &TALK *What have you noticed about my list of sources? What are its features? What should you think about when you create your own list of sources?*

Analyze

STEP 3: Reread and reflect.

Possible Think-Aloud: *Let's look at my list of sources that I cited. It looks clear and organized, and I think it will help my readers to know about the various resources I used when writing my piece. It also gives my readers a list of other books to read if they want to know more about my topic. Citing my sources was easy when I used the list of resources from my research notebook.*

Sum It Up

When we are writing nonfiction texts, it's a good idea to cite our sources. That way, our readers will know that our information is credible and reliable. As you return to your own nonfiction writing, work to create a list that showcases the many resources you utilized.

VARIATIONS

For Less Experienced Writers: Less experienced writers may need more explicit instruction on locating and citing reliable sources from which to gather information. Provide additional models and guided practice as you work with a common topic.

For More Experienced Writers: Show students how to create a more formal bibliography. Challenge them to list the title, author, place of publication, publisher, and date of publication for each source as they are researching. Then, coach them as they place the information in bibliographical form.

Add Captions to Visuals

WHEN TO USE IT: To help writers learn to integrate captions into their nonfiction writing

Model

STEP 1: Show students a caption in an enlarged text or one provided on the Resources CD-ROM, highlighting the complete sentence and the surrounding text box.

Possible Think-Aloud: *A caption is a sentence or two that explain the content of a photograph, a drawing, or other visual. It is usually placed inside a text box. Let's examine this visual and caption. Do you notice how the author has utilized a text box? I notice that the caption is a complete sentence. Labels can be a word or two, but a caption is a sentence.*

TURN &TALK *Compare what you know about a label to what you know about a caption. How are they alike? How are they different?*

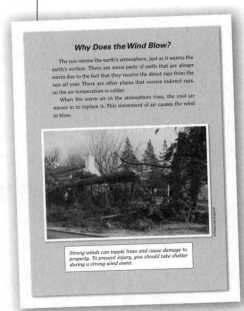

Why Does the Wind Blow?

The sun warms the earth's atmosphere, just as it warms the earth's surface. There are some parts of earth that are always warm due to the fact that they receive the direct rays from the sun all year. There are other places that receive indirect rays, so the air temperature is colder.

When the warm air in the atmosphere rises, the cool air moves in to replace it. This movement of air causes the wind to blow.

Strong winds can topple trees and cause damage to property. To prevent injury, you should take shelter during a strong wind event.

STEP 2: Use a computer and a projection device to model the addition of a caption to a previously constructed piece of writing.

Sample Modeled Writing

Possible Think-Aloud: *I have crafted a couple of paragraphs about wind. I have included a photograph, but there isn't a caption. I know that a caption should explain or tell about a visual, and it needs to be at least one complete sentence. I also know that it needs to be in a text box. Watch as I create a text box underneath the photograph. When I examine the photograph, it helps me think about what to say. I will write, "Strong winds can topple trees and cause damage to property." That's one sentence, but it isn't enough. I should tell my reader how to stay safe when encountering strong winds. Captions can have more than one sentence.*

TURN &TALK *Think together. Construct a sentence that I could use to finish this caption.*

Analyze

STEP 3: Reread and reflect.

Possible Think-Aloud: *Let's look again at the photograph and double-check my caption. There are two complete sentences in a text box. I also notice that the caption tells about the visual. That is what good captions are supposed to do! Because I've inserted a text box, I can drag it around on my page to decide where I want it. I could move the text box under the photograph, or the text box could be placed to the side of the visual. I prefer the caption underneath this photograph, so I'm going to drag the text box there.*

Sum It Up

Captions are important supports for photographs, illustrations, maps, and diagrams. They explain the content of the visual and help a reader understand the text. Captions are usually included in addition to the regular writing on the page. Sometimes they restate the same information. Sometimes they add a new fact or idea. Today as you return to your writing, try adding some captions to your visuals!

VARIATIONS

For Less Experienced Writers: Provide a small-group experience with leveled nonfiction selections. Guide the students in using sticky notes to write captions and insert them into the pages of the book.

For More Experienced Writers: Have experienced writers review previously constructed pieces of writing and add captions to enhance their work.

LINKS TO CD-ROM:
• Visuals: Lightning

Bulleted List

WHEN TO USE IT: When writing includes lists

Model

STEP 1: Demonstrate how to create a bulleted list.

Possible Think-Aloud: *Today I want to show you how to include a bulleted list in your writing. I have started a piece about the solar system. I am going to tell my reader that there are seven other planets in our solar system. I could make one long sentence, but instead I'm going to use a bulleted list. One planet is Mercury. I indent a few spaces, make a dot, leave two spaces, and write "Mercury." Notice that the bullet sits slightly above the line. The next planet on my list is Mars. I will move to the next line, indent, make a bullet, skip two spaces, and then write "Mars."*

TURN &TALK *Partners, think together. Do you prefer a bulleted list to one long sentence? How does a bulleted list help you as you read about the solar system?*

Earth is not the only planet in our solar system. There are seven other planets that also revolve around our sun:

- Mercury
- Mars
- Venus
- Earth
- Saturn
- Jupiter
- Uranus
- Neptune

Sample Modeled Writing

STEP 2: Continue creating a bulleted list.

Possible Think-Aloud: *The next item on my list is Venus. Watch as I indent, make my bullet, leave two spaces, and write the word "Venus." Think together: What are the other planets I should include in my list? I'll add those items next. Each time I'll indent, make a bullet, and leave two spaces.*

TURN &TALK *Partners, think together. What do you think of my bullets? Why do you think they make a list easier to read?*

Analyze

STEP 3: Reread and reflect.

Possible Think-Aloud: *Let's read my writing so far. What do you think? Did I use a bullet with each item on the list? I like using a bulleted list because it breaks up my writing, and it gets the attention of the reader. It's an easy way to include information in a list.*

Sum It Up

Today we learned how to include bullets in our writing. As you begin writing, see if you can include some bullets in your pieces. Remember to indent, make the bullet, leave two spaces, and then write your word or words. Let's begin!

VARIATIONS

For Less Experienced Writers: Provide the group with several nonfiction texts. Encourage them to look for bulleted lists. Guide a discussion about each author's purpose for using a bulleted list.

For More Experienced Writers: Demonstrate how to use bullets for longer phrases. For example:

The earth is able to support human life because:

- Its atmosphere includes the right mix of gases.
- It is not so close to the sun that high temperatures are too hot.
- It is not so far away from the sun that low temperatures are too cold.
- Its orbit keeps it a constant distance from the sun.

Text Boxes

WHEN TO USE IT: To help writers learn to experiment with page layout and placement of visuals

Text boxes allow the writing and the visuals to be manipulated on the page. The goal of this lesson is to teach students how to use text boxes to find a page layout that is visually pleasing and informative.

Model

STEP 1: Explain that writers can use text boxes to enhance page layout.

Possible Think-Aloud: *When I am ready to present my writing to an audience, I want to think about the layout of my page. I also want to consider the visuals that will help make the information clear for my reader. Today I want to show you how you can place parts of your writing into text boxes on the computer. Once they are in a text box, you can move the writing around the page, change the size and shape of the box, and insert diagrams and photographs*

TURN &TALK *Think together. How would placing sections of your text inside a text box improve the layout and help make your writing look more professional?*

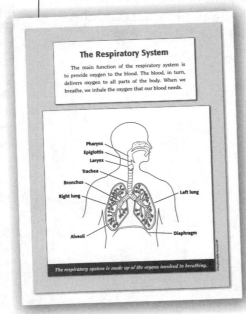

STEP 2: Demonstrate how to create a text box, experiment with page layout, and insert visuals.

Sample Modeled Writing

Possible Think-Aloud: *I'm ready to create a text box for this section of my writing about the respiratory system. Once I create the text box, I can add the text. I'll write, "The main function . . . our blood needs." Now I can take my cursor and drag the text box containing my writing to a new position. I can also enlarge this diagram that I downloaded from the Internet. I'll add a smaller text box below to serve as a caption for the diagram.* (Continue modeling options with page layout and placement of text boxes.)

Analyze

STEP 3: Reread and reflect.

Possible Think-Aloud: *Let's examine my page now. What do you think about the size of the diagram? Do you agree that the text boxes are placed in the most appealing location? I'm pleased with how my page looks. I think it will help make the information understandable to a reader, and it looks polished and professional!*

Sum It Up

Today we learned how to place sections of our writing into text boxes on the computer. Once the writing was in a text box, we could move the writing around on the page, change the size and shape of the box, and insert supporting visuals. As you return to your writing today, take some time to experiment with page layout to create a visually pleasing arrangement. I can't wait to see your polished work!

VARIATIONS

For Less Experienced Writers: Gather a small group of writers, and guide them in examining the pages of several nonfiction resources. Help students find ideas and possibilities that they would like to try when experimenting with layout and visuals.

For More Experienced Writers: Stretch these writers to experiment with other ways to visually represent their writing. These might include creating a PowerPoint presentation or an electronic book.

Punctuation and Capitalization

Controlling the Pace and Flow of Messages

Well-designed punctuation and capitalization control the flow of a message, helping the reader understand nuances of meaning, and make the texts we construct more interesting. At grades three, four, and five, writers need to learn that interesting phrasing and complex sentences depend on internal punctuation to control pace and meaning. A key feature for writers to understand is that punctuation and capitalization should be considered during drafting to add interest and support meaning. Waiting until editing to work on punctuation and capitalization is not likely to lift sentence quality or improve sentence fluency.

LESSON	3	4	5	RELATED LESSONS
1 Commas: Separating Phrases in a Series	●	●	●	*Sentence Fluency:* Lesson 9, Use the Rule of Three
2 Comma: Opening Element	●	●	●	*Sentence Structure:* Lesson 4, Opening Element
3 Punctuating a Direct Quote	●	●	●	
4 Punctuating Onomatopoeia	●	●	●	*Word Choice:* Lesson 11, Use Onomatopoeia
5 Using a Dash		●	●	*Sentence Fluency:* Lesson 7, Using a Dash
6 Capitalize Headings and Titles	●	●		*Text Features:* Lesson 1, Powerful Titles *Text Features:* Lesson 2, Effective Headings

Commas: Separating Phrases in a Series

WHEN TO USE IT: When writers begin writing complex sentences with phrases in a series

FOCUS THE LEARNING

As intermediate writers move into increasingly complex writing structures, lists of detailed descriptions can add action, enhance sensory imaging, and enrich sentence fluency.

Model

Write the first two sentences on a chart before the lesson begins.

STEP 1: Demonstrate how to visualize and then write in a way that shows a sequence of actions or observations.

Possible Think-Aloud: *I have started to write about a frog, newly awakened from his winter sleep. I visualize that although he is very hungry, he sits absolutely still—as frogs seem to do. Then, a worm comes into view. I remember from a video that the frog's toes twitched right before he moved. I also know from reading that the long sticky tongue of a frog snaps out with lightning speed. Watch as I write: "Then, his toes twitch, a long sticky tongue snaps out, . . . his throat." Since I am using a series of descriptions to highlight the action, notice that I inserted a comma after "twitch" and another one after "out."*

> **TURN &TALK** *Think together. Read my writing without the commas, and then read it again with them. What do you notice about your ability to visualize? What is the impact of the commas between the phrases?*

STEP 2: Continue writing a series of descriptions, inserting commas as appropriate.

> The newly awakened frog is groggy but enormously hungry. He waits patiently. Then, his toes twitch, a long sticky tongue snaps out, and the wiggling delicacy slips down his throat.

Sample Modeled Writing

Possible Think-Aloud: *We all know how to use commas for a series of words. What is exciting about creating a series of detailed descriptions is that we create a movie of sorts that speeds up the action and links observations more closely together. So the frog's toes twitched, his sticky tongue snapped out—I know! The worm is wiggling and moving, but the sticky tongue holds tight and the frog munches the worm down. For my next description, I will write, "and the wiggling delicacy slips down his throat." I don't need a comma here, as this is the end of the sentence. This time I use a period.*

TURN &TALK *The challenge is on. Think together and visualize a frog, thinking of all the things he can do. He can take a gigantic leap, soar to a lily pad, bunch his strong legs to escape from a predator, or . . . ? Construct a sentence with three actions or three observations in a row. Pump up those descriptions!*

Analyze

STEP 3: Reflect and extend.

Possible Think-Aloud: *You have shared some fantastic sentences with a series of descriptions that really bring action, observation, and visualization together. The key is to remember that the phrases need to be separated by commas—just as in my writing. I am passing out sentence strips so you and your partner can record your fabulous sentences. Notice that I am including two colors of felt pens. One is for your sentence, and the other is for your punctuation. Work together to be sure that you insert commas to separate your phrases. When you finish, we will share these in learning teams of six.*

Sum It Up

When writers use a series of descriptions to share observations or visualizations or to focus on action, commas play an important role. They separate the phrases to allow a reader time to connect to the action and the detail in the writing. As you begin writing, I will be hoping to see that you are creating some sentences with phrases in a series connected by commas.

VARIATIONS

For Less Experienced Writers: Guide these writers in designing descriptions in a series focused on an experience that they have shared at school. Have them begin by visualizing details, and then have them consider phrases or clauses that will have maximum impact.

For More Experienced Writers: Focus on elevating the detail that is included when writers string lengthier clauses, rather than phrases, in a series. Strive for richly constructed sentences, such as "The turtle quickly flattened himself to the ground, pulled his legs and head into the safety of his shell, and waited for the hungry possum to pass."

Comma: Opening Element

WHEN TO USE IT: To support use of complex sentences

FOCUS THE LEARNING

Introductory elements make writing more interesting while supporting sentence fluency. When sentences open with an introduction and the subject of the sentence floats to midstream, writing is enriched with texture and detail.

Model

Display a pocket chart with two base sentences: "The runaway peers into the moonless night. He can see that a quilt hangs from the porch railing and a lantern glows in the window."

STEP 1: Use a pocket chart to demonstrate the power of an opening element and comma.

Possible Think-Aloud: *I have started a piece of writing about a runaway on the Underground Railroad. My first sentence, "The runaway . . . night," is okay. But I think I can make it better by focusing on the setting with an opening element. Watch as I insert a strip that says, "Crouched in the shadows." Watch as I add a comma before "the runaway." This really changes the visualization. Now I know that the runaway was crouched down hiding in a shadow. That adds important information. You noticed that I started with a basic sentence. Then, I added an opening element with a comma. This change moved the subject of the sentence, the runaway, to the middle of the sentence.*

TURN &TALK *Analyze my new sentence. Consider the benefits of an opening element and a comma, before the subject and verb are introduced.*

STEP 2: Extend understanding by modeling another sentence expansion.

Crouched in the shadows, the runaway peers into the moonless night. In spite of the dim light, he can see that a quilt hangs from the porch railing and a lantern glows in the window. With his heart beating like a drum, he pulls the darkness around him and runs silent as a shadow to the front door.

Sample Modeled Writing

Possible Think-Aloud: *Adding the introductory element and a comma added detail and deeper understanding to the last sentence. Let's try it again. The next sentence in the chart is, "He can see that a quilt hangs from the porch railing and a lantern glows in the window." That's a pretty good sentence, but I would like to see if an opening element plus a comma will make it better. Watch as I add "In spite of the dim light." Now I will add a comma after "light" to separate the opener from the main sentence.*

TURN & TALK *Read this second sentence together, and analyze the introductory element. Did this add an important detail or perspective? Why is the comma important?*

Analyze

STEP 3: Reread and reflect.

Possible Think-Aloud: *This time I am going to start with an introductory element and then write the rest of the sentence. I am visualizing this runaway, impossibly frightened. He thinks this may be a safe house, but he can't be absolutely sure. Come in close as I write, "With his heart beating like a drum. . . ." That adds some tension and tells how frightened he is. But this isn't a sentence. I need to add a comma, and then we can add a subject and tell what the subject does. Put your heads together. What should I write after the comma?*

Sum It Up

Introductory elements followed by a comma add power to sentences. They add detail, action, a focus on the setting, or direct attention to the time. But they wouldn't work without commas. Commas set an introductory element apart—causing a reader to take a breath—and make the writing strong.

VARIATIONS

For Less Experienced Writers: Have writers search the work of their favorite authors for introductory elements and commas. They can present their findings on sentence strips along with a citation that tells the source, and then discuss how to use this structure in their own writing.

For More Experienced Writers: Help these writers to categorize introductory elements. Which ones focus on time, focus on place, add detail, or focus on action? What kinds of words launch each of these kinds of introductory elements? How can writers help themselves to remember the all-important comma when they write these richly constructed sentences?

Punctuating a Direct Quote

WHEN TO USE IT: When inserting a quotation into writing

FOCUS THE LEARNING

Maturing writers need to learn correct punctuation when inserting quotations to support key points in their nonfiction drafts.

Model

STEP 1: Discuss the use of quotations to support key points. Model insertion of the quote.

Possible Think-Aloud: *I am working on a persuasive argument about why reading is important and how everyone should spend more time each day reading! In a piece like this, it is often helpful to use a quotation from a famous person to support the point you are trying to make. I selected a quote from Dr. Seuss. We all remember reading* The Cat and the Hat *and other books he wrote for young children, but Dr. Seuss wrote scholarly adult articles for magazines, too. Watch as I insert a quote into my persuasive writing.* (Write the first two sentences.) *To insert my quote, I place a comma after "he said." Now I place a quotation mark (") to show that the quote is beginning. Since this is a quotation, I need to be very careful to write it using exactly the words Dr. Seuss wrote. I can't modify his text or it isn't a quotation. As I finish the quotation, I place a period and then a second set of quotation marks ("). That makes it clear that the quotation has ended.*

Everyone needs more time for reading! We all know that reading is important. But Theodor Seuss Geisel, the beloved Dr. Seuss, may have worded it best when he said, "The more that you read, the more things you will know. The more that you learn, the more places you'll go."

Source:
Dr Seuss. 1-Famous-Quotes.com, Gledhill Enterprises, 2011. http://www.1-famous-quotes.com/quote/3316, accessed Thu Jul 7 08:55:46 2011

Sample Modeled Writing

TURN & TALK *Notice that the quotation mark at the end of the quote was set outside the period. Why do you think that is the correct format?*

STEP 2: Show how to cite the source.

Possible Think-Aloud: *When using direct quotations in writing, we need to be sure that the punctuation sets the quote apart from the writing that is our own. It needs to be very clear that the quotation is from another person. Did you also notice that I named the source right in the sentence when I wrote, "But Theodor Seuss Geisel, the beloved Dr. Seuss, may have worded it best when he said . . ." I need to cite the source right in the text and use punctuation to be sure a reader understands the source and exactly which words are those that belong to Dr. Seuss versus those that are mine.*

TURN &TALK *Summarize what you know about punctuating a direct quotation. What do you need to remember?*

Analyze

STEP 3: Reread and reflect.

Possible Think-Aloud: *The last step when including a quotation in a piece of writing is to cite the actual source where you found the quotation. I found this quote on the Internet on a site that specializes in quotes from famous people. On a separate sheet of paper, I need to keep track of my sources. Watch as I write: "Source: Dr Seuss. 1-Famous . . . 2011." Notice that there is a colon after the word "Source" and a period after "Dr. Seuss," the author of the quote. Next, the website is listed. Notice the dashes in the website name and the period before "com." Those are important, too. Next comes a comma and the name of the publisher. This is a time to be very careful and triple-check to be sure all components of the citation are written correctly.*

Sum It Up

Quotations can add power and credibility to arguments or points we are trying to make in our writing. The trick is to select a quote carefully to be sure it supports your position. Then, surround it with quotation marks so it is clear that this is a statement from someone besides yourself. In addition, you need to explain the source within your writing and carefully list the citation in a reference or a source list. This is a time when punctuation is critical.

VARIATIONS

For Less Experienced Writers: Make photocopies or print the URL information for source lists so these writers can focus on their written messages and the integration of quotes rather than getting bogged down by reference lists.

For More Experienced Writers: Experiment with placing quotes in different portions of a nonfiction section. Sometimes a well-chosen quote can create a powerful beginning or ending to a piece of writing.

Punctuating Onomatopoeia

WHEN TO USE IT: When writers are including onomatopoeia in their writing

FOCUS THE LEARNING

Onomatopoeia occurs when words sound like the real-life sounds they represent. "Kerplink, kerplunk, kerplink" sounds like something dropping into a tin can. "Clip, clop, clip, clop" clearly sounds like a hoofed animal, such as horse, walking briskly across a hard surface.

Model

Find a copy of *Caves* by Stephen Kramer or another nonfiction title that includes onomatopoeia. Also have students bring a writer's notebook or clipboard for this lesson.

STEP 1: Clarify understanding of onomatopoeia and its relationship to life sounds.

Possible Think-Aloud: *Onomatopoeia uses words that sound like real sounds in life. Look closely at the opening page of Stephen Kramer's book* Caves. *Notice the way he finishes page 1: "Drip. Drip. Drip." He used onomatopoeia and placed a period after each word. That period causes me, as a reader, to stop after each word. Notice how dramatic that sounds. "Drip. Drip. Drip." How would it sound if he had used hyphens and written it "Drip-drip-drip"? Punctuation can be used with onomatopoeia in other ways, too. Watch as I write: "Whoosh!" In real life that could be wind or a bird flying too close. Notice the exclamation point. That reminds a reader to say it fast, with emphasis. I am going to write it again, but this time notice that I change the punctuation: "Whoosh . . . ." This time I added an ellipsis that tells a reader to take it slowly.*

TURN &TALK *Read each of these examples of onomatopoeia and consider the impact of the punctuation. How does the punctuation affect you as a reader? Are there any other punctuation marks you might try?*

STEP 2: Experiment with different punctuation combinations.

Whoosh!

Whoosh . . .

Drip. Drip. Drip.

Drip-drip-drip

Crrrack!

Cr . . . ack!

Whoo . . . Whoo . . . Whooing!

Clickety, clickety . . . shhh!

Sample Modeled Writing

Possible Think-Aloud: *Life is full of sounds, so one of the challenges we face as nonfiction writers is to bring those sounds to life on the page as we write. Sound is an essential component of nature and the settings on which our nonfiction writing is focused. So onomatopoeia and well-chosen punctuation can enhance sensory imaging and bring a reader more fully into the situation or setting you describe. Let's experiment some more. Let's try "crack." In a windstorm, we hear that sound a lot. I could write it as "Crrrack!" That tells my reader to emphasize the first syllable and say it very slowly. Or how about "Cr . . . ack!" Did you notice that this time I used an ellipsis in the middle of the word to really stretch it out and then bolded the second syllable?*

TURN &TALK *Read both versions of "crack," and talk about the way the punctuation changes your reading. How does it change the sensory image you construct? Name a situation in life where each of these sounds might occur as it is written.*

Analyze

STEP 3: Reread and reflect.

Possible Think-Aloud: *Punctuation and onomatopoeia work well together to deepen links to the setting and involve a reader. The trick is to find the right punctuation to match your meaning and the real-life sounds you are trying to depict. We all know a bit about wind storms or the sounds made by animals in the night— coyotes howling, owls whooing, cats screeching. Identify a situation and consider the sounds that are real and natural to it. Then, list words with onomatopoeia that you might be able to use in writing about the setting. Experiment together with different types of punctuation until you find one that you think will help a reader to read it in a way that most closely matches the sound in real life.*

Sum It Up

A bit of onomatopoeia can draw a reader more deeply into the setting. But it needs to be used wisely so the writing maintains the integrity of its nonfiction focus. Well-chosen onomatopoeia supported by punctuation that fits the meaning is a powerful tool for nonfiction writers.

VARIATIONS

For Less Experienced Writers: For writers learning English as an additional language, support their understanding by providing an experience that is naturally filled with sound. You might want to pop popcorn. You could also place different items into tin cans and cover them with foil, and then shake them and describe the sounds. You might also have them go outside to the school yard, just listen, and then record the sounds they hear.

For More Experienced Writers: Use onomatopoeia with interesting punctuation to launch nonfiction poems.

Using a Dash

WHEN TO USE IT: To draw attention to a specific point

FOCUS THE LEARNING

A dash is a unique writing tool that helps writers draw attention to something they particularly want a reader to notice. It is stronger than parentheses and causes a longer pause than a comma, so it is good for dramatic effect.

Model

Before the lesson, find a copy of *Black Whiteness* by Robert Burleigh or another nonfiction selection that includes dashes for dramatic emphasis.

STEP 1: Present mentor texts that demonstrate the use of a dash.

Possible Think-Aloud: *A dash works somewhat like a parenthesis or a comma, but we use them where we want a more dramatic effect. Here are two great examples: Watch as I project them using a document camera. The first is in* Black Whiteness, *a biography about Admiral Byrd and his scientific expedition to Antarctica. At the point where Admiral Byrd had become very ill and may be dying, the book says, "He does not stand—he wobbles. He does not walk—he creeps."*

TURN &TALK *Analyze the impact of the dash. How did it affect you as a reader? Why might this be a powerful tool for you to use in your writing?*

STEP 2: Display another mentor text, and then model a dash in writing.

High in a tree, the red-eyed tree frog rests quietly on a leaf. A cat-eyed snake glides forward in silent menace—intent on a juicy meal.

Sample Modeled Writing

Possible Think-Aloud: *Let's look at one more. In Jonathan London's* Voices of the Wild, *there is a poem about the otter. Jonathan London writes, "Something in my blood's memory warns me to flee. The man will only see a quick, sleek movement among stones—and I am gone." For me, the dash causes me to stop and really think, to slow down and process what is happening. As a reader, it has a lot of control over the way I interact with the text. Now watch as I try it in my own writing. I will set the stage by writing about the situation: "High in a tree . . . leaf." Now I am ready for a sentence with a dash: "A cat-eyed snake glides forward in silent menace—" Notice that I could have used a period instead of a dash. The sentence is complete. The dash allows me to add a thought to grab the attention of a reader.*

TURN &TALK *I need something after the dash. A powerful punch that makes it clear the snake is after the sleeping frog. Put your heads together. Think of a powerful ending for this sentence.*

Analyze

STEP 3: Reread and reflect.

Possible Think-Aloud: *Let's reread my writing and then vote to select the best possible ending for the second sentence. Using a dash is an exciting opportunity because you know a reader will really tune in and notice. The trick is to use dashes sparingly. Too many dashes will have a reader yawning in a hurry.* (After rereading and selecting an ending.) *Writers, if you were to write directions on how to use a dash, what would you include in the directions? What does a writer need to remember?*

Sum It Up

A dash is a powerful tool to use when emphasizing something important or especially interesting. Dashes are also great for supporting sentence fluency, as they give a very unique rhythm to the sentences in which they occur. A caution: Use dashes sparingly. Overuse is not a good thing.

VARIATIONS

For Less Experienced Writers: Use a pocket chart to present some basic sentences, and then show writers how you can strengthen the sentences and the sensory imaging by adding a dash plus a powerful ending.

For More Experienced Writers: Have writers rewrite textbook-like nonfiction passages and rev them up with dashes and powerful ending statements.

LINKS TO CD-ROM: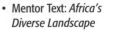
• Mentor Text: *Africa's Diverse Landscape*

Capitalize Headings and Titles

WHEN TO USE IT: To support correct format in published work

FOCUS THE LEARNING

Writers need to learn the correct format for capitalization of titles and headings to address conventional form.

Model

Prepare a chart with the text for each section, but omit the title and headings so those can be added as students observe.

STEP 1: Model writing.

Possible Think-Aloud: *Titles and headings get special attention when it comes to capitalization. With titles and headings, like the title of a book or a song, you need to identify the most important words and capitalize them. That means that smaller words used to link ideas, like "in," "a," "an," and "the," are not capitalized **unless** they are the first word in the title or heading. In the title for this piece on earthquakes, I need to capitalize "The" because it is the first word in the title. "Earth's" and "Crust" are central ideas, so they need a capital letter, too. Now consider "in," for "in action": I won't capitalize "in" because that word links "action" to "crust," but "Action" needs a capital for sure. Action in the crust is what causes earthquakes.*

TURN &TALK *My first heading is "Plates Float on the Mantle"—five words. Analyze the heading and decide which words need to be capitalized.*

The Earth's Crust in Action

Plates Float on the Mantle
Tectonic plates in the earth's crust fit together like pieces of a giant jigsaw puzzle, floating on a layer of molten liquid rock called the mantle.

The Pressure of Magma
The mantle's boiling magma is always in slight motion, placing pressure on the tectonic plates above it. When the pressure becomes too great for the joints where the tectonic plates meet, the plates move and shift, causing the ground above to move.

Shock Waves Rumble
As the plates and the earth above them shift, shock waves rumble through the earth. An earthquake is born.

Sample Modeled Writing

STEP 2: Continue analyzing headings and think aloud about which words to capitalize.

Possible Think-Aloud: *Heading one, "Plates Float on the Mantle," is also five words. I can see right away that I don't need to capitalize "on" or "the," as they are supporting words. Watch as I write the heading and capitalize the key words "Plates," "Float," and "Mantle." In heading two, I need to be careful. It starts with a secondary word, "the," but since it is the first word, "The" gets to have a capital letter.*

TURN &TALK *Think together. The next heading is "Shock Waves Rumble." What should be capitalized and why? Support your thinking.*

Analyze

STEP 3: Reread and reflect.

Possible Think-Aloud: *Let's reread the piece now and confirm that we have made the right choices in capitalizing the title and the headings. We want to check carefully to ensure that we only capitalize words that are important to the content or the first word in each title or heading.*

Sum It Up

The rule for capitalizing titles and headings requires that a writer identify words in a heading that are important to the content and make those capitals. This is also true for the very first word in a title or heading even if it is a supporting word such as "the." One more capitalization issue to check on is the use of proper names such as the name of a person, a town, and a country. Those need to be capitalized both in titles and in the body of a writing selection.

VARIATIONS

For Less Experienced Writers: Assist these writers in designing headings before they write, as this will help them to organize their writing around key words and ideas. This will also help developing writers to identify key words in titles and headings.

For More Experienced Writers: Stretch these writers to examine nouns and proper adjectives such as "Chinese inventors" or "Kleenex tissues" and discuss rules for capitalization.

Grammar

Structures and Patterns that Support Messages

The rich conversations we have with children all day long are essential building blocks of grammar development. Within the context of the language we hear in our lives and the works of our favorite authors, our ears become attuned to what "sounds right." When focusing on grammar, take cues from your students. Listen to their oral language patterns, and look closely at the grammar within their writing. With careful attention to the patterns that are already in place, you can open their eyes to structures and forms within a read-aloud or a favored nonfiction selection—helping young writers to apply the more formal registers of English that are seen in published books and expected of proficient writers and language users.

Maintain Consistent Verb Tense

WHEN TO USE IT: When writers accidentally change verb tense in the middle of a piece

For the most part, intermediate writers need to learn to select a verb tense and maintain it throughout a writing selection.

Model

STEP 1: Review verb tenses and think aloud about consistency.

Possible Think-Aloud: *I am going to write about the old apple tree at my grandmother's house and the way my sister and I liked to play in the branches when we were kids. This was a long time ago, so watch as I use past tense verbs to show that this already happened. "When my sister . . . tree." Watch as I go back and underline those past tense verbs. If I had been writing in the present tense as though this were happening today, I would have used "go" instead of "went." I would have written, "When my sister and I go to visit our grandma."*

TURN &TALK *Think together. The verb "spent" in the second half of the sentence is past tense. If I wanted to switch it to present tense as if this event were happening right now, what verb would I have chosen instead of "spent"?*

STEP 2: Continue to monitor verbs for past tense form.

When my sister and I <u>went</u> to visit our grandma, we <u>spent</u> as much time as we could in her old apple tree. We <u>hung</u> from the branches, breathe^d the fragrance of the sweet apples, and <u>filled</u> ourselves with the thrill of being nine feet off the ground.

Sample Modeled Writing

Possible Think-Aloud: *In my second sentence, I am going to focus on the things we did in the tree. Watch as I write: "We hung . . . ground." Now I am ready to go back and check my verbs. I started in the past tense, so I need to make sure I maintain past tense throughout. As I underline each verb, be prepared to decide if it is past or present tense. The first one is "hung." If this were present tense, it would say "We hang," so "hung" is correct. Next, "breathe the fragrance."*

TURN &TALK *Partners, analyze my verb. To maintain past tense in this sentence, have I used the correct verb?*

Analyze

STEP 3: Reread and reflect.

Possible Think-Aloud: *Being consistent in verb tense throughout a piece of writing is important for nonfiction writers. I am going to ask that you reread with me and double-check once again to be sure that I have underlined all the verbs and that each verb I used is written in the past tense so that I maintain the same tense throughout the writing.*

Sum It Up

Writers have an important decision to make with every piece of nonfiction writing. They need to decide if they are going to make their readers feel like the action is happening right now or if they will describe it as though it already happened. As you begin writing today, take a minute to look back through your writing and determine if you have written in the past or present tense. Then, check to be sure you have maintained that same verb tense throughout the writing.

VARIATIONS

For Less Experienced Writers: Guide writers in reading a variety of books and identifying whether they are written in present, past, or future tense. Then, conduct the same analysis of their writer's notebooks or writing folders to see which tenses they use most often and to analyze how effectively they have maintained the tense throughout a single piece.

For More Experienced Writers: Demonstrate the use of flashback and flash forward, and show how, even in nonfiction, these can be powerful literary devices that require a conscious and deliberate application of verb tense.

LINKS TO CD-ROM:
• Irregular Verbs: Present, Past, Past Participle

Use Prepositions to Enrich Descriptions

WHEN TO USE IT: To add precision to descriptions

FOCUS THE LEARNING

Prepositions and prepositional phrases add precision and clarity to descriptions.

Model

Provide students with the list of prepositions on the Resources CD-ROM, so they can contribute suggestions during this lesson.

STEP 1: Demonstrate how to enrich descriptions with prepositional phrases.

Possible Think-Aloud: *I am writing about an owl and the intensity of his nighttime hunt. To add precision to my description, I will open with the preposition "in" to focus on where the owl initiates his hunt. Watch as I write: "In the misty. . . ." There are several things you will want to notice about this sentence. First, my preposition allowed me to create an introduction to the sentence that tells exactly where the owl was sitting. "In the misty shadows. . . ." This includes a lot of specific detail that is important to visualizing the situation. Then, I used a comma before I started the main sentence.*

TURN &TALK *Think together about the mental image you were able to create with that sentence. Share your images. What do you visualize as a result of this sentence? Use your list of prepositions, and experiment with some different prepositions as openers to this sentence.*

STEP 2: Model the use of additional prepositions.

> In the misty shadows of a towering pine, the owl begins his watch. As dusk turns into dark, he sees the first sign of movement in the bushes below. The mouse pauses and the owl plunges through the shadows straight to his prey.

Sample Modeled Writing

Possible Think-Aloud: *In my first sentence, I used the preposition "in" to help me focus readers on understanding where the owl stood his watch. Now watch as I use a preposition to bring the same precision to a focus on time. "As dusk turns into dark. . . ." The preposition "into" enabled me to create a phrase that focuses on time. Prepositions are helpful in many ways!*

TURN &TALK *Use your lists of prepositions, and construct a sentence that would make a good next entry for this piece of writing. Remember to focus on precision in the details that you offer to your readers.*

Analyze

STEP 3: Reread and reflect.

Possible Think-Aloud: *Prepositions can be used in a lot of ways. For my next sentence, I am going to save my preposition for later in the sentence. My goal is to help a reader understand that the movement in the bushes is a mouse, so the owl must dive through the shadows to catch it. Watch as I write: "The mouse pauses and the owl plunges through the shadows straight to his prey." Notice how the prepositional phrase "through the shadows" gives exact details about "where" for a reader. Now reread the modeled writing together, and analyze the prepositions. Analyze my choices and consider other prepositions that might have been helpful.*

Sum It Up

Nonfiction writing can be greatly enhanced when we include prepositions that are thoughtfully used to add precision to descriptions—showing time and place. While prepositions can take on many functions in writing, today we have focused on ways that prepositions can enrich our descriptions. I know that as you begin to write today, you will pay special attention to opportunities to add precise information about where and when by using prepositions.

VARIATIONS

For Less Experienced Writers: During one-on-one conferences, guide less experienced writers in looking for ways to enrich sentence structure and improve descriptions with prepositions that focus on time and place.

For More Experienced Writers: Stretch these writers by introducing them to the understanding that some prepositions function as subordinate conjunctions in complex sentences. Prepositions such as "after," "as," "before," "since," and "until" lead smoothly into nouns, pronouns, or gerunds to set up complex sentences. Examples: "After the team loaded its gear, they climbed wearily onto the bus." "Gorillas are generally peaceful creatures, except when threatened."

LINKS TO CD-ROM: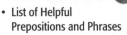
• List of Helpful Prepositions and Phrases

Select Precise Verbs

WHEN TO USE IT: To add precision and imagery to sentences

FOCUS THE LEARNING

Verbs can deliver more powerful descriptions than adjectives or adverbs if we guide writers to focus on verbs as the "engines" of sentences and tools for creating imagery.

Model

STEP 1: Think aloud as you emphasize precise verbs.

Possible Think-Aloud: *Verbs are often called the "engines" of sentences, so as I write today, I am going to focus on using verbs that are very precise so they build sensory images for a reader. First, I want to emphasize that once sealed, the interior of a pyramid was absolutely silent—until explorers and treasure hunters entered. I could say their footsteps ruin the stillness, shatter the stillness, or crack the stillness.*

TURN &TALK *Visualize absolute silence in a tomb that is suddenly transformed by people. "Then, footsteps _____ the silence." What verb would really power up this sentence with precision and imagery?*

STEP 2: Continue modeling and directing attention to precise verbs.

> For thousands of years there were no human sounds. Then, footsteps shattered the silence. Voices ricocheted through the tunnels and flashlight beams split the darkness, casting light on a strange and amazing sight—the sacred chamber at the very heart of the pyramid.

Sample Modeled Writing

Possible Think-Aloud: *Next, I need to select a verb that will highlight the impact of voices in this space that was silent. Watch as I write: "Voices ricocheted. . . ." "Ricocheted" helps me visualize the sound coming in waves, bouncing off stone walls, varying in intensity as the people moved through the tomb. Now close your eyes, and visualize absolute darkness in the tomb. There is no source of light. Then, suddenly a flashlight beam enters. I am thinking it could slash the darkness, cut the darkness, split the darkness. I will write "split the darkness" because I think the light would be just a slim strip cutting through the intense darkness all around.*

TURN &TALK *Analyze the verbs I have included in my writing. Evaluate the imagery and precision they create.*

Analyze

STEP 3: Reread and reflect.

Possible Think-Aloud: *Let's reread my writing and consider verbs we could select to add further precision and imagery to this selection. As we reread, think about the attributes of a powerful verb. Which verbs really bring you visual images? Which ones help you "see" exactly what I am trying to describe?*

Sum It Up

Verbs are amazing tools that can energize writing. They add precision and support imagery, and when used thoughtfully, they can make a bigger difference than adding adjectives. As you get ready to write today, it is your turn to grab some powerful verbs to serve as "engines" of your sentences and add imagery. Be sure to give yourself time to consider lots of options, and then use only the *best* verbs you can identify.

VARIATIONS

For Less Experienced Writers: Work with small groups of writers to create posters of fabulous action verbs they can reference to power up the verbs in their sentences. These writers may also benefit from taking time to visualize before writing so their verb choices are guided by imagery.

For More Experienced Writers: Demonstrate how to identify passive verbs and how to rewrite sentences that are powered by action and imagery. Once writers understand how to rework sentences that are encumbered by passive verbs, coach them in revising previously written pieces.

LINKS TO CD-ROM:
• Cloze for Powerful Action Verbs

Using Specific Adjectives

WHEN TO USE IT: When writers need to add specific details to descriptions

FOCUS THE LEARNING

Adjectives, when carefully selected, improve writing by fine-tuning sensory details while adding rhythm and flow to writing.

Model

Before the lesson, prepare an image of a real tiger with a close-up of the head, making the golden eyes and pink nose visible for your writers, or use the image on the Resources CD-ROM.

STEP 1: Think aloud about selecting specific rather than general adjectives.

Possible Think-Aloud: *Adjectives are helpful tools, but we need to be careful because adding adjectives that are general rather than specific can weaken a piece of writing. For example, I am going to write about three tigers hunting together. I could say "Three big tigers hunt . . . ," but the adjective "big" is really general. It doesn't offer a reader much detail. Instead, I need to select an adjective that is more specific and provides more detail. Listen as I think of adjectives that provide more specific details about my hunting tigers: "muscular," "huge," "powerful," "commanding," "dominant," "starving," "famished," "ravenous." I will select the specific adjective "powerful" because I want to emphasize their muscular bodies and power. Watch as I write: "Three powerful . . . forest."*

TURN &TALK *Think together. Analyze the adjectives I named, and then experiment by inserting different adjectives into the sentence in place of "powerful." The goal is to add detail by choosing very specific adjectives.*

STEP 2: Continue thinking aloud and modeling the selection of specific adjectives.

Three powerful tigers stalk the midnight forest— their pink, fist—sized noses sniffing the air. Keen—sighted, amber—flecked eyes gleam in the darkness, seeking food for greedy stomachs.

Sample Modeled Writing

Possible Think-Aloud: *Watch as I use a dash and insert adjectives that describe their noses: "pink, fist-sized." Using a compound adjective, such as "fist-sized," is another way I can be sure that my adjectives are highly specific rather than general. With "fist-sized" as an adjective, I can hold up my fist and see exactly the size of a tiger's nose. That's helpful! Listen as I try another compound adjective to describe their eyes. Tigers have excellent vision and eyes that are a distinct golden color with bits of green and brown. Adjectives for the eyes might include "yellow-gold," "golden-hued," "amber-flecked," "honey-colored," "keen-sighted."*

TURN &TALK *Look closely at this image of a tiger's head. Think together about highly specific adjectives that would describe eyesight that is six times better than a human's and eyes that are the color of golden honey with flecks of green and brown.*

Analyze

STEP 3: Reread and reflect.

Possible Think-Aloud: (Continue writing and thinking aloud through the third sentence.) *Watch as I underline the adjectives in my writing. Underlining is a tool writers can use while drafting to help themselves think about specific elements of the writing. Now that I have underlined the adjectives that are my writing target today, let's reread and analyze the adjectives. Remember, the goal is to avoid general adjectives such as "big" and focus on adjectives that really add specific details. Show me a thumbs up when you and your partner have read and analyzed the adjectives. When I see that everyone is ready, I am going to ask that you form teams of four and share your thinking with each other.*

Sum It Up

Adjectives are powerful tools, but we need to remember that they are not all created equal. Our job is to push toward higher levels of specific detail by selecting precise adjectives that support a reader in developing strong visual images and understanding the details that are important to the subject.

VARIATIONS

For Less Experienced Writers: Engage these writers with richly written mentor books such as *Bat Loves the Night* by Nicola Davies, and collect fabulous adjective/noun phrases as they move through the text. Compare and contrast the images that are created with phrases such as "beady eyes," "pixie ears," "thistledown fur," and "coat-hanger feet."

For More Experienced Writers: Challenge experienced writers to utilize a thesaurus while writing nonfiction to raise the specificity of the adjectives they are infusing.

LINKS TO CD-ROM:
• Photos of tiger head

Add Action with Gerunds

WHEN TO USE IT: To add sentence complexity and rich description

FOCUS THE LEARNING

Seymour Simon, the highly esteemed author of more than 250 nonfiction books, says that "*-ing*" words and comparisons are the two top tools for nonfiction writing.

Model

Gather several resources with information on tornadoes. It would be especially helpful to have at least one with large photographs for easy viewing.

STEP 1: Model inserting "*-ing*" words.

Possible Think-Aloud: *In looking at this book on tornadoes, I am reminded of the amazing power of these storms. Watch as I make a list of "-ing" words, or gerunds, that describe what a tornado can do. I want to include "twisting," "exploding," "howling," "smashing," "flattening," "lifting," "blasting," "destroying," and "roaring." Notice that each of these gerunds is based on a verb. So "twist" turns into "twisting," "explode" turns into "exploding," and so on. Look closely now as I weave two gerunds into a sentence about tornadoes. "Twisting and howling, the tornado ripped through the field." Notice that I used a comma after the two gerunds were used as an introductory phrase. I am not sure if you have tried this, but writers can even use three gerunds in a series to open a sentence. Watch as I try one of those: "Twisting, howling, and roaring, the tornado sped across the field."*

TURN &TALK *Think together and create sentences that open with one, two, or even three gerunds!*

STEP 2: Model how to insert gerunds into the body of a sentence.

Twisting and howling, the tornado ripped through the field.

Twisting, howling, and roaring, the tornado ripped through the field.

The tornado, twisting and howling, roared across the field.

The tornado roared across the field, shredding and destroying everything in its path.

Sample Modeled Writing

Possible Think-Aloud: *Gerunds make fabulous sentence openers, but they can be utilized in other ways as well. Watch as I use gerunds to create an appositive, or interrupter. "The tornado, **twisting and howling**, roared across the field." The gerunds gave the interrupter a lot of punch because they added specific information about the tornado.*

TURN &TALK *Give it a try. Experiment with a sentence that slips gerunds into an interrupter, forming an appositive.*

Analyze

STEP 3: Reread and reflect.

Possible Think-Aloud: *There are endless ways to slip gerunds into sentences to power up descriptions. Here is another one. Watch as I write: "The tornado roared across the field, **shredding and destroying** everything in its path." This time, did you notice that I could have placed a period after "field?" That was a complete sentence. But instead, I used gerunds as a closer to the sentence—adding more information and clarity. Let's reread and analyze the various places where gerunds were inserted into these sentences.*

Sum It Up

Gerunds are based on verbs, but they act like nouns and allow us to create highly engaging sentences that have great sentence fluency and lots of specific detail. When you are writing today, be sure to focus on action by using "*-ing*" words in a variety of ways. As you get ready to add this important tool to your thinking, remember this tip: You always need to check your sentence to be sure that if you remove a cluster of gerunds, you still have a sentence. Every sentence must have a subject and a verb.

VARIATIONS

For Less Experienced Writers: Show these writers how to start by adding a single gerund and a comma to create an interesting sentence opener. Example: "Twisting, the tornado surged toward the field."

For More Experienced Writers: Have these writers review previously completed pieces of writing and insert gerund clusters into various portions of sentences. Then, analyze the sentences to consider the benefits of the added action and the impact on sentence fluency.

Pronouns and Their Antecedents

WHEN TO USE IT: When pronoun-antecedent relationships are not clear in the writing

FOCUS THE LEARNING

Even very accomplished writers sometimes fail to connect pronouns to their antecedents, which can leave readers confused and irritated. Young writers in particular need lots of practice with pronouns and frequent opportunities to develop the habit of always checking for antecedents.

Model

Before the lesson begins, write the first draft of the poem on a chart, leaving room for an additional line to be added at the top

STEP 1: Think aloud and model how to be sure pronouns are clearly connected to an antecedent.

Possible Think-Aloud: *One of our goals as a writer is to be sure that readers are not confused by the pronouns we use. When we use pronouns such as "he," "she," "we," "they," or "it" in our writing, we need to check and be sure our readers know who or what we are describing. I am writing a poem about night. I start with the line "She cushions the stars." I have a pronoun, "she." But it's not clear at all what I am referring to! This pronoun does not have a clear antecedent. I need to add a line before this one: "Night is a velvet pillow." Now the antecedent is clear. "She" refers to "night."*

TURN &TALK *The next line begins with "her." Identify the antecedent for the pronoun "her." What does the pronoun "her" reference? How do you know?*

Night is a velvet pillow
She cushions the stars

Her darkness soothes the Earth
                    a new day
All too soon, it beams through the shadows
      Night
She must go

For a while

Sample Modeled Writing

STEP 2: Continue modeling and thinking aloud about pronouns and antecedents.

Possible Think-Aloud: *The third line says, "All too soon, it beams through the shadows." There is a pronoun, "it," so I need to check and be sure the antecedent is clear. As I reread, I realize that there isn't an antecedent. This will really confuse a reader. This line is about the sun and a new day, and the pronoun just won't work. Watch as I cross out "it" and insert "a new day."*

TURN &TALK *Analyze the last two lines. Check for pronouns and be sure that the antecedent for each is very clear. Be prepared to report your thinking with another team.*

Analyze

STEP 3: Reread and reflect.

Possible Think-Aloud: *Because this is a draft, it is okay to be a bit sloppy, so I am going to draw a line from each pronoun to its antecedent to be sure that I have this right. It just isn't an option in a piece of writing to have pronouns that aren't clearly supported by an antecedent. Let's reread together. When we come to a pronoun that I need to check, signal me with a thumbs up. Then, I will find its antecedent and draw a line to connect them.*

Sum It Up

Pronouns are an important part of speaking and writing, but when we use them, we have an obligation to be sure that a reader or a listener is very clear about the antecedent. They need to know who or what we are talking about! As you prepare to write today, I challenge you to stop yourself every time you start to use a pronoun and be sure that the antecedent is very clear.

VARIATIONS

For Less Experienced Writers: Provide sentences with pronouns, such as "I left it right here, but now it's gone" and "Their pencils scribbled furiously, and they finished their test with only a few minutes to spare." Guide writers in analyzing the sentences and considering ways to add specific nouns so the pronouns have a specific reference.

For More Experienced Writers: Read aloud a passage from a mentor text, deliberately replacing all the names with pronouns. Ask students to discuss how their understanding is impacted when only pronouns are used in sentences. Read aloud another section of the text, replacing the pronouns with their antecedents. Challenge writers to carefully check their own writing to be sure that they are showing the references between pronouns and antecedents.

Single vs. Double Subjects

WHEN TO USE IT: To adjust the use of double subjects in oral and written language

FOCUS THE LEARNING

The use of double subjects such as "my mom, she" or "the alligator, he" is a very common error in oral and written language. To move toward more formal registers of language and grammatically correct use, writers need to pause to consider ways to avoid this error in their writing.

Model

STEP 1: Think aloud about identifying a subject only once in each sentence.

Possible Think-Aloud: *The subject is the part of the sentence that tells us who or what is doing something. As writers, we need to learn to tell who or what a sentence is about only one time in each sentence. In my writing today, I want to say, "Harriet Tubman, a conductor on the Underground Railroad. . . ." I would not say, "Harriet Tubman, she was a conductor." "Harriet" and "she" are the same person, so that would be telling who the sentence is about twice! I can name the subject just one time. My second sentence will be about her own escape from slavery. I will start with "As a young woman." Now I need a subject for the sentence. I need to use Mrs. Tubman's name or a pronoun—not both.*

TURN &TALK *Analyze this sentence: "Ms. Tubman, she escaped from the slavery of her childhood. . . ." Is there a double subject? If so, improve the sentence by eliminating one of the subjects.*

STEP 2: Continue thinking aloud and modeling.

> Harriet Tubman, a conductor on the Underground Railroad, was a very brave woman. As a young person, she escaped from the slavery of her childhood by following the Underground Railroad herself. Then, Ms. Tubman repeatedly returned to the region where she had been indentured and helped others escape.

Sample Modeled Writing

Possible Think-Aloud: *Here comes sentence three. I used the pronoun "she" in the last sentence, so in this one I will use her name, Ms. Tubman. Watch as I write: "Then, Ms. Tubman. . . ." When we work to avoid double subjects, we also need to create balance between naming the subject and using a pronoun. Too much of either gets boring for a reader.*

TURN &TALK *If you were to teach others about how to avoid using double subjects, what would you teach them? What would you want them to learn?*

Analyze

STEP 3: Reread and reflect.

Possible Think-Aloud: *Let's reread this writing and check for two important things. We need to be sure that there are no double subjects. And we need to check for balance between naming the subject and using a pronoun. We don't want to bore a reader by naming the subject or using a pronoun over and over in the same piece of writing.*

Sum It Up

Remember, when you write about someone or something, use either the subject's name or a pronoun for the name in the same sentence. Don't use both the name and the pronoun in one sentence. That's doubling up! Also be sure to create balance between naming the subject and using a pronoun.

VARIATIONS

For Less Experienced Writers: During the writing workshop, remind students to check their subjects to be sure they didn't "double up." Help writers apply what they know as they craft writing selections.

For More Experienced Writers: Have each student identify a favorite biography selection. Then, have them analyze the balance between naming the subjects and using pronouns within the selections.

Subject-Verb Agreement

WHEN TO USE IT: When writers have not yet acquired subject-verb agreement

Subject-verb agreement can be challenging for some writers, especially if they are learning English as an additional language or speak non-standard English at home. Support this important concept with lots of modeling and positive coaching.

Model

STEP 1: Model how to shift verbs to match singular and plural forms.

Possible Think-Aloud: *We know that every sentence needs to have a subject and a verb. But once the sentence has both parts, it is important to be sure that those parts agree with each other. I am writing about manatees. My first sentence is "Wild manatees swim. . . ." Since this sentence focuses on manatees in general, a plural, I need to be careful with the verb. It could be "swim" or "swims." Listen as I try it out: "Manatees swim" or "Manatees swims." With a plural subject, "Manatees," I don't need the "s" on "swim." If I was talking about a single manatee, then I would need to say, "A manatee swims."*

TURN &TALK *For my next sentence, I want to explain that they are gentle. So I need to get the verb right. Think together. If I use "they," should the verb be "are" or "is"? Be ready to explain your thinking.*

> Wild <u>manatees</u> **(p)** swim in warm coastal waters eating over 60 different species of plants—up to 9% of their body weight each day. Mana<u>tees</u> **(p)** are gentle and slow-moving creatures, often sleeping or resting through many <u>hours</u> **(p)** of the day. Sadly, their greatest threat **(s)** is from people. A mana<u>tee</u> **(s)** is often killed or injured by boats, fishing line, fishing nets, and pollution, which all pose threats to this gentle creature.

Sample Modeled Writing

STEP 2: Continue modeling and thinking aloud.

Possible Think-Aloud: *Sentence two definitely needs to use the verb "are," because the pronoun "they" means "many." It is a plural. The next sentence is tricky. I want to explain that their greatest threat can be people. Listen as I say it out loud. That is a helpful way to test. "Their greatest threat are from people." "Their greatest threat is from people." That helped. "Threat" is singular so the verb needs to be "is." And it sounds right! If I had used the term "threats," then that would be a plural, meaning many, and I would need to use the verb "are." Subject-verb agreement can be tricky!*

TURN &TALK *If you were going to write directions for how to create subject-verb agreement in writing, what would you include in the directions? What should writers think about and do?*

Analyze

STEP 3: Reread and reflect.

Possible Think-Aloud: *This is a tricky topic, but I think you are getting it. If the subject is singular, you need a singular verb. If the subject is plural, you need a plural verb. Get ready to analyze. I am going to go through each sentence and underline the subject. Above it, I will insert a little "s" or a "p" for singular or plural. Then, we can think together about the verbs to be sure they agree. Watch closely.*

Sum It Up

If you write about a singular subject, you need to use a singular verb, such as "is," "was," or "has," or an action verb that ends with an "s." If you write about a plural subject, you need to use a plural verb, such as "are," "were," or "have," or an action verb with no "s" added.

VARIATIONS

For Less Experienced Writers: During writing conferences or small-group reading sessions, ask students to point out singular subjects and verbs in mentor texts and in their own writing. Ask, *"What do you notice about the verbs?"*

For More Experienced Writers: Encourage students to find examples of singular subjects and verbs in agreement in content area texts, such as science lab procedures, and math story problems. Then, have them check their own work to be sure they have monitored subject-verb agreement.

Spelling Consciousness

Thinking Strategically—Making My Message Accessible to Others

When writers approach spelling tasks strategically, they have a sense of when to rely upon themselves and their knowledge of morphemes, root words, affixes, and word parts or when to return to other resources for support. Strategic spellers pay attention to the way the words look, and the search for patterns in words. These spellers have a distinct sense of spelling consciousness that guides them as they write.

LESSON	3	4	5	RELATED LESSONS
1 Notice When Words Are Not Spelled Correctly	●	●		*Editing:* Lesson 5, Use Spelling Consciousness
2 Strategic Spellers Try Different Spellings for Words	●	●	●	*Editing:* Lesson 5, Use Spelling Consciousness
3 Use Root Words		●	●	
4 Navigating Homophones	●	●	●	

Notice When Words Are Not Spelled Correctly

WHEN TO USE IT: To help writers develop a system for noticing misspelled words

FOCUS THE LEARNING

In writing, the most important goal is always to extend and expand communication. However, work that is presented or shared with others demands that attention be given to spelling and noticing when words don't look quite right.

Model

Have the first two sentences already written on a chart before beginning this lesson. Please note that the spelling errors are intentional.

STEP 1: Model how to underline words that don't look quite right while maintaining a focus on the message.

Possible Think-Aloud: *Spelling is important, but a first draft is mostly a time to focus on the message—the meaning. If we are going to pause and think about spelling during a draft, it needs to be quick. That is why spelling consciousness is such a helpful strategy. With spelling consciousness, writers notice spellings that don't look quite right and quickly draw a line under those words. That's a reminder to go back and check the spelling when the message is complete. This is not the time to get a dictionary and look up words, as you might lose momentum with the writing. Watch as I take a look at the word "spred" in the first sentence. The middle of the word doesn't look right to me, so I'm underlining the word to remember to check it later. I'm wondering about "unpredictibility," too. It's such a great word! I don't want to put in a simple word just because I'm not sure how to spell "unpredictability." Great writing deserves great vocabulary! So I'm underlining that word to remind me to check the spelling later.*

Forest fires spred quickly, raging through dry forests, grasslands, and farmers' fields. Fire is an inferno of unpredictibility that sucks oxigen from the air, gobbls up everything in its path, and even creates its own wind. The raidient heat from an advancing fire is so intens that it can kill people even before the fire line is visable.

Sample Modeled Writing

TURN &TALK *Partners, think together as you evaluate this strategy. Why is it a good idea to use spelling consciousness and simply underline words during a first draft? Why is this better than stopping to look up words in a dictionary?*

STEP 2: Continue modeling and thinking aloud about spelling consciousness.

Possible Think-Aloud: *I am ready to write sentence three about the intensity of the heat. I will write, "The raidient heat from an advancing fire." "Raidient" looks strange to me. Watch how I quickly underline it and keep going with "is so intens that it can kill people even before the fire line is visable." I really like the way this writing is flowing. Forest fires are a big problem in this country, so I need to keep my attention mostly on the message so my writing conveys the importance of the topic. I do think, however, that a few of these words may need attention when I am ready to edit.*

TURN &TALK *Think together and apply spelling consciousness—notice words that need attention. Observe and wonder together. Are there any words in this last sentence that should be underlined?*

Analyze

STEP 3: Reread and reflect.

Possible Think-Aloud: *I am feeling good about the message now. So let's go back to the top and read it again to apply spelling consciousness through the entire piece. Remember that we won't fix the words now. Underlining is a great reminder to work on the words when this piece is edited. As I read sentence one, I will touch each word, as that slows down my reading and helps me to notice the spelling.* (Begin reading sentence one.) *Oops! Look at "thrugh." I missed this one the first time. That doesn't look right, so I definitely want to underline it.* (Continue rereading and underlining words as you think aloud.)

Sum It Up

Spelling consciousness is a really important strategy, as it helps us to stay focused on the message—the heart of the writing—but also gives us a way to quickly leave behind a reminder to work on certain words during editing.

VARIATIONS

For Less Experienced Writers: Encourage less experienced writers to use spelling consciousness to underline words of concern and then select five or six to investigate and correct. By limiting the number of words they repair at any one time, you may actually increase the writers' ability to remember the correct spellings.

For More Experienced Writers: Lead a discussion about the resources writers use to support spelling accuracy. Students may want to discuss the benefits of looking up content-specific words in a science or social studies resource, using Portable Word Walls (see the Resources CD-ROM), lists of homophones (see Resources CD-ROM), or Spelling Checklists and self-assessments.

LINKS TO CD-ROM:
- Spelling Strategies Self-Assessment
- Portable Word Wall

Strategic Spellers Try Different Spellings for Words

WHEN TO USE IT: To assist writers in attending to visual awareness of spelling

FOCUS THE LEARNING

While writers may rely on the spelling patterns they have learned, part of the secret is for each writer to learn to trust his or her own intuition about words.

Model

Writers will need scratch paper, personal whiteboards, or writer's notebooks for this lesson.

STEP 1: Model how to experiment with alternative spellings in the margin or on scratch paper.

Possible Think-Aloud: *I am writing about the importance of exercise. My first sentence begins with "Many people clame that they don't have time." I am going to stop writing, as I don't think "clame" looks right. Watch as I work in the margin of this rough draft and experiment with different ways to spell the word. I know that you can create a long "a" sound with "ay," "ai," and "ey" (as in "hey"). Watch as I try those spellings in the margin: "claym, claim, cleym." That helped! "Claim" looks right. I will cross the others out and insert "claim" into my draft.* (Finish the sentence.) *Here is another opportunity to try margin spelling—"exercize." That looks pretty good, but I am not sure.*

TURN &TALK *Use your whiteboards and try out different spellings for "exercize" while I try some possible combinations in the margin of my draft. Think together about possible ways to spell this word, and then select the one that you think "looks right."*

STEP 2: Think aloud as you continue to experiment with word spellings in the margin.

Many people <u>clame</u> that they don't have time to <u>exercize</u>. While it would be <u>ideel</u> to <u>dedeicate</u> time every day to it, you can get in movment without going to the gym.

Claym
Claim
Cleym
Exsercise
Exercise
Exersise

Sample Modeled Writing

Possible Think-Aloud: *When we think about common word patterns and then experiment with spelling, it helps us apply what we know about good spelling. It is important to notice that I only take a moment or two to experiment. I don't want to get off track and forget what I was writing about. My next sentence is "While it would be ideel. . . ." I don't think the middle is right. Watch as I try "ideal, idele, idyle." I've got it. "Ideal" looks best to me. "Dedeicate" is a word that I may want to work with a bit, but I am not going to take time now. Watch as I quickly draw a line under it and finish my thought. I don't ever want spelling to get in the way of my best thinking, so I will wait to work on that word.* (Finish the passage.)

TURN &TALK Think together. What are some different ways that you might approach the spelling of "dedicate"? Try several patterns and analyze them to find the best one.

Analyze

STEP 3: Reread and reflect.

Possible Think-Aloud: *It is really helpful to experiment with different ways of spelling words. You can try word patterns out using the margin of a sloppy copy, scratch paper, whiteboards, or a special section of your writer's notebooks. I am going to make a list of steps to follow when experimenting with words. Watch as I write: "1. Underline words that don't look quite right. 2. Decide if taking time will cause you to forget your message. If so, keep writing. Come back to the spelling later. 3. If you think you can remember your message, begin trying different possible spellings." Writers, analyze the strategy of trying out different spellings. Think together about ways that this strategy might be helpful in your writing.*

Sum It Up

When writers approach spelling tasks strategically, they learn to rely upon themselves and their knowledge of spelling patterns and what "looks right" visually. So notice the way words look, pay attention, and underline words that don't seem quite right. If time allows, and it won't interfere with your message, try out some different spellings and select the one that "looks right."

VARIATIONS

For Less Experienced Writers: Provide coaching during writing conferences to individuals who need assistance in exploring different spelling patterns.

For More Experienced Writers: Teach these writers that in addition to experimenting with spelling patterns in margins and on scrap paper, they can consciously attempt to visualize words with different spelling patterns.

Use Root Words

WHEN TO USE IT: When writers need support for spelling and understanding word meaning

FOCUS THE LEARNING

Knowing the building blocks of the English language can help writers understand word meaning and offer clues to spelling.

Model

Pass out copies of the Roots and Bases Chart, from the Resources CD-ROM.

STEP 1: Model and think aloud about using root words as a link to spelling.

Possible Think-Aloud: *Did you know that if we take time to consider the root or the base of some words, we can unlock both meaning and spelling? Here is an example: In the word "aquarium," there is a root, "aqua." Find it on your chart of root words. As you slide your finger to column 2, you will see that it means "water." An aquarium is a container for water. So if I wasn't sure about how to spell "aquarium," I could use the root word chart to help me get the first syllable, "aqua," correct. Since I am writing about how to set up an aquarium, this is really helpful. I begin with "To set up an. . . ." If I hadn't thought about the root word, "aqua," I would be tempted to begin aquarium with "ac." That is a sound my ear can hear. But the root word sets me straight. That is helpful!*

TURN &TALK *Look at the Roots and Bases Chart and identify roots that are in words that you find familiar. Think about how you might use these roots in reaching for better spelling.*

STEP 2: Continue modeling and thinking aloud about using root words while spelling.

> To set up an <u>aquarium</u>, we must focus on an <u>ecologically</u> balanced system. Healthy fish need <u>aquatic</u> plants, <u>aeration</u>, a <u>thermometer</u>, and a system for <u>removing</u> waste.

Sample Modeled Writing

Possible Think-Aloud: *I am ready to write "ecologically." If I start by thinking of syllables, I first hear "eco" and then "logic." I am going to check the root word chart and see if that will help. Join me as I scan my chart for "eco." There it is! "Eco" means environment or house. That fits perfectly with my meaning, so I know that "ecologically" will start with "eco" rather than "eko."*

TURN &TALK *Join me in searching for "logic" or something close to it in the root word chart. If you find something that might fit, check the meaning and see if it fits with "ecologically." Talk about what you are learning.*

Analyze

STEP 3: Reread and reflect.

Possible Think-Aloud: (Continue writing and guiding writers in searching for roots for the underlined words.) *This is like being a word detective. It is really fun to see which words have roots that will help me spell more effectively. The next sentence tells that the system needs "<u>aquatic</u> plants, <u>aeration</u>, a <u>thermometer</u>, and a system for <u>removing</u> waste." Join with me in searching for roots that may help us confirm the spelling for these important words. Partners, think together and be ready to report your findings.*

Sum It Up

Knowing the building blocks of the English language can help writers understand word meaning and offer clues to spelling. All you need to do is think about possible root words that can help lead you to correct spelling and that link to meaning as well. Root words are fascinating because they appear in so many different words. Once you begin to pay attention, you will find them everywhere. Be sure to keep your root word chart in a handy place in your writer's notebooks so you can refer to it again and again.

VARIATIONS

For Less Experienced Writers: Experiment with creating a variety of words from a basic root or base word. The root "mot" is especially good for this, as you can create "motor," "motorcycle," "locomotive," "motion," "commotion," "promotion," "remote control," "motivation," "emotion," and so on. Provide English Language Learners whose native languages derive from Greek or Latin roots opportunities to make connections to words in their first language that share a root or base with the English cognate.

For More Experienced Writers: Focus on pre- fixes and suffixes (see Resources CD-ROM).

LINKS TO CD-ROM:
- Roots and Bases Chart
- Prefixes Chart
- Suffixes Chart
- How Suffixes Change Words

Navigating Homophones

WHEN TO USE IT: When you see evidence of homophone confusion in your students' work

FOCUS THE LEARNING

Homophones are words that sound the same but the spelling and meanings are different (examples: "their," "there," "they're"; "chili" and "chilly"; "bored" and "board"). Homophones are particularly challenging for spellers because they must think about meaning to select the correct spelling.

Model

Writers will need two things for this lesson: a copy of the Spelling Reference: Homophone Sheet and a writing folder, writer's notebook, learning log, or some other collection of writing. Prepare the modeled writing on a chart before the lesson begins.

STEP 1: Demonstrate how a homophone reference can help when adjusting spelling.

Possible Think-Aloud: *As writers, we always focus on meaning. In doing so, we need to be especially careful with homophones—those pesky words that sound alike but have different spellings and meanings. Each of you has a copy of a spelling reference for homophones. We will practice with it today, and then I know you are going to want to keep it handy in your writer's notebooks or writing folders. On this chart, I have an example of what happens to writers when they forget to pay attention to homophones. Listen as I begin reading: "I have been weighting an our. . . ."* *I am going to stop here because I already see two homophones that we need to check on. Scan down the homophone sheet, and find the homophones "wait" and "weight." There is a sentence to help you identify the meaning of each. "Wait" means to spend time anticipating that something will happen. "Weight" refers to heftiness, total pounds or kilos. The example sentences help me to know that "weight" should be changed to "wait."*

TURN &TALK *Think together using the chart to check on the homophone "our" and "hour." Use the sentences to find the one with the meaning that we need for this sentence about how long someone has been waiting.*

> I have been weighting an our
> four the plumbers to arrive
> with there tools to fix our
> faucet. They are busy, but
> I am two. This isn't fare.

Sample Modeled Writing

STEP 2: Continue identifying homophones in your modeled writing and analyzing whether spelling matches meaning.

Possible Think-Aloud: *The next one that catches my eye is "there." We all know that "there," "their," and "they're" are tricky. In the sentence I wrote, "there" refers to tools, so I need the form that is a possessive and shows that something belongs to someone. This chart has helped me confirm that this word should be spelled t-h-e-i-r. Watch as I make the change.*

TURN &TALK *You know what to do. Work together and analyze this writing. Find the homophones and identify each form that is needed to make the spelling and the meaning match up.*

Analyze

STEP 3: Reread and reflect.

Possible Think-Aloud: *You get the idea, and you now have a tool that will really help you to conquer homophones and other tricky words that sound alike but mean different things. This is a chance for you to reread some of your own work and check words that might need to be adjusted so that meanings and spellings match up. When you find a place in your own work where you can make an adjustment, share it with your partner and talk about what you are going to do with the spelling.*

Sum It Up

To help us be the best spellers we can, we need to learn the meanings of a variety of homophones and focus on using the spelling that matches the meaning of our writing. Over the next few weeks, I challenge you to become hypersensitive to homophones in both reading and writing. We can all learn to control homophones if we remember that they are tightly linked to meaning.

VARIATIONS

For Less Experienced Writers: During individual writing conferences, coach writers in analyzing their work for homophones that are challenging them, and make personal reminder notes to help writers remember to get these under control.

For More Experienced Writers: Guide these writers in working with homonyms in which the spelling is the same but the pronunciation and meaning are different. Examples: "minute," "bow," and so on.

LINKS TO CD-ROM:
• Spelling Reference: Homophone Sheet

CD-ROM INDEX

Section	Lesson Number	Title
Record Keeping Forms		Class Record-Keeping Grid
		Trait Scoring Guide
		Demonstration Lesson Tracker: Research
		Demonstration Lesson Tracker: Planning
		Demonstration Lesson Tracker: Drafting
		Demonstration Lesson Tracker: Revising
		Demonstration Lesson Tracker: Editing
		Demonstration Lesson Tracker: Presenting
		Demonstration Lesson Tracker: Ideas
		Demonstration Lesson Tracker: Organization
		Demonstration Lesson Tracker: Word Choice
		Demonstration Lesson Tracker: Sentence Fluency
		Demonstration Lesson Tracker: Voice and Audience
		Demonstration Lesson Tracker: Sentence Structure
		Demonstration Lesson Tracker: Text Features
		Demonstration Lesson Tracker: Punctuation and Capitalization
		Demonstration Lesson Tracker: Grammar
		Demonstration Lesson Tracker: Spelling Consciousness
Research	1	Rating Tool for Print Sources
	2	Alphaboxes
	3	Amelia Earhart
	4	Key Word Strategy
	5	Octopus
	7	'Ecological Nightmare'
	8	'All Wrapped Up'
	Modeled Writing	Examples of Modeled Writing from each lesson.

Section	Lesson Number	Title
Planning	1	Reduce Reuse Recycle PowerPoint Water Conservation PowerPoint Poster 1: Let's Save Some Water Poster 2: Keeping it Green Poster 3: Water Crisis Poster 4: Composting
	2	The Water Cycle Planning an Explanation Understanding Text Structures
	3	Cause/Effect Organizer 1 Cause/Effect Organizer 2
	4	Generalizations Planning Sheet
	5	Steam Train
	7	Planning Investigation: Blob Fish Facts Planning Investigation: Motorcross
	8	Flowchart Framework
	Modeled Writing	Examples of Modeled Writing from each lesson.
Drafting	4	Transition Words and Phrases to Use When Inserting Examples
	7	Mentor Text: *The Last Living Symbol of the American West*
	8	Mentor Text: *Africa's Diverse Landscape*
	9	Mentor Text: *Africa's Diverse Landscape*
	10	Features of a Persuasive Text
	Modeled Writing	Examples of Modeled Writing from each lesson.
Revising	1	Using Precise Descriptions
	2	Strong and Weak Leads
	3	Strong and Weak Endings
	5	Sentence Fluency Checklist

Section	Lesson Number	Title
Revising *(cont.)*	8	Revision Checklist A Revision Checklist B Revision Checklist C
	10	Cut and Paste Revision
	Modeled Writing	Examples of Modeled Writing from each lesson.
Editing	1	Writer's Self Reflection
	2	Editing Checklist I Editing Checklist II Editing Checklist III Editing Checklist IV Editing Reflection Sheet: Capitalization and Punctuation
	3	Express Lane Edit
	4	Peer-Editing Checklist Peer-Editing Celebration
	5	Spelling Consciousness Checklist A Spelling Consciousness Checklist B
	6	Editing a Paragraph T.I.P.S. When to Start a New Paragraph
	7	GPS Text Copyediting Symbols
	Modeled Writing	Examples of Modeled Writing from each lesson.
Presenting	4	The Layers of the Atmosphere PowerPoint
	5	Modeled Writing Example Without Page Breaks
	Modeled Writing	Examples of Modeled Writing from each lesson.
Ideas	1	Nonfiction Topic List
	2	Mustangs Mentor Text: *The Last Living Symbol of the American West*

Section	Lesson Number	Title
Ideas *(cont.)*	3	Jaw-Dropping Details Organizer
	4	Details Chart
	5	Main Idea and Details Reflecting on Main Ideas Writing Samples (Dear Mom and Dear Katie)
	6	Venus Flytrap Anticipating Reader Questions
	8	Blue Whale Comparison Diagrams
	9	Persuasive Framework Mentor Text: *Reversing a Heavy Trend* Writing Samples (Dear Mom and Dear Katie)
	10	Informational Narrative Poems
	Modeled Writing	Examples of Modeled Writing from each lesson.
Organization	1	Spider Style Organizer
	2	Timeline
	3	Comparison Chart Venn Diagram
	4	Main Idea and Details Writing Samples (Dear Mom and Dear Katie)
	5	Mentor Text: *Animal Architects*
	6	Books with Strong Leads Mentor Text: *Africa's Diverse Landscape*
	7	Mentor Text: *Africa's Diverse Landscape*
	8	T.I.P.S. When to Start a New Paragraph
	9	Mentor Text: *Reversing a Heavy Trend* Persuasive Framework Planning Page Writing Samples (Dear Mom and Dear Katie)
	Modeled Writing	Examples of Modeled Writing from each lesson.

Section	Lesson Number	Title
Word Choice	1	Eagle's Beak
	2	Powerful Verbs, Powerful Writing
	3	Linking Words and Phrases
	4	Words to Use When Describing What You See, Hear, Taste, Smell, and Touch Mentor Text: *The Last Living Symbol of the American West*
	5	Mentor Text: *Animal Architects*
	6	Similes
	8	Mentor Text: *The Last Living Symbol of the American West*
	9	Words and Phrases that Show Order or Sequence Planning Sheet for Sequencing Events
	10	Compound Descriptors Mentor Text: Penguins: *Belly-sliding, Fast-swimming, Birds!*
	11	Onomatopoeia Mentor Text: Penguins: *Belly-sliding, Fast-swimming, Birds!*
	12	Self Assessment: Persuasive Language Mentor Text: *Reversing a Heavy Trend* Writing Samples (Dear Mom and Dear Katie)
	Modeled Writing	Examples of Modeled Writing from each lesson.
Sentence Fluency	1	Varying Sentence Length Checklist
	2	Strong and Weak Sentence Fluency
	3	Sentence Beginnings Checklist
	4	Personal Sentence Planning Chart Prepositions
	5	Adverbs and Adverb Phrases
	6	Two-Word Sentences
	7	Mentor Text: *Africa's Diverse Landscape*
	8	Linking Words and Phrases
	Modeled Writing	Examples of Modeled Writing from each lesson.

Section	Lesson Number	Title
Voice and Audience	6	An Enticing Title
	9	Wash Your Hands!
	12	Self-Assessment for Voice
	Modeled Writing	Examples of Modeled Writing from each lesson.
Sentence Structure	1	Mentor Text: *The Last Living Symbol of the American West*
	3	Combining Sentences
	4	Mentor Text: *Arabian Horses—A Proud and Versatile Breed*
	Modeled Writing	Examples of Modeled Writing from each lesson.
Text Features	1	Thinking about Titles
	2	Mentor Text: *Africa's Diverse Landscape*
	4	Weathering and Erosion
	5	Earthworm Cutaway Volcano Cross-Section
	9	Lightning
	Modeled Writing	Examples of Modeled Writing from each lesson.
Punctuation/ Capitalization	5	Mentor Text: *Africa's Diverse Landscape*
	Modeled Writing	Examples of Modeled Writing from each lesson.
Grammar	1	Irregular Verbs: Present, Past, Past Participle
	2	List of Helpful Prepositions and Phrases
	3	Cloze for Powerful Action Words
	4	Photos of tiger head
	Modeled Writing	Examples of Modeled Writing from each lesson.

Section	Lesson Number	Title
Spelling Consciousness	1	Spelling Strategies Self Assessment Portable Word Wall
	3	Roots and Bases Chart Prefixes Chart Suffixes Chart How Suffixes Change Words
	4	Spelling Reference: Homophone Sheet
	Modeled Writing	Examples of Modeled Writing from each lesson.

INDEX